Remaking Market Society

Neoliberalism has been one of the most hotly contested themes in academic and political debate over the last 30 years. Given the global and persistent influence of neoliberal ideas on contemporary styles of governance, social-service provision, and public policy, this intensive interest is understandable. At the same time, the use of the term has become loose, vague, and over-extended, particularly in the extensive critical literature. Rather than engage in further critique, or in the reconstruction of the history of neoliberalism, this volume seeks to bring analytical clarity to the ongoing debate.

Drawing inspiration from the work of the Hungarian economic historian, Karl Polanyi, *Remaking Market Society* combines critique, original formulations, and case studies to form an analytical framework that identifies the key instruments of neoliberal governance. These include privatization, marketization, and liberalization. The case studies examine the development of neoliberal instruments (reform of the British civil service); their refinement (reform of higher education in England and Wales); and their dissemination across national borders (EU integration policies). Rather than look back nostalgically on the post-war welfare-state settlement, in the final chapter the authors ask why the coalitions that supported that settlement broke down in the face of the neoliberal reform movement.

This highly original work offers a distinctive transdisciplinary approach to political economy, and therefore is an important read for students and academics who are interested in political economy as well as social theory and political philosophy.

Antonino Palumbo is a political theorist who works on globalization, the transformation of governance and the implications of changes in state steering for modern representative democracies. Since 2002 he has been teaching at Palermo University (Italy), where he is an associate professor in political philosophy.

Alan Scott is Professor in the School of Behavioural, Cognitive, and Social Sciences, University of New England, Australia, and Adjunct Professor of Sociology at the University of Innsbruck, Austria. He has taught and researched at universities in the UK, Austria, Australia, and France, and his main research interests are in the fields of political sociology and social theory.

Routledge Frontiers of Political Economy

For a full list of titles in this series please visit www.routledge.com/books/series/SE0345

227. The Political Economy of Emerging Markets
Edited by Richard Westra

228. The Social Construction of Rationality
Policy Debates and the Power of Good Reasons
Onno Bouwmeester

229. Varieties of Alternative Economic Systems
Practical Utopias for an Age of Global Crisis and Austerity
Edited by Richard Westra, Robert Albritton and Seongjin Jeong

230. Money as a Social Institution
The Institutional Development of Capitalism
Ann E. Davis

231. Remaking Market Society
A Critique of Social Theory and Political Economy in Neoliberal Times
Antonino Palumbo and Alan Scott

232. Political Economy and Natural Theology
Smith, Malthus and their Followers
Paul Oslington

233. Sharing Economies in Times of Crisis
Practices, Politics and Possibilities
Edited by Anthony Ince and Sarah Marie Hall

234. Philosophy in the Time of Economic Crisis
Pragmatism and Economy
Edited by Kenneth W. Stikkers and Krzysztof Piotr Skowroński

Remaking Market Society

A Critique of Social Theory and Political Economy in Neoliberal Times

Antonino Palumbo and Alan Scott

Routledge
Taylor & Francis Group
LONDON AND NEW YORK

First published 2018
by Routledge

2 Park Square, Milton Park, Abingdon, Oxfordshire OX14 4RN
52 Vanderbilt Avenue, New York, NY 10017

Routledge is an imprint of the Taylor & Francis Group, an informa business

First issued in paperback 2019

British Library Cataloguing in Publication Data
A catalogue record for this book is available from the British Library

Library of Congress Cataloging in Publication Data
Names: Palumbo, Antonino, author. | Scott, Alan, 1956- author.
Title: Remaking market society : a critique of social theory and political economy in neoliberal times / Antonino Palumbo and Alan Scott.
Description: Abingdon, Oxon ; New York, NY : Routledge, 2017. | Includes bibliographical references and index.
Identifiers: LCCN 2017003322 | ISBN 9780415837736 (hardback) | ISBN 9780203796375 (ebook)
Subjects: LCSH: Neoliberalism--Social aspects. | Social policy. | Social sciences--Philosophy. | Political science--Economic aspects.
Classification: LCC HB95 .P2866 2017 | DDC 303.48/201--dc23
LC record available at https://lccn.loc.gov/2017003322

ISBN: 978-0-415-83773-6 (hbk)
ISBN: 978-0-367-86803-1 (pbk)

Typeset in Times New Roman
by Taylor & Francis Books

Contents

Illustrations

Figure

Tables

Introduction

Much ink has been spilt on the theme of neoliberalism. As one reviewer of a recent volume on the topic noted: 'if arguments were won on the basis of tonnage, free-market philosophies would have fallen long ago under a weight of words' (Birch 2015: 330). This introduction, by way of a justification for adding to this weight of words, will seek to locate our arguments and aims within the extensive – and ongoing – literature and debate.

Much of the work Birch had in mind takes the form of a *critique* of neoliberalism on one, or both, of the following grounds:

1 social effects: neoliberalism has exacerbated economic and spatial inequalities, weakened public service provision, and over-commercializes and over-marketizes (e.g. Brenner and Theodore (eds) 2002; Peck 2012; Brown 2015);
2 political effects: neoliberalism has undermined democratic politics, democratic values, and the quality of democratic institutions (e.g. di Palma 2013; Streeck 2014; Brown 2015).

The 2008 Global Financial Crisis (GFC) gave further impetus to these critical efforts even though, or precisely because, initial hopes that neoliberalism was in terminal crisis were soon dashed: 'almost as suddenly as it had arrived, this sense of a progressive new dawn evaporated. Worse than this, it soon became clear that the global crisis had set the stage for another neoliberal counter-offensive' (Peck *et al* 2012: 266). A related area of critical academic endeavour has focused on the history and dissemination of neoliberalism (e.g. Mirowski and Plehwe (eds) 2009); on neoliberalism as a hegemonic project in Gramsci's sense (Plehwe *et al* (eds) 2006), as a discourse (Springer 2012), as culture and 'structure of feeling' (McGuigan 2016). Some of this critical work was aimed at a broader audience, and has – deservedly – found its way into public debate (e.g. Harvey 2005, Crouch 2011, Streeck 2014).

In taking Polanyi's *The Great Transformation* as our starting point, we clearly align our arguments with these critical endeavours. However, it is our intention neither to offer a critique nor a history of neoliberalism. Our aim is narrower: to develop a distinct analytical framework for a debate that has not yet run its course. We depart from much of the critical literature in one key respect: our preference for political over economic readings of neoliberalism. Much of that literature has been framed in terms of a radical – which usually means neo-Marxist – political economy. This framing can be seen at the most basic level, in standard definitions of neo-liberalism as:

> the elevation of the market – understood as a non-political, non-cultural, machine-like entity – over all other modes of organization.
>
> (Mudge 2008: 204)

> the extension of competitive markets into all areas of life, including the economic, politics, and society.
>
> (Springer *et al* 2016: 2)

> enacting an ensemble of economic policies in accord with its root principle of affirming free markets.
>
> (Brown 2015: 28)

There are two potential problems with such definitions: (i) over-stretching the concept and (ii) conflating neoliberalism's practices and policies with its intellectual self-understanding. To take these points in turn. The elevation of the market over other modes of organization, its extension into other (or all) areas of social life, and a preference for free markets are certainly characteristics of neoliberalism, but they are ones shared with a broader pro-market stance. These principles each find a particularly radical and robust expression in neoliberal arguments, but they are not specific enough to identify neoliberalism as a circumscribed ensemble of theory and practice.

The overstretching of the concept – at worst to the point of including 'all aspects of state governing in contemporary liberal democracies and the majority world beyond them' (Dean 2014: 150) – or its use as a 'sloppy synonym for capitalism itself, or as a kind of shorthand for the world economy and its inequalities' (Ferguson 2009: 171) weakens its analytical usefulness. This point has recently been made with respect to urban studies in which much of the transformation of cities – from gentrification to financialization – has been explained in terms of neoliberalism. In such approaches Le Galès (2016: 156) detects the presence of 'a contradiction between a rather deterministic macro framework relying upon a very fluid and constructivist definition of neoliberalism' and confusion 'about the relationship between liberalism, globalized capitalism, and neoliberalism.' The result is the ascription of all manner of urban change to a rather nebulous and overblown notion of 'neoliberalization' in which the latter operates as a *deus ex machina*. Such conceptual over-reach erases all differences between liberalism and neoliberalism. As Michael Storper (2016: 249) has noted, this 'polysemic' usage 'facilitates an indiscriminate critique of capitalism, and represents liberalism as somehow inherently hostile to states, to public goods, to regulation, and to social and economic equality and opportunity and in favour of plutocratic power and cronyism.' Storper traces this tendency to conflate varieties of liberal thought by reducing them all to neoliberalism to the 'widespread hostility to markets (i.e. to liberalism) of many authors on neo-liberalism and nostalgia for 20th-century welfare states' (Storper 2016: 258) accompanied by 'an ominous anti-capitalist drumbeat' (Storper 2016: 243).

One radical response to this loss of analytical purchase has been to call for a moratorium on the use of the term on the grounds that it has been irredeemably damaged due to over, and over-extended, use, is under specified, and encourages 'abstract critique' in place of 'constructive engagement' (Harding 2007: 456). As Harding notes (again with respect to urban studies):

> It would be particularly helpful, in this regard, if commentators who use the words neoliberal, neoliberalism and neoliberalization [...] were prepared to say precisely what they mean by them, which economic and social interests advance them, through what mechanisms and with what effects. In the absence of such clarity, the danger is that they continue to be used as catch-all terms of abuse by 'progressive' critics rather than concepts that are useful to empirical research.
>
> (Harding 2007: 455)

A less drastic response would be to take up Harding's challenge and offer a more precise and circumscribed definition (cf. Dean 2014), specify the interests, actors, and mechanisms at work, and identify the resulting effects. This is the path we shall seek to take, but before specifying how we understand neoliberalism, we need to consider the second potential weakness of standard definitions: the tendency to take its self-understanding at face value.

The brief definitions listed above all – rightly – cast neoliberalism as a shift in the relationship between the state and the market. However, they do so in such a way as to imply a zero-sum game in which any extension of the market is necessarily at the expense of the state and the breaking down of 'institutional pillarization' between market and state is to the latter's detriment. Such a reading equates neoliberalism not merely with privatization and marketization, but also with deregulation. To view neoliberalism in this way is to accept the terms in which it has framed its project: as a rolling back of the state. In contrast, here we shall develop the argument that neoliberalism is not merely economic policy and practice, but also a technique for state actors to rule through the market in a way that can strengthen rather than weaken state power and authority. We thus view neoliberalism as – to use a rather old-fashioned term – a form of *statecraft*: the means, skills, and knowledge required for the purpose of government.

In reading neoliberalism as a form of government or rule, our position has a clear affinity with the school of thought that provides the major alternative to radical political economy, namely that influenced by Michel Foucault's interpretation of neoliberalism as a specific 'art of government' or 'governmental rationality' (Foucault 2004). This understanding of what Rose (1999) has called 'advanced liberalism', in which rule increasingly takes place at a distance and subjects are 'responsibilized', has produced an influential and innovative body of literature on 'governmentality'. We are sympathetic to the aim of this approach: to shift the terms of debate away from dualistic notions of state retreat and market domination, and partially agree with one of its conclusions, namely that 'what we observe today is not a reduction of state sovereignty and planning capacities but a displacement from formal to informal techniques of government and the appearance of new actors on the scene of government' (Lemke 2007: 57–58).[1] However, we shall not adopt the language of this poststructuralist perspective for the following reason: its understanding of neoliberalism is grounded in a conception of power as network-like, highly defused, and decentred. This view emerged out of an understandable impatience with the more standard 'modernist' emphasis upon the increasing concentration, centralization, and monopolization of power in organizational hierarchy in which there is the ever-present danger of reifying 'the state'. Foucault's response was not to abandon the notion of state altogether, but to translate it into state effects and to view it as a 'transactional reality' in which the distinction between state and government becomes fluid. However, in some subsequent governmentality literature this turns into an anti-state bias. This tendency has been noted by Foucauldian scholars themselves, notably by Villadsen and Dean (2012: 416) who argue that, for example in the work of Nikolas Rose, Foucault's critique of neoliberal 'state-phobia' merges into an 'anti-state rendering of Foucault's thinking on the state'; a move which, under contemporary conditions, draws the governmentality approach into the compass of neoliberalism. Since the story we shall relate is one of the concentration and refinement of power, the governmentality framework is not appropriate to our endeavour. Thus, despite a common stress on neoliberalism as an 'art of government', the position that we shall develop here takes its cue not from poststructuralism, but from modernist approaches; from classical rather than contemporary social theory. Rather than adopt the (relatively) new neologism 'governmentality', we prefer, as already noted, an old one: statecraft.

Having spent some time dwelling on what this book will not do and where its arguments are not to be located, it is time to say something about what we shall be doing.

Arguments and structure of the book

Rather than interpret neoliberalism as a – more-or-less – coherent doctrine and programme, we view it as a somewhat eclectic – and therefore flexible – toolkit of ideas, policies, and instruments.[2] We are thus less interested in neoliberalism at the level of ideas than as a practice deploying specific measures and instruments; above all those associated with so-called New Public Management (NPM). For the purposes of the arguments developed in this volume, we define neoliberalism as a programme of government made up of three components: privatization, liberalization, and marketization. We adopt the term 'liberalization' in preference to deregulation because, in our Polanyian reading, neoliberalism requires more, and a greater variety of types of, regulation; a view supported by some recent political-science analysis. While liberalization entails a withdrawal of regulatory power, this is, we shall argue, followed by its reaffirmation and a shift in modes of regulation. Privatization, liberalization, and marketization are the three components of the neoliberal programme of government and form the parts of a policy set we shall call the New Public Management 'template'. This template is not mechanically or rigidly applied. Rather the three policy components can be adopted in varying degrees, and in a different order, according to context and to the preferences of political principals. To capture the flexibility of the application and adaptation of the NPM template we use a metaphor, which we hope is vivid but at the risk that some readers may find it merely fanciful: the 'fruit machine'. Like a fruit machine, the component elements can be spun and re-spun. Our point here is not merely that this capacity for recombination may account for the oft-noted global variations in neoliberal policies (e.g. Brenner *et al* 2010), but also that it has a strategic purpose: pre-empting or disrupting the gaming of new rules. Without this flexibility new rule regimes would be highly vulnerable to what Christopher Hood (1998) has called 'functional disruption' and 'reverse effects'.

In analyzing neo-liberalism at this policy level we seek to contribute to the literature on so-called 'new policy instruments' (e.g. Lascoume and Le Galès 2007; Kassim and Le Galès 2010). But there is a second level of analysis requiring a further specification: that of agents and agency. Here we understand neoliberalism as a 'three-level game' played out between (i) political principals and those in charge of service delivery; (ii) the suppliers involved in the production line together with public service users; (iii) public sector and civil society. This will entail developing a typology of actors and classes of activity, and understanding the distinct logics and dynamics at work at each of these three levels in order to better appreciate both the diverse and shifting strategies available to actors and their distinct utility functions and preferences. This move marks a further shift away from neo-Marxist structural and functionalist explanation.

In developing this framework we structure the argument as follows.

Part I is intended to set the scene and sketch in outline the approach we adopt. Chapter 1 offers a close reading of Polanyi's *The Great Transformation*. Our aim here is to locate our arguments within the third critical perspective on neoliberalism – one whose influence has grown significantly in the wake of the GFC. In our reading, Polanyi offers an alternative and not a supplement to neo-Marxist political economy. He breaks with the latter in fully acknowledging the state's active role as market maker and in shaping the 'market subject' rather than viewing it as an instrument or apparatus for reproducing capitalist relations of production. In contrast to 'state theories of reproduction of capitalism', Polanyi offers an account of the state that ascribes to it a central not peripheral role in the constitution of 'market society'.[3] Our adoption of a Polanyian perspective is not, however, uncritical. Against the main thrust of his own analysis, Polanyi tends to argue – or simply assume – that the 'double movement' (marketization followed by reregulation in order to defend society against the effects of the disembedded market) was the final round of the historical development he traces. Gareth Dale thus summarizes the logic underlying *The Great Transformation* as follows:

> E-D-E', where E and D represent embedded and disembedded society. The new form of society, E', represents the end of history, in which the market elements that had emerged to dominate 19th-century society became integrated (or sublated) within a regulated synthesis.
>
> (Dale 2012: 14)

Subsequent historical experience has demonstrated that this dynamic is cyclical; not so much a 'great transformation' as – Dale's coinage – 'a great oscillation'.[4] Here – as elsewhere – we also seek to avoid the element of nostalgia evident in much contemporary critical literature (cf. Storper 2016) by tracing this cyclical dynamic to the failure of re-embedding via regulation to meet its democratizing promise, and to the long-term decline in support consequent upon this failure.

In Chapter 2 we review a debate which – at a high level of theoretical abstraction – formulates notions of reflexivity, detraditionalization, and negotiated identity; namely theories of a 'reflexive' or 'second' modernity. These meta-theoretical – or, less politely, speculative – reflections had effects downstream – for example in the extensive literature on governance. They articulated a set of ideas and assumptions that have framed much contemporary socio-political analysis: the declining power of hierarchy (of 'command-and-control'), the weakening of old solidarities in the light of growing 'individualization', and the emergence of less institutionalized forms of 'sub-politics'. Against these 'weakly postmodernist' arguments we seek to defend a modernist reading of contemporary social and political change; one that reaffirms Weber's equation of modernity with increasing rationalization rather than one that posits an epochal break with the logic of modernity.

If Chapter 2 has a largely critical and negative role, Chapter 3 tries to provide more positive support for our commitment to modernist social theory. We start from recent arguments in political science that support the view that privatization and marketization are accompanied by more – and more formalized – regulation, and are thus to be understood in terms of a 'high' rather than 'second' or 'post' modernity. We then draw on Weber and on the sociology of professions in order to show that these arguments apply equally at the meso level of organizations. Here – as in the case of the state – the centralization of power is not threatened by rule and target negotiation and the growing emphasis on quasi-voluntary instruments emphasizing compliance rather than – as in the Weberian account of bureaucratic hierarchy – obedience. Good governance codes, light-touch regulation, and 'soft' law/rules supplement; strengthen rather than displace; traditional modes of command-and-control. At both the level of the state and within organizations, a modernist logic remains at work, and the scope, validity, and effectiveness of hierarchical power is reinforced by rule proliferation and 'hyper-innovation' (Moran 2003). The chapter concludes with the model of power proposed by the German political sociologist Heinrich Popitz according to whom the ability to establish factual – i.e. physical – realities represents the highest and most stable expression of power relations. We extend this notion of 'fact-setting power' to include social technologies of the kind to be analyzed in Part II.

Part II opens with an Introduction in which we present the framework that will inform the three case studies that comprise the second part of the book. Here we introduce systematically (i) the idea of the New Public Management template; (ii) the analogy between the implementation of that template and a fruit machine; (iii) the three-level game. In line with the modernist perspective we have adopted, we propose a depoliticization thesis as the most plausible characterization of the NPM template. The Introduction to Part II concludes with an account of the dovetailing of the three case studies that will follow. Here we would wish to emphasize that these case studies are not simply an application of our framework. Rather we fully and systematically develop that framework in the course of the case studies.

The three case studies – reform of the British civil service along network-governance lines; the imposition of a corporate structure on higher education in England and Wales; good governance programmes within the EU – are thematically distinct. In the first we analyze a pioneering effort to develop the NPM template; in the second we see its refinement within a specific policy area; and in the third we trace its dissemination across national borders. We have taken two UK cases because it is in the UK that, in our view, the NPM template has been most enthusiastically embraced, rolled out, and rigorously deployed. In this sense the UK is both the 'canary in the coal mine' (Vernon 2011) and a laboratory in which policy instruments and rules have been invented, and from which they have been exported, imitated, and disseminated. In each of the case studies, we examine not merely the instruments but also their effects in terms of deprofessionalization, the replacement of traditional lines of accountability, modes of regulation, and forms of social interaction; and dissatisfaction with the outcomes that occasionally leads to (collective) voice but more usually to (individual) exit. In contrast to accounts of neoliberalization in terms of impersonal social and economic forces, in our case studies we focus on agents and actors, and in particular on the role of meta-regulators within the reform process. The case studies seek to avoid repetition and drive the argument on not merely via their varied thematic emphasis (respectively, on innovation, refinement, and dissemination) but also by shifting the focus onto distinct levels and players within what we have called the three-level game.

In the concluding chapter (Chapter 7) we come full circle and revisit the issue thematized, but left hanging, in Chapter 1: the tensions within Polanyi's own formulation of the 'Polanyian approach' that has shaped our analysis. After the publication of *The Great Transformation*, Polanyi turned to historical-anthropological studies in order to support the disembedding thesis. This deprives us of his account of the further development of market society during the rest of his lifetime, and, in particular, of the implication of the post-Second World War reinstating of the market order for the framework proposed in his 1944 magnum opus. Where might a Polanyian analysis have gone had the shortcomings of the re-embedded regulatory order and the consequent decline in support for it been more fully acknowledged? Here we conclude with a novel claim: the work of Polanyi's Columbia colleague C. Wright Mills in the late 1940s and 1950s provides some significant clues for answering this question. We do not imply a direct influence; indeed, as far as we know, Mills makes no reference to Polanyi. Our claim is rather that Mills, with some prescience, was concerned with themes and started to articulate the outlines of answers to matters that are of contemporary concern: the decline in support of organized labour for social-democratic regulation; the vulnerability of salaried professionals to reform pressure (and the strategies they adopt in light of this); changes in the class structure; the rise of managerialism and 'managerial demiurge'. The reference to Mills is of more than historical interest. Since his themes – and unwittingly also his arguments – address the preconditions for the implementation of the NPM template and the weakness of a countermovement to it they are of continuing relevance to any understanding of the state-driven reforms of the last decades. Our concluding arguments then are (i) that Mills can be used to adjust the Polanyian approach in order to address some of the shortcomings of its original formulation and (ii) that he identified – at least *in nuce* – the preconditions for the success of neoliberal and NPM-inspired reform.

Notes

1 Our agreement is partial in that we also argue that informal (soft) 'techniques of government' are of growing importance. However, in our view, these supplement rather than displace formal (hard) rules. See Chapter 3.

2 For this reason, we shall not follow Storper in drawing a clear distinction between the 'resolute modernist sociology of Hayek, Mises, Schumpeter, and Lippman' (2016: 249) – neo-liberalism properly understood – and its contemporary successor, which Storper dubs 'crony-plutocratic doctrines'. What we have called the neoliberal programme of government cannot be reduced to such doctrines.

3 The distinction between the theory of the state and 'state theories of reproduction of capitalism' is taken from Przeworski, 1990: 85. In the latter 'functionalist analysis' 'the state as an institution is never present' (Przeworski, 1990: 88).

4 Something that became evident to Polanyi after the post-war restoration of market society rather than the continuation of the New Deal, which he viewed as a nascent form of socialism (Polanyi 1947). His commitment to the logic characterized by Dale led him to ascribe this development to our 'obsolete market mentality' rather

than undertaking a reassessment of his analysis in light of these developments. Contemporary commentators (e.g. Peck 2010) who argue that neoliberalism is in its 'zombie phase' – i.e. still operating but devoid of any intellectual rationale – are unknowingly repeating this move and thus in danger of making a similar error of judgement.

Part I

Modernity: continuity and change

1 Social theory as critique of political economy

The Polanyian synthesis and its influence

1.1 Introduction

The framework and arguments that we shall develop in this volume draw, selectively, on classical – modernist – social theory, and in particular on the work of one of its last representatives: the Hungarian economic historian Karl Polanyi. In this chapter, via a close reading of Polanyi's arguments, particularly as set out in *The Great Transformation*, first published in 1944, we outline the broad perspective to be developed and filled out in subsequent chapters.

In the wake of the 100th anniversary of the outbreak of the First World War, the West is facing three major crises – economic, political, and ecological – uncannily similar to those responsible for that catastrophic conflict and the subsequent dissolution of the nineteenth century world order. In this context it is not at all surprising to witness a rekindled interest in Karl Polanyi, the thinker who, more than anyone else, attempted to chronicle, rationalize, and evaluate the changes that eventually led to the collapse of that order. This time around, the attention is, however, largely restricted to Polanyi's critique of political economy contained in his masterpiece *The Great Transformation*, rather than the economic anthropology he contributed to later in the 1950s, and for which he is still remembered.[1] In a kind of cultural countermovement against the hegemony of current neoliberal thought, a new Polanyian moment is gathering pace and we wish to contribute to it by presenting his analysis of market society and the theory of social change he developed out of it.

Although post-Second-World-War social theorists have always maintained an ambivalent attitude towards Polanyi, and in particular towards *The Great Transformation*, he is currently inspiring a widespread interdisciplinary debate concerning his legacy and his ability to supply a heuristic framework for understanding the present, prolonged post-GFC crises.[2] In this chapter we propose a reading of Polanyi's work that views it as a remarkable effort to arrive at a synthesis of classical social theory the aim of which was to develop an alternative to political economy and to counter its vision of market society. The critique of classical political economy proposed by Polanyi harks back to the radical socialist tradition, but departs in crucially important ways from Marxist perspectives, above all in its anti-materialistic stance. While stressing these differences and their heuristic value for assessing the neoliberal reforms of the last three decades, we also point out that Polanyi's notion of crisis remains unfortunately bound to a Marxist reading of market society as riddled with internal contradictions that will inevitably bring about its dissolution, rather than viewing crisis as part of cyclical dynamics allowing for both consolidation and renewal.

1.2 The Whig interpretation of social progress: political economy as heuristics and as ideology

Polanyi advances a reading of classical political economy as composed of two main strands: a heuristic framework concerned with understanding the basis of social change, and a prescriptive theory (the liberal creed) interested in influencing both the direction and pace of change. Building on the utilitarian philosophies of the eighteenth-century Scottish School, classical political economy supports a naturalistic account of the development of market society as the outcome of the individual's propensity to produce and barter commodities. It is upon this propensity that the division of labour unfolds *within* given social groups, and trade relations are established *between* them. Moreover, it is claimed that left to itself this propensity would promote a continuously expanding dynamic able to progressively encompass any social group and field of activity, leading eventually to the expansion of the market pattern onto a global scale. Underpinning this natural propensity is the expectation of the potential material gains that could accrue to the individuals and groups actively engaged in the production and distribution of commodities. According to this account, a market society is not only humanity's natural condition, but also one that can satisfy the sentiment of social justice in the most effective way. Hence, since Mandeville, a long line of political economists has attempted to show that the 'unintended consequences' of self-seeking and maximizing behaviour would indeed be the promotion of public benefits.[3]

Upon these two beliefs – in the naturalness of market exchanges and the unintended positive consequences of the profit motive – political economy has erected a liberal creed committed to showing the derivative nature of moral virtues and social norms, while denouncing any attempt to enforce them directly through exhortation, cultivation, or statecraft. While virtuous behaviour and selfless cooperation have come to be described by liberal theorists as ineffectual or unsustainable, political action and statecraft are systematically depicted as interferences that reduce individual freedom and undermine the self-regulating power of market society. Political economists are thus led to view politics not only as superfluous in fostering collective action, but also as a highly disruptive activity that needs to be cut down to size and subordinated to the requirements of market society. Consequently, underpinning the liberal ideology erected by generations of political economists is a common justificatory framework employed to assess social changes, institutions, actions, and values. This framework became a matter of public debate; one based on criteria of 'feasibility' able to tell us what kind of society and which institutional arrangement are compatible with the individual's natural propensity to produce and barter freely, and in doing so unintentionally promote public happiness and social justice. Criteria of 'desirability', employed by the old moral economy, and of 'electability', advocated by market democrats, are progressively discarded as being unsound, or arbitrary, or hubristic, or some combination thereof.[4]

Recalling and synthesising the main insights of classical social theory, Polanyi painstakingly tries to dismantle this narrative of social change and question its ideological authority. His feat was to develop a powerful challenge to political economy's epistemic hard core: its account of unintended consequences and theory of feasibility. For Polanyi, the attempt to build a market society is utterly utopian in that it is predicated upon the disembedding of the economy from its wider social milieu; an endeavour that could only produce negative unintended consequences having cumulative catastrophic effects on society and nature alike. This is the reason why, according to Polanyi, far from being self-regulating, the market pattern requires persistent external interventions to protect its working not only from the reaction of those who will lose out – those whose 'social standing', 'social claims', and 'social assets' are threatened (cf. Polanyi 2001 [1944]: 48) – but also from the inner competitive dynamic unleashed by the profit motive among the business classes: 'even capitalist business itself had to be sheltered from the unrestricted working of the market mechanism' (Polanyi 2001 [1944]: 201). The utopian nature of market society rests therefore on its own structural infeasibility; its inability to create and maintain the preconditions for its self-reproduction, and the social costs any attempt to prop it up politically is likely to generate.

Polanyi employs a blend of historical and analytical arguments to refute the idea of the naturalness of market society. History shows us that:

> The logic of the case is, indeed, almost the opposite of that underlying the classical doctrine. The orthodox teaching started from the individual's propensity to barter; deduced from it the necessity of local markets, as well as of division of labor; and inferred, finally, the necessity of trade, eventually of foreign trade, including even long-distance trade. In the light of our present knowledge we should almost reverse the sequence of the argument.
>
> (Polanyi 2001 [1944]: 61)

Analytically, he makes clear that:

> A market economy can exist only in a market society. [...] A market economy must comprise all elements of industry, including labor, land, and money. [...] But labor and land are no other than the human beings themselves of which every society consists and the natural surroundings

> in which it exists. To include them in the market mechanism means to subordinate the substance of society itself to the laws of the market.
>
> (Polanyi 2001 [1944]: 74)

The market economy and the set of social relations and institutions it requires to work properly cannot, consequently, be the outcome of a spontaneous order but are the result of repeated and sustained political attempts to bring them into existence and maintain them. The Industrial Revolution was, on this account,

> merely the beginning of a revolution as extreme and radical as ever inflamed the minds of sectarians, but the new creed was utterly materialistic and believed that all human problems could be resolved given an unlimited amount of material commodities.
>
> (Polanyi 2001 [1944]: 42)

In relation to land, one of the three fictitious commodities discussed, he lists several 'stages in the subordination of the surface of the planet to the needs of an industrial society'. These stages are then identified as (i) 'commercialization of the soil, mobilizing the feudal revenue of the land'; (ii) 'forcing up of the production of food and organic raw materials to serve the needs of a rapidly growing industrial population on a national scale'; (iii) 'the extension of such a system of surplus production to overseas and colonial territories'. With this last step, Polanyi notes, 'land and its products were finally fitted into the scheme of a self-regulating world market' (Polanyi 2001 [1944]: 188). Similar analyses are also carried out in relation to labour and money – hence, Polanyi's stark conclusion that 'while *laissez-faire* economy was the product of deliberate state action, subsequent restrictions on *laissez-faire* started in a spontaneous way. *Laissez-faire* was planned; planning was not' (Polanyi 2001 [1944]: 147).

Such a proposition is much more than an attack on the extravagant claims of liberal ideologues old and new. First of all, it is an indictment of political economy as an intellectual discipline committed to the explanation of social change. As he puts it:

> Nowhere has liberal philosophy failed so conspicuously as in its understanding of the problem of change. Fired by an emotional faith in spontaneity, the common-sense attitude toward change was discarded in favor of a mystical readiness to accept the social consequences of economic improvement, whatever they might be. The elementary truths of political science and statecraft were first discredited, then forgotten.
>
> (Polanyi 2001 [1944]: 35)

In an almost Nietzschean manner, Polanyi develops a counter-genealogy of 'the origins of our time' based on the assumption that:

> A blind faith in spontaneous progress had taken hold of people's minds, and with the fanaticism of sectarians the most enlightened pressed forward for boundless and unregulated change in society. The effects on the lives of the people were awful beyond description. Indeed, human society would have been annihilated but for protective countermoves which blunted the action of this self-destructive mechanism.
>
> (Polanyi 2001 [1944]: 79)

This counter-genealogy will serve Polanyi's aim to develop an alternative account of change based on his notion of 'double movement' that will be the focus of the next sections.

A second, and possibly more destructive, charge against political economy is related to the political role the latter played in *The Great Transformation*. Besides its epistemic and heuristic shortcomings, it is the ideological cover supplied by political economy as discipline that Polanyi is keen to expose. To start with, he points out that the allegedly principled opposition to state intervention is a cultivated liberal myth:

> Strictly, economic liberalism is the organizing principle of a society in which industry is based on the institution of a self-regulating market. True, once such a system is approximately achieved, less intervention of one type is needed. However, this is far from saying that market system and intervention are mutually exclusive terms. For as long as that system is not established, economic liberals must and will unhesitatingly call for the intervention of the state in order to establish it, and once established, in order to maintain it. [...] The accusation of interventionism on the part of liberal writers is thus an empty slogan, implying the denunciation of one and the same set of actions according to whether they happen to approve of them or not. The only principle economic liberals can maintain without inconsistency is that of the self-regulating market, whether it involves them in interventions or not.
>
> (Polanyi 2001 [1944]: 155)

Moreover, the interventions called for by liberals sought to base society 'on a motive only rarely acknowledged as valid in the history of human societies, and certainly never before raised to the level of a justification of action and behavior in everyday life, namely, gain' (Polanyi 2001 [1944]: 31). Indeed, so forceful is Polanyi's disdain towards political economy that he gives the misleading impression that the changes set in motion by the Industrial Revolution are the result of its ideological activism: 'the most violent outburst of religious fervor in history' (Polanyi 2001 [1944]: 31) – rather than a concerted plan devised and carried out by a coalition of political and economic forces interested in imposing a novel and subtler form of domination at national and international level. In short, Polanyi's opposition to mere materialistic explanations of change leads him to overstating his case, blaming the messenger for the message.

1.3 Elements of a nonmaterialistic social and political theory of change

As an analysis of the transformations brought about by the Industrial Revolution and heuristics of change in a market society, Polanyi's masterpiece undoubtedly belongs to the 'long' nineteenth century, 'extending from the Age of Enlightenment to the end of the First World War' (Özveren 2007: 552). In many ways, it could actually be considered its closing act. *The Great Transformation* shares three main features with many of the classic works of that time: (i) the heroic ambition to retain a broad synoptic vision on complex social phenomena while subscribing to positivistic scientific values; (ii) the no less ambitious desire to derive useful normative prescriptions that aspire to be unprejudiced; (iii) a rich and fluid linguistic structure that engages the reader in creative interpretations. These characteristics render the classic texts of social theory vulnerable to critique concerning their indeterminacies and inconsistencies, especially when seen from the perspective of today's highly professionalized and specialized research communities. However, their craftsmanship makes them akin to geological sediments that can be mined repeatedly without exhausting their ability to surprise and stimulate. In this section we present the main elements composing Polanyi's theory of change by investigating their intellectual derivation and their usefulness for understanding the transformations at the roots of our own time.

1.3.1 Polanyi and classical social theory

The main influence acknowledged in Polanyi's text is that of Max Weber. From the latter's work in economic history, Polanyi derives the core element of his critique of political economy:

> The outstanding discovery of recent historical and anthropological research is that man's economy, as a rule, is submerged in his social relationships. He does not act so as to safeguard his individual interest in the possession of material goods; he acts so as to safeguard his social standing, his social claims, his social assets. He values material goods only in so far as they serve this end.
>
> (Polanyi 2001 [1944]: 48)

Other Weberian themes can be easily spotted in the text, even where not formally acknowledged. For instance, the similarities between Polanyi's remarks on the shortcoming of the Marxist theory of class conflict and his far more nuanced account of collective identity and action are too close to Weber's to be coincidental: 'class interests offer only a limited explanation of long-run movements in society. The fate of classes is much more often determined by the needs of society than the fate of society is determined by the needs of classes.' From this he concludes that 'neither the birth nor the death of classes, neither their aims nor the degree to which they attain them; neither their co-operations nor their antagonisms can be understood apart from the situation of society as a whole.' (Polanyi 2001 [1944]: 159). As with Weber, but much more forcefully than Weber himself, Polanyi rejects any materialistic account of change, be it utilitarian, historical, or dialectical, and with it both the artificial separation between economic and political domains and the attempt to subordinate the latter to the former. In essence, his work can be read as an endeavour to flesh out Weber's narrative of modernity as a process of progressive rationalization. But in doing this he focuses mainly on Weber's more pessimistic and Nietzschean passages, thus proposing an examination of rationalization as a novel form of domination; a view that will subsequently be popularized by critical theorists in Marxist hue and, arguably, find its most sophisticated expression in Foucault's studies on governmentality.[5]

While Weber may have been a key source for Polanyi's analysis, the latter's evaluation of capitalist modernity seems in important respects to be closer to that of Émile Durkheim, despite the lack of explicit reference to Durkheim in Polanyi's work. Indeed, even the intellectual development of Durkheim and Polanyi display striking similarities. Both started with a concern about the moral crisis brought about by market economy and tried to derive normative prescriptions to reduce the negative impact of social change. Later in their careers, however, they put on one side the more political aspects of their work to concentrate on the positive analysis of research ambits that could reinforce their epistemic critique of political economy: in Durkheim's case the study of elementary forms of religious life (1995 [1912]); in Polanyi's case the study of pre-modern forms of economic life. In doing so they used, in a similarly careless manner, organic metaphors and systemic terms, which have contributed to countless misunderstandings concerning their methodology and politics.

Here we would like to draw attention to a feature of Polanyi's critique of market society that shows his affinity to Durkheim and his school. In what sense does a market economy pose a mortal danger to society? For Marxist thinkers, the pivotal concept is an economic category, 'exploitation', and the various forms of 'alienation' it promotes (hence the liberal attempts to refute Marxist criticisms by showing the contribution brought about by markets to social welfare). For Polanyi such an explanation is heuristically wanting:

> a social calamity is primarily a cultural not an economic phenomenon that can be measured by income figures or population statistics. [...] Not economic exploitation, as often assumed, but the disintegration of the cultural environment of the victim is then the cause of the degradation. The economic process may, naturally, supply the vehicle of the destruction, and almost invariably economic inferiority will make the weaker yield, but the immediate cause of his undoing is not for that reason economic; it lies in the lethal injury to the institutions in which his social existence is

> embodied. The result is loss of self-respect and standards, whether the unit is a people or a class, whether the process springs from so-called 'culture conflict' or from a change in the position of a class within the confines of a society.
>
> (Polanyi 2001 [1944]: 164)

Echoing Durkheim, Polanyi's main concern seems to be 'anomie', a state of normlessness due to the absence, or weakness, of institutions and rules regulating social intercourse. By destroying pre-modern norms and values and replacing them with egotistic preoccupations and competitive pressures, market society is a formidable source of anomie. Far from being transitional and restricted to specific social and geographical contexts, the expansionary logic of the market pattern ends up imposing a generalized and permanent anomic condition that will, eventually, tear society apart. On this point, extremely insightful are the passages comparing the effects of Western imperialism to those of the British enclosures:

> To the student of early capitalism, the parallel is highly significant. The condition of some native tribes in modern Africa carries an unmistakable resemblance to that of the English laboring classes during the early years of the nineteenth century. [...] [T]he true cause of their degradation could not be more aptly described than by their existing in a "cultural vacuum" – the term used by an anthropologist to describe the cause of the cultural debasement of some of the valiant black tribes of Africa under the influence of contact with white civilization. (Polanyi 2001 [1944]: 165)

The 'cultural vacuum' Polanyi refers to is part of that general modern *malaise* Durkheim labels 'anomie', and whose negative influence far outweighs 'exploitation' as a heuristic category. Thus, Polanyi spells out that:

> it is precisely this emphasis put on exploitation which tends to hide from our view the even greater issue of cultural degeneration. If exploitation is defined in strictly economic terms as a permanent inadequacy of ratios of exchange, it is doubtful whether, as a matter of fact, there was exploitation. The catastrophe of the native community is a direct result of the rapid and violent disruption of the basic institutions of the victim (whether force is used in the process or not does not seem altogether relevant). These institutions are disrupted by the very fact that a market economy is foisted upon an entirely differently organized community; labor and land are made into commodities, which, again, is only a short formula for the liquidation of every and any cultural institution in an organic society.
>
> (Polanyi 2001 [1944]: 166–67)

1.3.2 Reaction: countermovement and double movement

The enduring and most influential part of Polanyi's *magnum opus* is undoubtedly his thesis of the 'double movement': a rationalization of the dialectical relation between the forces of change and the reaction of those opposing it. And, obviously, this also is the feature of his work that has attracted the critical attention of successive generations of social and political theorists. Polanyi's account of the double movement is introduced in Chapter 6 in a passage that is worth quoting in at length, even if in abridged form:

> To allow the market mechanism to be sole director of the fate of human beings and their natural environment, indeed, even of the amount and use of purchasing power, would result in the demolition of society. [...] Robbed of the protective covering of cultural institutions, human beings would perish from the effects of social exposure; they would die as the victims of acute social dislocation through vice, perversion, crime, and starvation. Nature would be reduced to its elements, neighborhoods and landscapes defiled, rivers polluted, military safety jeopardized, the power to produce food and raw materials destroyed. [...] But no society could stand the effects of such a system of crude fictions even for the shortest stretch of time unless its human and natural substance as well as its business organization was protected against the ravages of this satanic mill.
>
> (Polanyi 2001 [1944]: 76–77)

From this he concludes:

> Indeed, human society would have been annihilated but for protective countermoves which blunted the action of this self-destructive mechanism. Social history in the nineteenth century was thus the result of a double movement: the extension of the market organization in respect to genuine commodities was accompanied by its restriction in respect to fictitious ones. [...] Society protected itself against the perils inherent in a self-regulating market system – this was the one comprehensive feature in the history of the age.
>
> (Polanyi 2001 [1944]: 79)

A sympathetic reading of this passage would treat Polanyi's account as a rhetorical way of evaluating the market economy according to criteria of feasibility similar to those employed by political economists, while turning their conclusions upside down. A market economy, according to this perspective, requires a continuous and permanent process of disembedding that would undermine the prerequisites of a stable social order. Without external interventions to prop it up, in periods of systemic crisis a market society would, therefore, be an unstable social construct prone to implosion. Polanyi is indeed so keen to attack political economy on its own epistemic turf that he emphasizes the inconsistencies to which the latter is led when attempting to explain the waves of regulation that have arisen in the wake of the Industrial Revolution:

> Unable to adduce evidence of any such concerted effort to thwart the liberal movement, he [the liberal economist] falls back on the practically irrefutable hypothesis of covert action. This is the myth of the antiliberal conspiracy which in one form or another is common to all liberal interpretations of the events of the 1870s and 1880s.
>
> (Polanyi 2001 [1944]: 155)

Besides Polanyi's naïve optimism concerning the ability of the countermovement to neutralize the anomic effects of the market mechanism via regulation, the blend of dramatic expressions, organic metaphors, and systemic language used here raises epistemic problems that even the most sympathetic reader cannot easily ignore. We maintain that the systemic language used is misleading and that Polanyi's account can be restated in less controversial epistemic terms. Moreover, we believe the double movement supplies us with a plausible heuristic of the social changes that accompanied the rise and fall of nineteenth-century attempts to create market society. We will consider whether Polanyi's thesis supplies a useful framework for understanding and assessing the changes occurring in the post-Second World War period in the final section.

The first element worth noting in Polanyi's social history is that the countermovement is not a unitary phenomenon, but a process composed of many phases, each of which has at its 'core' distinct social actors and rationales. Polanyi identifies and discusses three main stages: (i) Speenhamland period (1795–1834); (ii) 'the hardships caused by the Poor Law Reform, in the decade following 1834'; (iii) 'the deleterious effects of a competitive labor market after 1834, until in the 1870s the recognition of the trade unions offered sufficient protection.' He notes that 'chronologically, Speenhamland antedated market economy; the decade of the Poor Law Reform Act was a transition to that economy. The last period – overlapping the former – was that of market proper.' (Polanyi 2001 [1944]: 86).[6] Speenhamland, the historical case at the centre of Polanyi's book (Chapters 7 and 8), deals with the Agricultural Revolution that preceded industrialization.[7] Here the countermovement, the resistance against the commodification of land and rural labour, is led by two main social actors, local landlords and commoners. According to Polanyi,

> the allowance system will appear as a device contrived by squirearchy to meet a situation in which physical mobility could no longer be denied to labor, while the squire wished to avoid such unsettlement of local conditions, including higher wages, as was involved in the acceptance of a free national labor market.
>
> (Polanyi 2001 [1944]: 93)

Thus, 'the supremacy of squire and parson was even enhanced […] Politically, the squire's pull with the village poor was strengthened by Speenhamland while that of the rural middle class was weakened' (Polanyi 2001 [1944]: 100–101).

At the same time, he develops a powerful analysis of the unintended consequences brought about by what will be the last act of resistance of a traditional rural order against a rising new industrial urban order. First, as already noted, there is the destruction of the rural middle class:

> The bulk of yeomanry had long vanished in the vicissitudes of the Agricultural Revolution, and the remaining lifeholders and occupying-proprietors tended to merge with the cottagers and scrap-holders into one social stratum in the eyes of the potentate of the countryside.
>
> (Polanyi 2001 [1944]: 100)

Second, a vicious dynamic undermining of the work ethic of rural labour, leading to the blurring of the distinction between working poor and paupers, is set in motion:

> Under the Speenhamland Law a man was relieved even if he was in employment, as long as his wages amounted to less than the family income granted to him by the scale. Hence, no laborer had any material interest in satisfying his employer, his income being the same whatever wages he earned […]. Within a few years the productivity of labor began to sink to that of pauper labor, thus providing an added reason for employers not to raise wages above the scale.
>
> (Polanyi 2001 [1944]: 83)

Finally, the unviability of the remedies promoted by the countermovement led to the implosion of the rural social coalition driving it, rekindling the industrial revolutionary fire that will, eventually, burn that traditional order to the ground. As if this analytical reconstruction of social change was not already complex enough, Polanyi continues to stress the differences with the countermovement that followed the Industrial Revolution first, and the one that will follow the collapse of the nineteenth century order in the 1930s. And then, adding a last twist to this narrative, he engages in a comparative analysis of European social history explaining the differences between British and Continental responses to change, and the 'social origins of dictatorship and democracy' on the old continent. These are themes that would only re-emerge in social theory some 20 years later in the work of Barrington Moore Jr. (1966) who, however, makes no reference to Polanyi's pioneering efforts.[8]

It is not our intention to mount an all-out defence of Polanyi, but it seems clear to us that the charges moved against him concerning his historical inaccuracies, and the use of simplistic binary categories (e.g. Steiner 2009) somehow miss the point and fail to do him justice. Polanyi's social history is meant to supply a rationalization of change, not its chronicle; as such, it is already far too detailed and ambitious. From time to time, this overwhelming richness leads him to summarize his arguments using simplistic organic metaphors and systemic categories. Furthermore, the tension criss-crossing the whole book between assessing social change and the shortcomings of the interpretation supplied by political economy compounds the problem and encourages misunderstanding.[9] It was perhaps the magnitude of the task and the awareness of the problems involved in accomplishing it that explains Polanyi's later intellectual development: the narrowing of his research field to economic anthropology and his choice to write only essays based on more manageable case studies (Polanyi *et al* (eds) 1957).

Such misunderstandings aside, Polanyi's account of social change is nevertheless marred by limitations that make it problematic as an analytical framework for explaining the phoenix-like ability of the liberal order to rise from its ashes. Our contention, as noted above, is that Polanyi's notion of crisis remains bound to a Marxist reading of market society as riddle with internal contradictions that will inevitably bring about its dissolution, rather than viewing crisis as part of cyclical dynamics allowing for both consolidation and renewal. In addition, we believe that Polanyi's confidence in the power of welfare policies to counterbalance the anomic effects of the market mechanism is not only unwarranted, but also inconsistent with both his theory of the state and his analysis of the perverse side-effects of regulation highlighted by the Speenhamland case study discussed above.[10]

1.4 The politics of the market: crisis, consolidation and renewal of the liberal order

1.4.1 Market self-regulation

Let us start with the first half of Polanyi's double movement: the building of a self-regulating market mechanism. Polanyi claims that a self-regulating market mechanism can work properly only within a market society; that is, a society in which labour, land, and money have been thoroughly commodified and all social institutions subordinated to the economic imperative. Like Weber (2005 [1906]) in his account of the distinct logics of the 'old' and the 'new' economy, Polanyi believes this attempt to be unique in human history: 'all economic systems known to us up to the end of feudalism in Western Europe were organized either on the principle of reciprocity or redistribution, or householding, or some combination of the three' (Polanyi 2001 [1944]: 57). To establish a market society congenial to a self-regulating market, Polanyi maintains that the behavioural traits of the classical *homo economicus* – self-interest, propensity to produce and barter, and limited sympathy – are insufficient. Thus, for him, the process requires political interventions that can remove any obstacle that could create friction within the market mechanism:

> Self-regulation implies that all production is for sale on the market and that all incomes derive from such sales. [...] Neither price, nor supply, nor demand must be fixed or regulated; only such policies and measures are in order which help to ensure the self-regulation of the market by creating conditions which make the market the only organizing power in the economic sphere.
>
> (Polanyi 2001 [1944]: 72)

This commits the political authorities engaged in the construction of market society to devise negative integration policies directed at dismantling social regulation in spheres of activity untouched by the market pattern, and preventing social re-regulation in those spheres already submitted to the market. Within this analytical scheme, the trust Polanyi places in countermovements pressing for a welfare state is misplaced. Since market forces operate in close partnership with those political forces willing to expand the market pattern, it is unlikely that the latter will intervene during periods of crisis in ways that put the self-regulating mechanism in jeopardy. Rather, political forces will be keen to preserve it from imploding in order to reactivate it at a later stage.[11]

1.4.2 Crisis: from protecting society to protecting the market order

During a crisis the movements wishing to protect society from anomic disintegration are likely to find themselves in a double bind. On the one hand, they are forced to rely on the external intervention of those very political institutions engaged in the building of market society. Unless these movements are able to renew those institutions from the ground up and maintain a tight control over them the risk is that political intervention will try to weather the crisis only to restart its pro-market activities once the danger is past. The problem faced by Polanyi on this point is even more acute than that confronting Marxists because the state here is not an epiphenomenon with limited autonomy from market forces, but a social actor that is, at the same time, independent from, and crucial for, the functioning of the market mechanism. In the Polanyian social history, the state is indeed depicted as a first mover; as a guardian and a reactivator of the liberal utopian dream; as 'market maker'. Moreover, an economic crisis that puts in danger the actual existence of the self-regulating market mechanism lends enormous political leverage to the forces that dominate state policy *vis-á-vis* the economic forces responsible for it; a leverage that can reinforce their dominant role within the liberal pro-market partnership. Thus, crisis represents an opportunity for a government to re-affirm its indispensability in defending society from the market and to activate a new cycle of market reforms; something recently and vividly illustrated in the period following the Global Financial Crisis of 2008.

On the other hand, externally enforced protective measures are liable to disrupt the market mechanism in ways that can further damage the constituencies calling for state protection, thus undermining, eventually, the social coalitions supporting the countermovement. Speenhamland is an exemplary case. Here, Polanyi notes that

> No measure was ever more universally popular. Parents were free of the care of their children, and children were no more dependent upon parents; employers could reduce wages at will and laborers were safe from hunger whether they were busy or slack; humanitarians applauded the measure as an act of mercy even though not of justice and the selfish gladly consoled themselves with the thought that though it was merciful at least it was not liberal; and even ratepayers were slow to realize what would happen to the rates under a system which proclaimed the 'right to live' whether a man earned a living wage or not.
>
> (Polanyi 2001 [1944]: 83–84)

A few pages later he explains, however, that

> This act of an ambiguous humanitarianism prevented laborers from constituting themselves an economic class and thus deprived them of the only means of staving off the fate to which they were doomed in the economic mill. [...] Speenhamland was an automaton for demolishing the standards on which any kind of society could be based. Not only did it put a premium on the shirking of work and the pretence of inadequacy, but it increased the attraction of pauperism precisely at the juncture when a man was straining to escape the fate of the destitute.
>
> (Polanyi 2001 [1944]: 103–104)

In other words, while a crisis puts the dominant political classes in a strong position *vis-à-vis* society and the market, the countermovement finds itself with little room for manoeuvre. Hence, rather than producing a generalized collapse of the liberal order, the end result of a crisis could well be the regeneration of that same order and the start of a new double movement in a cyclical fashion.

The failure of the countermovement supporting the Speenhamland legislation led to the dissolution of the rural coalition opposing the commodification of land and labour and to a restart of the political project to develop market society through industrialization. In the process rural society and its traditional power structure was neutralized and dissolved. The second phase revolves around the centralized imposition of a new round of negative integration policies that liberal propaganda has presented as *laissez-faire* solutions. Once again, Polanyi is ready to point out that 'laissez-faire itself was enforced by the state' (Polanyi 2001 [1944]: 145). In discussing the unfolding of this further double movement, he restricts his attention to the social legislation that was for him responsible for reshaping its inner dynamics along class lines: 'the Parliamentary Reform Act of 1832, which refused them [the working classes] the vote; the Poor Law Reform Act of 1834, which excluded them from relief and distinguished them from the pauper' (Polanyi 2001 [1944]: 174). Probably in an act of mercy towards the reader, Polanyi avoids discussing the parallel legislation that since the mid-1840s opened the way to the 'joint-stock company' with limited liability and legal personality (the modern business corporation), whose prominence will come to displace the model of business partnership that led the Industrial Revolution itself (Ireland 2010). The anomic effects these changes had on the work ethics of the business community of the time are no less important than those produced by the social legislation of the 1830s on the working classes.[12] Here we find the seeds of a new double movement that will lead, in time, to the deep depression of the 1930s and the attempt to restrain financial markets by 'embedding liberalism'.

The failure of the countermovement that eventually tried to contest these developments is at the root of the power politics embarked on by the various European colonial empires, which, as a side-effect, brought about the First World War. Polanyi's discussion of those events has been analysed in depth by Lacher (1999) and does not require repeating here. As for Lacher, we find Polanyi's political optimism in relation to the ability of the then incipient welfare state to solve the dilemma facing the two previous countermovements he so accurately analysed puzzling. It would have been more consistent to acknowledge the dilemma each crisis of the market experiment poses and the cyclical nature of the double movement. As Lacher puts it:

> this is the tragedy of modern history. Society's attempt to mitigate the economy's totalising demands, the defence of everything that makes us human, led to its deepest crisis and total breakdown of society precisely to the degree that this self-defence was successful.
>
> (Lacher 1999: 321)

This raises two final questions we want to mention in concluding this chapter (and to which we shall return in the concluding chapter, Chapter 7). The first, and frankly less important for us, concerns the reasons for Polanyi's surprising optimism with respect to the third instance of counter-reaction; that undertaken by society after the Second World War. This might be due to the fact that, in the end, his conception of crisis remains within the gravitational pull of Marxism and its Hegelian conception of dialectic movement. In spite of the fact that Polanyi does not subscribe to a philosophy of history, materialistic or otherwise, he tends to present the double movement as a process whose result is always a synthesis able to resolve the contradiction between thesis and antithesis; a resolution that is somehow progressive, rather than regressive or circular. This comes to the fore in the discussion of Speenhamland. The degradation of rural labourers notwithstanding, the allowance system had the effect of slowing down the pace of change and allowing the resettlement of surplus rural labour in the new urban economy. In turn, the second double movement, responsible for the industrialization of the country and its imperial expansion, caused the development of a distinctive class conscience and politics: labourism. Jointly, these two events came to preserve Britain from the fascist reaction of the 1930s.[13]

1.4.3 From double movement to cycle: on the limits of Polanyi's analysis

When we attempt to piece together the building blocks of Polanyi's theory of change: his own reading of the double movement as composed of two single macro stages, the building of a utopian market society, and the decentralized counter reaction summoned by the anomic effects produced in the process, the results are far too simplistic. A better and more accurate representation would be one where various double movements follow one another, and where countermovements are never sufficiently successful to derail the market-building partnership between the dominant economic and political forces committed to carry the project onwards. Each new cycle ends producing systemic crises whose devastating effects are progressively bigger and farther reaching, in a vortex-like pattern. The whole process comes neither to an end nor to the positive resolution sought by Polanyi's socialism. This is because a crisis represents an opportunity for the social agents composing the pro-market coalition to regenerate themselves and redefine the terms of their partnership. As we have already noted, political representative forces become the institutional reference point for countermovements looking for protection, while economic forces can carry out a process of consolidation that weeds out the most exposed forms of organization. We see this, for instance, in the irresistible hegemony acquired in the twentieth century by the modern corporation *vis-á-vis* not only the old business partnerships, but also any other alternative form of production and distribution. The rationale for the unfolding of this dynamic does not require controversial organic metaphors and systemic categories, but can be framed in sequences of micro-interactions between collective agents facing external threats and internal challenges. The important issue is not whether Polanyi's analysis can be reframed so as to avoid the various inconsistencies noted by his critics, but whether the revised version of the theory of change proposed here is at all helpful in understanding the transformation occurring in our own time. Firstly, can the evolution of the welfare state post-Second World War, its crisis, the dominant position acquired by neoliberal forces and the breakdown of the economic order they fostered in *les trente furieues* be read as the unfolding of a new (fourth) Polanyian double movement? Secondly, what can this reading tell us about the courses of action open to us that can help solve the current crisis without generating perverse side-effects that could pose an even greater risk for future generations?

Our reading here suggests that the reasons behind the breakdown of the post-war settlement supporting the welfare state are strikingly similar to those responsible for the collapse of Speenhamland. In both cases, the rights-based allowance system produced a growing popular discontent among both those who were benefiting and those who were bearing the financial burden that was in the end fatal. Even the timeline of the welfare crisis has uncanny similarities with the one that brought the Speenhamland system to an end. The erosion of public confidence in the protective measures devised started first within the constituencies that were supposed to benefit from them – rural labour in one case and industrial workers in the other – and then within the corresponding middle classes called to support it by either local rates or general taxation. Last but not least, we can observe the rise of parallel critical currents that highlight the defects of the entitlement culture fostered by those protective measures; critiques that will be crucial for repealing legislation supporting those measures and dismantling the institutions tasked with their enforcement.[14]

In a Polanyian spirit, it is possible to argue that, *mutatis mutandis*, the common reason for the collapse of those protective solutions and related countermovements is a general contradiction at the heart of the cultural enterprise that sought to restrain the market mechanism without changing the relation of social and institutional subordination required by market society. This relation of subordination is in effect retained by the main political forces supporting an ideal 'embedded liberalism', which could enjoy the benefits brought about by dynamic markets while neutralising its deleterious side-effects.[15] As we shall argue in the final chapter of this book, a resolution of that contradiction consistent with the Polanyian analytical framework proposed here would require more radical solutions. It would require a deep and wide ranging process of democratization of all ambits of social life that could not only preserve a variety of social and institutional forms, as advocated by Glasman (1996), but also rebalance the relations between them so as to eliminate any subordination to the market. In different ways, both Speenhamland and the welfare state failed to do that. Hence, we see the start of a new double movement with a further round of neoliberal pro-market policies leading to current economic, environmental, and political crises. Before engaging in this normative task, our aim is to investigate whether the development of social and political theory in the twentieth and early twenty-first centuries was at all able to overcome the limitations of the classical counterparts upon which Polanyi's theory of change rests. This will enable us to assess the latter's ability to arrive at a better account of the challenges we face in our times.

1.5 Conclusion

In this chapter we have offered a close but critical reading of Polanyi's account of the making of market society. The aim has been to sift those utopian (perhaps Christian socialist) elements from Polanyi's argument that lead him into an overly optimistic view of the powers of the double movement from the (Polanyian) analytical framework that we adopt – and seek to refine – in this volume. But the project started by Polanyi was hardly taken up by social theorists of the post-Second World War period. In the first half of the post-war period, social theory, and sociology in particular, seemed largely content to exclude economic phenomena from their purview, and to respect the disciplinary boundaries that economics had drawn around itself.[16] The publication of Mark Granovetter's 'Economic action and social structure' in 1985 marked a revival of economic sociology. However, while Granovetter drew explicitly on Polanyi's embedding/disembedding thesis, he inverted its analysis by seeking to show that even apparently disembedded economic relations remained, in fact, embedded. Such a move stripped Polanyi's argument of its critical aim and impulse (see Beckert 2009).

The second phase, from the late 1980s, which will form the prime concern of the next chapter, saw a postmodern and cultural turn in social theory. This move took social theory even further away from the modernist paradigm, of which Polanyi was a late representative. This line of analysis, we shall argue, falls behind the position advanced by classical – modernist – social theory even as it claims to have moved beyond it. This, in turn, results in a vacillation within much contemporary social thinking between a moralizing critique that has lost analytical purchase and an ambivalence that teeters on the brink of a celebration of capitalism's new cutting edge. The analytic framework we shall develop from Chapter 3 onwards emerges in opposition to this – still influential – style of analysis and seeks to revive classical social theory's critical engagement with the claims of political economy.

Notes

1 As Polanyi-Levitt and Mendell (1987: 34–35) note, 'Interestingly, it was this detour into economic anthropology which secured him a permanent place in the social sciences.'
2 This is exemplified in publications dedicated in whole or part to Polanyi's work (e.g. Blyth 2002; McRobbie and Polanyi-Levitt (eds) 2005; Nafissi 2005; Bugra and Agartan (eds) 2007; Harvey, Ramlogan and Randles (eds) 2007; Hann and Hart (eds) 2009; Dale 2010). Outside the field of Polanyian studies, there is a growing number of attempts to use his analytical framework for understanding current change (e.g. Harmes 2001; Jessop 2001; Ankarloo 2002; Helleiner 2003; Munck 2006; Levien 2007; Burgoon 2009; Caporaso and Tarrow 2009; Wang 2008; Cahill 2011; Raffer 2011).
3 A reconstruction of this tradition of thought from a neoliberal perspective can be found in Barry (1982). A philosophically more accurate account is proposed by Hamowy (1987). For a restatement see Sugden (1992).
4 The distinction between three types of justification is derived from Hamlin and Pettit (1989).
5 On these connections, and crucial differences, see Özveren (2007).
6 Roughly speaking, these three phases are related to the attempt to commodify land, labour and money, even if their chronology tends to overlap significantly. Every time the systemic crisis confronting society is explained as due mainly to the perverse side-effects produced by such an attempt in relation to each fictitious commodity. Note that this reconstruction is at odds with the one proposed by Block (2003), who singles out only two main systemic crises, considering the great depression of the 1870s and the great depression of the 1930s as part of a same double movement. In our account they pertain instead to two distinct double movements yielded by the commodification of labour and of money respectively.

7 Block and Somers (2003) have criticized Polanyi's account of Speenhamland for accepting much of the narrative set out in Royal Commission Report of 1834. Recent historical analysis, they argue, questions the assumption – common in both pro-market and left commentary – that under Speenhamland 'an income floor was inadvertently transformed into an income ceiling' (Block and Somers 2003: 284). In accepting this view, Polanyi's only recourse was to argue 'the Speenhamland incident could not be generalized to later cases of state action because it occurred before the working class was capable of mobilizing to defend its own interests' (Block and Somers 2003: 291).

8 The crucial passages, in Polanyi's nuanced account, are the following: 'The Continental laborer had not passed through the degrading pauperization of Speenhamland nor was there any parallel in his experience to the scorching fires of the New Poor Law. From the status of a villain he changed – or rather rose – to that of a factory worker, and very soon to that of an enfranchised and unionized worker. Thus he escaped the cultural catastrophe which followed in the wake of the Industrial Revolution in England.' (Polanyi 2001 [1944]: 184). And again 'Both in Germany and in Italy fascism could seize power only because it was able to use as its lever unsolved national issues, while in France as in Great Britain fascism was decisively weakened by its antipatriotism. [...] During the period 1917–23 governments occasionally sought fascist help to restore law and order: no more was needed to set the market system going. Fascism remained undeveloped. [...] In the period 1924–29, when the restoration of the market system seemed ensured, fascism faded out as a political force altogether. [...] After 1930 market economy was in a general crisis. Within a few years fascism was a world power' (Polanyi 2001 [1944]: 251).

9 Concerning the narrative, the impression is that Polanyi is using a literary devise that reminds of the montage technique (editing) theorised by Walter Benjamin in the 1930s.

10 Two slightly different accounts of Polanyi's relationship to Marxism have been offered by Block (2003) and Polanyi-Levitt and Mendell (1987). The former notes Hegelian influences similar to the ones we discuss below. His overall reconstruction of Polanyi's theory is however incompatible with the one proposed here. Block tries to defend Polanyi's politics (his support of regulation and the welfare state) against the heuristic structure of his own work. In contrast, we are trying to rescue Polanyi's theory of change from his optimistic political conclusions. Lacher (1999) develops a reading of Polanyi's double movement in which the protectionist policies adopted at the turn of the nineteenth century are understood as a response to the deep depression of the 1870s. This is compatible with the interpretation we are advancing here.

11 In more contemporary neo-institutional language, Polanyi views the state both as 'market maker' and 'market modifier'. See Caporaso and Tarrow (2009). Our argument focuses on the tensions in this dual role and on the fact that the former tends to trump the latter.

12 As early as 1862, these were neatly summarized by the then editor of *The Law Times*, in perceptive Polanyian terms: 'The Law of Partnership hitherto has been, that each partner shall be answerable for the debts and contracts of the other partners, within the reasonable scope of the business of the partnership. This law was founded upon the following principles: that he who acts through an agent ought to be responsible for his agent's acts; that policy, as well as justice, prescribes that he who shares the profit of an enterprise should be subject also to its losses; that there is a moral obligation, which it is the duty of the laws of a civilized and Christian nation to enforce, to pay debts, perform contracts and make reparation for wrongs. Limited Liability is founded on the opposite principle and is designed to enable a man to avail himself of his agent's acts, if advantageous to him, and

not to be responsible for them if they should be disadvantageous; to speculate for profits without being liable for losses; to make contracts, incur debts, and commit wrongs, the law depriving the creditor, the contractor, and the injured, of his rightful remedy against the property or the person of the wrongdoer, beyond the limit, however small, at which it may please him to determine his own liability. Thus it practically enables a trader to speculate for the chances of indefinite gain, without being liable for more than a small definite loss.' (Cox 1862: 1–2).

13 On this point we disagree with the reading proposed by Özveren (2007: 560), who attributes to Polanyi 'truncated dialectics', even if we agree with the overall thesis supported by the author in that article.

14 Townsend, Malthus and Ricardo are, for Polanyi, the main figures who contributed to the intellectual debacle of Speenhamland. The critical figures responsible for the intellectual reversal of the fortune of the post-war welfare consensus are undoubtedly Hayek (1982), Buchanan and Tullock (1962) and Friedman (1962). To these canonical champions of neoliberalism must be added Anderson (1978) – directly inspired by Polanyi's analysis of Speenhamland, and Mead (1992), whose work has had a more direct impact on policy.

15 For the notion of 'embedded liberalism' see Ruggie (1982); for a Polanyian defence of 'embedded liberalism' as a political ideal see Block (2003).

16 David Stark (2009: 7) refers to this stance as 'Parsons's Pact' – i.e. Talcott Parsons's exclusion of economics from the imperialistic ambition he had for sociology, and for structural functionalism in particular.

2 Theories of the second modernity

A critique

2.1 Introduction

In the previous chapter we set out the broad outlines of the position that we seek to develop and apply in this volume. Building on Polanyi's arguments, we provide a political, rather than economic, account of neoliberalism and of what we shall call the 'New Public Management template'. Thus our argument will not be grounded in political economy either in its liberal form, which emphasizes feasibility and the spontaneous order of the market, nor in what is normally taken to be its main rival: a political economy influenced by Marxist theory. Following Polanyi, we argued that the latter does not sufficiently break with liberalism's 'economic fallacy', the ahistorical view that the economy is separate from and prior to the broader social relations in which it is embedded. We also noted that Polanyi is himself vulnerable to the criticisms he makes of Marxism. Contra Polanyi (1947), given the cyclical nature of capitalism the belief that crises offer a genuine opportunity for a reinvigoration of markets is no mere expression of economic liberalism's 'obsolete market mentality'. However, these teleological tendencies in Polanyi's thought, rooted as they are in his ethical socialism, can be bracketed out without significantly affecting the analytical purchase that his arguments offer; indeed they run counter to the main thrust of that analytic framework.

The role of this chapter is to contextualize our position by identifying the influential strands of social theory that we seek to counter. The following chapter – Chapter 3 – will, in a more positive spirit, set out a sociological sketch of the modernist counter-narrative towards which we seek to contribute.

2.2 Contemporary social theory's critique and search for an alternative diagnosis

Contemporary social theory appears to offer a bewildering array of competing perspectives. Behind this diversity, however, lie some common themes and aims. It is with these commonalities rather than differences that we are concerned. Social theory's turn to a 'post-' or 'second' modernity is the focus here.

We might start by distinguishing between a strong and a weak postmodernist programme. The 'strong programme' – postmodernism in a strict sense – is sceptical of all grand narratives, which it associates with modernism and for which Lyotard's *The Postmodern Condition* (1984) provided the manifesto. The 'weak' postmodernist programme doubts the continued relevance of the modernist narratives that have been inherited from the late nineteenth and early twentieth centuries but does not abandon grand narrative, indeed seeks to offer one of its own.[1] While much of the intellectual excitement around postmodernist thought in the 1980s and 90s focused on the drama of the strong programme, and while this deeply influenced newer (inter- or trans-) disciplinary areas such as science and technology studies (STS), it was the weaker programme that exercised greatest influence on longer established social-science disciplines, notably political science and sociology. It is thus postmodernism in its weaker form that will be our prime concern.

The central assertion of the weak postmodernist programme is that the period leading up to and beyond the latest *fin-de-siècle* cannot be understood through concepts and categories borrowed from its predecessor. Such concepts live on but as 'zombie categories' which, while still holding sway over the imagination of social scientists, have little genuine contemporary relevance (Beck 2001). Since social theory is the product of late-nineteenth and early twentieth-century thought, such a claim amounts to a call for a radical rethink. This locks much contemporary theory into the rhetoric of historical discontinuity; into an epochal mode of analysis (Osborne 1998). The emphasis upon radical discontinuity demands a relabelling of our social condition. If classical social theory was an interpretation of *modernity*, then the task of contemporary social theory was to interpret what comes *after*. If the substantial focus of classical social theory was on industrial capitalism, urbanism, and the nation-state, then contemporary social theory must either update those categories or demonstrate their redundancy and replace them. Thus, even what we have called the weak postmodernist programme makes strong claims.

From the 1990s, social theory has provided us with a rich set of alternative labels for the social constellation that was said to have succeeded modernity: risk society (Beck 1992), reflexive modernity (Beck *et al* 1994), liquid modernity (Bauman 2000), network society (Castells 2005 and Castells 2009). But whatever the label, the structure of the argument remains the same. We shall thus take one of its most influential expressions as standing for the whole.

2.2.1 The second modernity thesis

In a collective volume that represented one of the highest profile statements of the second modernity thesis (Beck, Giddens and Lash 1994), Scott Lash (1994: 122) argued that the significance of the theory of reflexive modernity – in contrast to both modernization theory and 'postmodernist versions of critical theory' – was that it 'constituted a turn towards *zeitdiagnostische Soziologie*', sociology as a diagnosis of the times. If the political concern of the 1940s and 50s had been with the Great Depression, the rise of European fascism and the Second World War, then that of the late 1980s and 1990s was shaped by the collapse of communism, the decline of the working class as a political force in the post-industrializing societies of the West, and the emergence – post '68 – of New Social Movements, notably environmental movements and second-wave feminism. The theory of a second, or reflexive, modernity is one such response. In order to reconstruct the central claims of this position in a comprehensible fashion, we shall present the argument as a set of complementary theses – individualization, detraditionalization, and reflexivity – that seeks to identify a break with the first – 'simple' – modernity.

Individualization thesis

For Ulrich Beck (1994: 13), with whom the term is most closely associated, individualization means 'first, the disembedding and, second, the re-embedding of industrial society ways of life by new ones, in which the individuals must produce, stage and cobble together their biographies.' This shift reflects the hollowing out or fragmentation of those institutions – the welfare state, the large bureaucratic corporation, mass political parties – that provided both security and certainty: 'the disintegration of the certainties of industrial society' (Beck 1994: 14) and with it the displacement of risk from institutions onto individuals. With these new conditions one is compelled to be concerned with the 'manufacture, self-design and self-staging of one's own biography' (Beck 1994: 14) in face of the decline of historically transmitted, and long stable, institutions. Support for political parties, for example, becomes more volatile; neither a life-long affiliation nor a matter of self-understanding, identity, and belonging, but rather of shifting – and increasingly volatile – preferences.

Detraditionalization thesis

In his contribution to the same volume, Anthony Giddens focuses on the obverse side of individualization, namely on 'detraditionalization'. Here the argument is that while classical social theorists, from Marx through Tönnies, Durkheim and on to Weber, correctly saw that modernization entailed the destruction of tradition, they failed to see that this could only be partially achieved within the parameters of the first modernity because 'a *collaboration between modernity and tradition* was crucial to the earlier phases of modern social development' (Giddens 1994: 91, original emphasis). 'Early modern institutions', according to Giddens, are dependent upon both old and invented new traditions: 'formulistic truth, and associated rituals, were pressed into service in new arenas – the most important being the symbolic domain of the "nation"' (Giddens 1994: 93). It is only with the arrival of a global, reflexive, or what Giddens, rather confusingly, also calls 'high' modernity,[2] that we arrive at a truly 'post-traditional' society. The waters are somewhat muddied by the fact that Giddens claims that while there is a 'cultural evacuation' of community, traditions are not completely absent from post-traditional societies. They must, however, be 'discursively articulated' if they are to avoid descending into an 'embattled' rather than 'ascendant' fundamentalism (Giddens 1994: 100). The former – discursively articulated – course is illustrated by gender relations in which, we are assured, 'divisions between men and women, up to and including the most intimate connections between gender, sexuality, and self-identity, are publically placed in question' (Giddens 1994: 106).

Reflexivity thesis: the 'modernization of modernity'[3]

Reflexivity takes place both at the level of social structures – a reflection on rules and resources (Beck 1994: 115) – and, as Giddens (1991) in particular emphasized, at the level of the self and within the sphere of intimacy. Elements of the reflexivity thesis are already evident in the above theses. Those who are busily self-designing and self-staging their own biographies – constantly feeling their pulse, as Weber (2002 [1920]: 76) said of early Puritans – are presumably already leading something of an 'alert, conscious, and self-aware life' (Weber 2002: 72). Likewise, a tradition that has learnt to become 'discursively articulated' has presumably reached a level of reflexivity for which the term 'tradition' may no longer be appropriate – what room here for the appeal to custom; to having always done things this way; to the natural order; to all those sources of legitimation that make tradition tradition?

To the three theses developed in Beck *et al* (1994) must be added a fourth: *deterritorialization*, the weakening of the ability of nation-states and national societies to act as bounded containers (cf. Giddens 1985: 120) in the face of transnational flows of information and ideas, money, technologies, ideologies, and people, and their growing integration into transnational institutions and processes. The social sciences remain caught within 'methodological nationalism', the equation of society with the nation, and the state with the nation-state (Beck and Schnaider 2006). The onward march of globalization has turned the nation and the nation-state into further examples of zombie categories of declining relevance. At its extreme, this view requires abandoning the core category of sociology: society, which has become ineluctably and irredeemably equated with territorially bounded national societies (Urry 2000). Deterritorialization requires us to turn towards movement and mobility as the central qualities of an increasingly borderless, networked, and global world; a world in which society is dissolved into flows and 'scapes' (Appadurai 1990) (see §2.3.1).

The common theme running through the second modernity thesis is that individuals are increasingly freed from institutions, social structures, and traditions as these have become challenged by globalizing forces. Face-to-face trust is increasingly replaced by impersonal trust in expert systems (Giddens) or by a new scepticism – or at least fading deference – towards experts (Beck), the appeal to tradition gives way to reflexive argument, and old solidarities and collective identities are replaced – if at all – by new negotiated ones. Depending on whether one prefers to see the glass as half full or half empty, this either condemns us to choice, uncertainty, and individualized risk or empowers and responsibilizes us. But the fundamental message is that it does all of the above.

2.2.2 *Problematizing diagnostic sociology*

While some of the claims of second modernity theorists seem highly speculative, many of the developments that they were seeking to conceptualize were clearly taking place, and some have continued along the path identified by these authors. For example, Beck's argument concerning declining identification with political parties and the corresponding increasing volatility in voters' preference and behaviour has been confirmed by more empirically informed political science (see, for example, Mair 2013). What is more problematic is the framing of these developments and the sweeping conclusions drawn. We thus draw attention, firstly, to the problematic nature of *Zeitdiagnose* as a style of theorizing, and, secondly, we question the underlying claim that modernist analysis has been overtaken by such events and developments, and thus no longer supplies tools of analysis adequate to the task. The second, and more important, of these points we develop in §2.3.

With respect to the first issue, we might take our cue from an observation by Antonio Gramsci (1971: 171): 'it is absurd to think of a purely "objective" prediction. Anybody who makes a prediction has in fact a "programme" for whose victory he is working'. While it would be an exaggeration to say that social theory understood as *Zeitdiagnose* was working for the victory of a specific *programme*, the claim to *objective* diagnosis is hardly less problematic. *Zeitdiagnose* can – in retrospect – come to look more like a *Zeitsymptom*, a symptom of the times. This point has been forcefully made by Paul du Gay (2003) who argues that the logic of 'epochalism' in social theory – its assertion of a radical break[4] – has an affinity with influential and contemporaneous strands of management thought. More specifically, diagnostic social theory makes – albeit in a less heroic register – claims very similar to those made by the liberation management movement (e.g. Peters 1992).[5] Whereas for liberation management gurus the corrosion of those institutions that provided security (a job for life) unambiguously represents liberation – the chance to reinvent the self as an entrepreneurial self, a brand, or an *Ich-AG* (one-person concern) – for Beck (1992) it constitutes a '*Freisetzung*', a word with an apt double meaning: being set free and being made redundant. While the tone of second modernity theorists remains more ambivalent, and certainly less evangelical, than that of Peters and co., they share in common a dichotomous logic and an emphasis upon the inevitability of the decline of institutions. Both positions tend 'towards an overdramatic dichotomization that not only renders important contextual details insignificant, if not entirely invisible, but also makes the changes they outline appear largely inevitable and hence incontrovertible' (du Gay 2003: 667). Paul du Gay goes on to note the influence of such modes of thinking on administrative reform and policy – i.e. a more direct link to 'a programme' in Gramsci's sense.[6]

In our view theories of reflexive modernity are caught and vacillate between the affirmation of personal freedom critiqued by du Gay and a romanticism of civil society and non-conventional politics. With respect to the latter, we are told that reflexive modernity 'proffers a politics of radical, plural democracy, rooted in localism and the post-materialist interests of the new social movements. In brief, if simple modernity means subjugation, then reflexive modernity involves the empowering of subjects' (Lash 1994: 113). For Beck 'sub-politics', a bottom-up politics outside the institutions and conventions of normal politics, represents a form of 'self-organization': the '(reflexive) *sub-politicization of society*' (Beck 1994: 39; original emphasis). To this self-organization of civil society are ascribed moral qualities that the state, as a hierarchical structure of authority, is thought to lack. The former is more open, communicative, and democratic. In light of this, the state 'must practice self-restraint and self-abnegation' (Beck 1994: 41). The 'rule-directed' style of governing industrial society (with its simple axes of left–right/public–private) must give way to a 'rule-altering politics' in which, in the spirit of reflexivity, the very rules of the political game are up for negotiation. Only in this way can we reinvent politics as 'creative and self-creative politics' (Beck 1994: 38). As Paul Hirst (1996: 99) has noted, such an anti-statist elevation of civil society closely parallels economic liberalism's elevation of the market over the state: 'economic liberals like Hayek and post-Marxist radicals [...] seem unlikely bedfellows, but they share the belief that civil society is a spontaneous order.' Whereas, for the former, civil society is the sphere of private individuals and of private property, for the latter it is the site of progressive social forces.

In seeking to break with classical social theory, theorists of reflexive modernity have ended up retranslating some of the basic assumptions of economic liberalism into the language of social and cultural theory. Just as neoclassical justifications for the market (see Chapter 1) identified a spontaneous order in which a depersonalized force (the market's 'hidden hand') was at work, so theories of a second or reflexive modernity ascribe major social transformations to vaguely defined external forces such as 'globalization'. This tendency of social theory to 'depopulate' its texts and detach diagnosis from agency has recently been subject to something of a forensic linguistic examination by Michael Billig (2013). It is worth discussing some of his arguments here because they lend support to the general case we are making against diagnostic social theory and sociology.

The appeal of diagnostic and epochal mode of analysis – with its focus on selective trends and the inevitability of change in a specified direction – is that it lends theory authority and absolves (not least, powerful) actors of responsibility by ascribing causal powers to impersonal forces – globalization, post-Fordism, individualization, detraditionalization, etc. How this rhetorical move works is precisely Billig's concern in his detailed analysis and critique of this style of social-scientific writing (and thinking). The device that is, for

Billig, central to much of the social-scientific enterprise is the use of the noun in place of the verb (the myriad of 'izations'), which, together with a predilection for the passive over the active voice (i) removes human subjects except as recipients of external and impersonal forces – no-one is doing anything, social scientists (and social theorists) 'depopulate their texts'; (ii) gives a false impression of technical precision and thus lends authority to concepts that are 'imprecisely linked to human actions' and 'leave a gap between the concept and the world' (Billig 2013: 120 and 133); (iii) enables the social scientist or social theorist to treat abstract nouns as though they were real things with causal effects. We reify as we write, even, as Billig rather mischievously notes, as we write about something called 'reification'.

When he compares this style of social-scientific argumentation to other kinds of discourse Billig tends to refer to commerce and advertising since they – like the social scientist – have a product to promote (Billig 2013: 142). This is not wrong, but it is perhaps incomplete. Firstly, contemporary academics work in a highly competitive and international environment in which they must vie for attention in an increasingly crowded and noisy space. As Mary Douglas and Gerald Mars once observed (2003: 767), in such an environment 'anyone can compete to grab the megaphone, no holds barred; and the one who gets it also benefits from a cumulative advantage, namely that what the "superstar" says, goes'. Since the supply of megaphones is limited, finding a (new) label – a new adjective – for society is a tempting strategy, not least because it works. Secondly, in contrast to commerce and advertising, which have to kindle a desire for a particular commodity, social theorists also have to *persuade*. These are tasks that social theory has in common with a wide variety of activities beyond commerce and advertising: news commentators and bloggers, management gurus, and politicians. Each strives to have an effect on a specific audience; to make that audience see things in the way the author or speaker would wish them to. It is not merely that the label – reflexive or liquid modernity, risk society, *Erlebnisgesellschaft*,[7] etc. – gives the theory in question a brand, more importantly, the label can, if widely adopted, frame the terms of the debate.[8] The identification of impersonal, exogenous, and supposedly unstoppable forces lends the theorist authority while, as Billig points out, absolving them of the responsibility of identifying agents who, or institutions which, contribute to these processes.

But such strategies bring with them dangers and temptations. For example, the social theorist can all too easily be lured into objectifying and generalizing the experience of the milieu in which they are themselves located, and with which they are most familiar. The experience of a particular group – perhaps that which Weber (2005 [1906]) called the *Bildungsaristokratie*, the educational aristocracy – can all too easily be presented as a common experience, projected onto an entire era, and translated into a general diagnosis of the times. In speaking blithely for all of us, diagnostic sociology seems strangely unsociological.[9]

2.3 Metaphors of flows and networks

To the rhetorical moves criticised by Billig we would add one more: the use of metaphor. Social theory has always been a highly metaphorical enterprise. The metaphors found in classical social theory tended to be hard and mechanical (see Scott 1997).[10] Weber's famous 'iron cage' (or, less poetically but more accurately, 'steel-hard casing' in Kalberg's translation of *stahlhartes Gehäuse* – Weber 2002 [1920]: 123) is the most famous example of the former. Elsewhere, Weber contrasts Marx's 'dead machine' with the 'living machine' of bureaucracy, a form of 'congealed spirit' (*geronnener Geist*) (1994 [1918]: 158); a metaphor that Simmel (1996 [1911]) had already used to characterize modern culture. It is therefore not surprizing that, in the attempt to distance themselves from classical (modernist) social theory, theorists of a second modernity should reach for metaphors that were soft and fluid. Bauman's 'liquid' modernity and the ubiquitous 'network' in which information and social capital 'flow' have been the most prominent. We shall thus discuss these two central metaphors – liquidity and networks – because they have been influential – indeed, all but ubiquitous – in contemporary analysis across a broad range of themes and literatures, from organization studies through to the significant literature on (network-, partnership- or multi-level) governance in political science.

2.3.1 Metaphor 1: liquid modernity/soft capitalism

In recent social theory no one has made more of the metaphor of liquidity than Zygmunt Bauman in a series of texts (of which Bauman 2000 sets out the argument and his subsequent work has elaborated its sub-themes).[11] In the spirit of weak programme postmodernism Bauman asserts a periodization of capitalist modernity into a solid or heavy phase, and one – ours – that is liquid and 'light'.[12] Whereas the former emphasizes scale, predictability, and certainty, liquid modernity disposes of everything that stands in the way of the individual's freedom 'to choose and to act' (Bauman 2000: 5). The former represents durability, the latter is transient; the one is hardware, the other software. Liquid modernity is characterized by the loss of the modernist illusion that history has an aim (*Telos*) and by deregulation and privatization (Bauman 2000: 29). In this process big institutions – notably the state – have been weakened and – as for Beck – responsibilities have been devolved to individuals whose lives increasingly take the form of a 'task' for which they are (held) responsible. The statist logic of planning gives way to the market logic of choice, individual utility maximization, and pleasure-seeking; and to consumption. For Bauman this increase of individual *choice* is accompanied by growing powerlessness, loss of security, and civility (especially towards strangers). We must, we are told, learn to 'walk on quicksand' (Bauman 2005: ch. 6) as planning gives way to design and security declines.[13]

The most obvious contemporary influences on Bauman's analysis are Richard Sennett's account of the decline of the public sphere (1974) and changing nature of work (1998) and Beck's version of the individualization thesis and his notion of risk society. However, the single most important recent source of the 'liquid modernity' metaphor itself is possibly the work of the social geographer Nigel Thrift whom Bauman references on several occasions. Thrift (1997) speaks of 'soft', rather than liquid, capitalism, but the qualities imputed to this supposedly new phase of capitalism are very similar to Bauman's list: speed, flexibility, lightness, innovation; performativity and design rather than rules and plans. These are qualities that are embodied in the newer swifter organizational forms adopted by the contemporary firm and the kinds of managerial subjects they encourage (Thrift 2000), and are inscribed into its architecture and spatial design (Thrift 2006).

The similarities and differences between Bauman's and Thrift's take on liquid modernity/soft capitalism are instructive because they lie on the opposite sides of the normative watershed of periodizing diagnostic sociology. Firstly, Thrift emphasizes more the degree of continuity – at least of (profit) motive – as well as differences between the old and new. Secondly, and more importantly, the affinities at the level of diagnosis belie the differences at the level of evaluation, the normative assessment of these developments. The contrasting ways in which Bauman and Thrift use these metaphors illustrate the ambiguities of much contemporary social theory towards the developments it seeks to analyse.

Any assessment of Thrift's analysis of contemporary capitalism is hindered by the increasingly abstract language he has adopted and by his eschewal and almost complete lack of reference to what he most likely considers mainstream positions and literature both in social theory and social science (with selected exceptions such as Gabriele Tarde and Actor Network Theory). These are replaced by a synthesis of contemporary managerial texts and cultural theory, notably that of post-Heideggerians such as Peter Sloterdijk. While this makes it very difficult to work out exactly what Thrift's own perspective is, the move marks one advance over the strategy adopted by Bauman. While Bauman's analysis of contemporary society remains externalist – written out of an ethical/judgemental stance – Thrift, precisely because of his refusal to explicitly judge, brings us much closer to the language in which contemporary capitalism presents and understands itself. Faced with cases where the normative position of a thinker is unclear, commentators frequently take refuge in the term 'ambivalence'. But Thrift's position might be better captured by the more common-or-garden phrase begrudging respect. But it is a begrudging respect that occasionally borders on celebration of capitalism's ability not merely to incorporate critique (cf. Boltanski and Chiapello 2005 [1999]) but also to reach ever deeper into and tap our human – even pre-cognitive – capacities (Thrift 2006).

Capitalism, for Thrift, has moved beyond a phase in which land, labour, and capital (Polanyi's fictional goods) were the exclusive sources of profit to include knowledge, innovation, creativity, and talent (see also Chapter7). Thus, we are told, it is now 'talent pivot points', 'talent management', and 'talent marketplaces' that are the key to firms' profitability. Here Thrift's account on occasions comes close to the nostrums of contemporary management texts. The talented have to be identified and 'kept happy', space has to be designed in a way that facilitates 'the kinds of intensity which will allow creativity to expand', which in turn means 'adopting flat models of organization which can allow the rapid construction and prototyping of ideas' (Thrift 2008: 121). The aim is innovation: 'producing knowledge that cannot be known in advance' (Thrift 2008: 122).[14] But Thrift is too sophisticated a thinker to align himself exclusively with this position – which he can be read as merely describing – and there are observations that jar with a straightforward managerialist self-understanding: 'the rise of talent has also been paralleled by a rise in brutal, speeded-up administrative routine carried out in panoptic spaces of a very traditional kind' (Thrift 2008: 127). But this thought is left hanging. The crucial example of this comes in a shift in the argument after he makes the following claim:

> It would be quite possible to argue at this point that the world of talent was something of an illusion, restricted to the few and highly dependent upon the ministrations of a legion of people who never get an opportunity to display talent and indeed are actively dissuaded from doing so.
>
> (Thrift 2008: 129)

This line of argument is not followed up. Rather he immediately shifts attention to how the modern firm mobilizes the creative capacities of even those outside the charmed circle of those declared talented, or even those (e.g. consumers) outside the corporation.[15]

There is in Thrift's work an admirable attempt to avoid the tone of lament of much Critical Management Theory literature and social theory, but the balance is tipped too strongly in the opposite direction. What we get is an account of how a segment of contemporary business sees itself, and/or would like to be seen, filtered through and supplemented by the language of cultural theory. The equivocation in theories of a second modernity noted above – between an affirmation of new individual freedoms and civil society romanticism – here takes a different form: between the moral – perhaps almost theological – critique of Bauman and Thrift's ambiguity that can tip into – or be read as – a celebration.

Thrift's emphasis upon the innovative and creative potential of these new organizational forms can be seen in the second metaphor that has been central in contemporary social thought: the network.

2.3.2 Metaphor 2: the network

The notion of 'network' has been put to two distinct, mutually exclusive, but nonetheless sometimes confused, uses in the social sciences: as *network theory* and as an *adjectival attribution* – the network polity, network organization, network state, network society. For brevity's sake we shall refer to the latter as the *theory of networks*. *Network theory* has developed complex analytical models for broad application across a wide range of societal contexts. With some of its roots in Simmel's formal sociology (see Krackhardt 1998), it has been highly influential, particularly in economic sociology and organization studies, for example through the work of Mark Granovetter and Ronald Burt respectively. It is also closely associated and overlaps with another influential line of analysis, social capital theory (see Lin 2001 and Burt 2005) and has successfully established itself as a significant perspective within contemporary social science. It has developed highly sophisticated methodological and theoretical tools for analysing ties within and between networks and/or organizations, and the attendant advantages (or disadvantages) of an actor's location within and/or across them.

In contrast, the *theory of networks*, which is our concern, is closer to the epochal style of theorizing discussed above. Rather than seeking networks within a wide range of social contexts, the network here is understood as a distinct societal type; one that challenges alternative social arrangements, notably hierarchies and markets. In its strongest form (Castells 2009) the 'network society' and the 'network state' are, in a version of the deterritorialization thesis referred to above, said to *displace* their territorially bounded and hierarchical predecessors. In the more moderate version proposed by Grahame Thompson, which lies somewhere between network theory and the theory of networks, networks are viewed as means for coordinating social relations in a way that is distinct from hierarchies and markets, but one which supplements rather than replaces them, and which can 'organize and sustain the basic "social structure" of any society' (2003: 29). Rather than view networks as a distinct societal type (à la Castells), Thompson views them as a distinct order (Thompson 2003: 38) that can coexist alongside market and hierarchal orders. Nevertheless, for Thompson the 'network order' is of growing importance as industrial organizations, states, and the international system become increasingly reliant on this form of coordination to redress the limits and perverse effects of hierarchical and market orders. As will be evident in Chapter 3, we are perhaps somewhat more sceptical than Thompson in our suspicion that network (and indeed market) orders are frequently trumped by – and not infrequently put to the service of – hierarchical orders. But our main target here is not this moderate form of the theory of networks, but the kinds of epochal claims implicit – indeed, often explicit – in its stronger variant.

The distinction between what we have called 'network theory' and the 'theory of networks' is frequently elided in the literature. This becomes evident when we trace what has happened to the concept of the network between the classical formulation provided by Mark Granovetter (1985) and its current usage – for example in the work of Manuel Castells (e.g. 2005 and 2009) – as an adjective identifying a putative epochal break and to characterize contemporary society. Granovetter's usage displays a strong degree of continuity with American post-war organizational sociology. Philip Selznick, to take one prominent example, sought to show that formal organizations were shot through with 'informal and unavowed ties of friendship, class loyalty, power cliques, or external commitments' (1948: 27). While this posed a potential threat to formal organizations (e.g. the danger of corruption or cronyism), these informal social relations (or networks, as we would now call them) were also necessary supplements to formal structures; the latter in key respects being parasitic on the former. Networks were thus nested within organizations of many different types. Granovetter essentially retains this logic: the universality of network-like relations and their utility. A second stage arises when networks come to be seen not as supplements but as alternatives to formal hierarchical organizations (notably, Powell 1990 and Ansell 2006). This in turn sets the stage for the final move: the network becomes a societal type. This third stage is motivated by a normative as well as an analytical agenda: the implicit assumption, or explicit claim, that networks are superior; that they are less prone to the kinds of failure that dog markets and hierarchies respectively. This normative agenda was particularly evident in the early phase of governance literature in the UK where policy networks and partnership governance were thought superior to traditional and hierarchical – 'command-and-control' – styles of government (e.g. Rhodes 1997 and Ansell 2000).[16]

In this strong form, network theory translates the assumptions of reflexive modernity theorists into a concept that can be put to more direct use across a variety of fields of research in political science (e.g. policy networks), sociology (network society), and organization studies (network organizations). Castells' work has been so influential that it has come to be all but equated with the notion of the network state and network society, and has therefore drawn criticism (including from one of the authors of this volume – Palumbo 2015: 168–71). Rather than go over the network state/society debate again here, we shall take an influential account of post-hierarchical organizational form – David Stark's *The Sense of Dissonance* (2009) – as our illustration of the power of the network metaphor. This work both develops Thrift's themes of creativity and innovation, and provides a foil for our argument in Chapter 3.

What distinguishes Stark's work from the more speculative 'diagnostic sociology' discussed above is that it is grounded in thorough and long-term ethnographic research. Stark is also a highly sophisticated theorist well aware of the ambiguities in the uses of the term 'network'. He therefore characterizes the kinds of post-hierarchical organizations he analyses not as a network but as 'heterarchy'[17]: 'an organizational form of distributed intelligence in which units are laterally accountable according to diverse principles of evaluation', and which, in contrast to hierarchy, is characterized by 'more crosscutting network structures, reflecting the greater interdependencies of complex collaboration' (Stark 2009: 19). Borrowing from the language of the economy of conventions (Boltanski and Thévenot (2006) [1991]), such organizations are said to contain multiple and coexisting 'orders of worth', competing conceptions of value, justice and fairness, and criteria of judgement and evaluation.

Stark's prime concern is how such a pluralistic organizational form can be harnessed to increase the likelihood of innovation and entrepreneurship. The 'dissonance' created by competing orders of worth is not simply a source of potential conflict, but also a precondition for innovation, which Stark, following Dewey, understands as the result of 'search' 'during which you do not know what you are looking for but will recognize it when you find it' (Stark 2009: 1). Stark's entrepreneur is not a broker in Burt's (2005) sense – i.e. someone who transmits information across the 'structural holes' that lie between networks – but someone able to recombine assets in a way that facilitates 'new knowledge' (Stark 2009: 17). The heterarchy is the framework best suited to innovation and entrepreneurship and embarks 'on a radical decentralization in which virtually every unit becomes engaged in innovation' (Stark 2009: 21). It is thus the antithesis of the formal organization understood as a hierarchy based upon principles of centralization, command, and control:

> because of the greater complexity of these feedback loops [in heterarchical firms], coordination cannot be engineered, controlled, or managed hierarchically. The results of interdependence are to increase the autonomy of work units from central management. Yet, at the same time, more complex interdependence heightens the need for fine-grained coordination across increasingly autonomous units.
>
> (Stark 2009: 21)

Dissonance too needs to be organized, but this cannot be done via 'traditional' bureaucratic or Taylorist means that apply the same (rational efficiency) criteria across all activities, but rather by reporting systems that are both 'flattened' and pluralistic: 'sites of heterogeneous systems of accounting for worth' (Stark 2009: 25). The role of management here 'becomes the art of facilitating organizations that can reorganize themselves' (Stark 2009: 26). Heterarchy thus 'denotes a form of governance' (Stark 2009: 31) in which coordination is the outcome not of command-and-control but of ordered interactions.

The detailed ethnographies upon which his analysis is based – work within a socialist factory, a new-media start-up during the dot-com boom, and an arbitrage trading room – lend Stark's account considerable plausibility and authority. The heterarchical organizational form is also very appealing. It stands not only in contrast to command-and-control and to Taylorism, but also to the kinds of organizational forms encouraged by New Public Management (with which we shall be concerned later in this volume). All of the above seek to tame uncertainty – via, in the case of NPM, target setting, measurement, and the notion of a principal agent with unambiguous preferences – whereas heterarchy embraces uncertainty, viewing it as a precondition for innovation; for allowing 'distributed intelligence' to do its work. But how generalizable are these cases? Can 'heterarchy' be exported or adopted by formal organizations? Is it *the* suitable organizational form within a putative second, reflexive modernity?

Stark is cautious here noting that heterarchy is 'not a panacea' (Stark 2009: 31). But there is a danger that the text could be read precisely in this way, and there are aspects of his approach that encourage such a reading. Firstly, the three cases, while richly reported and fascinating, are perhaps atypical in that they are located in contexts where central control was declining (the Hungarian economic model – centralized planning with market elements), had not yet a chance to emerge (start-ups), or was operating in an exceptionally anarchic environment (arbitrage trading). Secondly, Stark himself does not always resist the temptation to generalize from these cases:

> Old metaphors like 'the reins of power' are misleading. So, too, is the notion that power is 'exercised' – as if it were some kind of organizational calisthenics. These metaphors of power as something that can be held or grasped are comforting, for they suggest that if power could be seized by others who do not currently hold it, then things could be righted and brought back under control. But such notions are falsely comforting, for power in its heterarchical form is suffused throughout the organization, distributed rather than concentrated.
>
> (Stark 2009: 210)

Touché! But there is an equal and opposite danger, taking order for granted and downplaying its institutional preconditions. This point has been noted by Jens Beckert when he asks 'how can one conceptualize the simultaneous occurrence of dissonance and stability in one theory?' and notes:

> The coordination of economic activities in firms and in markets presupposes both social structures that actors can take for granted and behaviour that is not completely random. Stark may take too much order for granted without explaining it from the conceptual premises he develops.
>
> (Beckert 2011: 610)

Heterarchy can too easily come to be viewed in the way markets have frequently been: as a spontaneous order. Whereas the market's 'hidden hand' creates order out of the anarchy of competing individual preferences and utilities, so Stark's heterarchy appears to create order out of multiple interactions through little more than a general acceptance of a plurality of worth and the ability to recombine in imaginative and innovative ways. Finally, Stark comes close to a more conventional diagnostic sociology – one very similar to Thrift's 'soft capitalism' – by introducing something of a *deus ex machina* into the story: 'hyperentrepreneurial capitalism' with its 'relentless search not only for new domains of activity but also for new sources of creativity'; a creativity that works best where 'unbound from hierarchical control' (Stark 2009: 206). Hyperentprepreneurial capitalism is a new label for a familiar, and much older, process: commodification and commercialization. We might well accept

Stark's argument that the breaking down of hierarchy is a means to this end where the aim is to tap sources of stifled creativity. But there are other – we shall suggest more typical – contexts where precisely the opposite is required: the concentration, stabilization, and centralization of power; more, not less, hierarchy. As we shall seek to demonstrate in the rest of this volume, where, for example, commercialization requires reclaiming state-sponsored commons (e.g. in health or educational services) for commercial purposes a very different means must be sought; one which hierarchy facilitates rather than hinders, and where creativity plays a more marginal, and less valued, role; where what is required is not creativity but compliance.

Our subsequent argument in this volume will be that the NPM template with which we shall be concerned reproduces the anti-hierarchical and anti-bureaucratic language of heterarchy, but the means adopted are distinctly 'modern' – i.e. technical and increasingly rational – and thus diverge sharply from the organizational forms reported by Stark. Before that we need return to the theme discussed earlier and make more explicit our reasons for preferring a modernist over what we have called the weak postmodernist programme.

2.4 The inescapabilty of the modernist paradigm

In Chapter 1 we presented Polanyi as perhaps the last modernist theorist, and therefore as being well placed to provide a synthesis of the intellectual tradition of which he was a late representative. Since our own position draws on this modernist strand of thought, we need to explain why we do not accept the core assertions of weak postmodernism and prefer those of its predecessor. Our argument is that in seeking to go beyond the modernist theorists of the late nineteenth and early twentieth centuries, reflexive modernity and network theorists have fallen behind the theoretical advances and critical stance of their predecessors in two respects. Firstly, in the search for novelty they have misascribed characteristics to a putative second modernity that had long been recognized as features of modernity as such. Rather than break from classical social theory, theorists of the second modernity have revisited many of its core concerns. Secondly, classical social theory took a more nuanced view. Both these points can be made with reference to the individualization thesis.

While the idea that individualism lies at the heart of modernity does not originate with Simmel – Marx's critique of the Robinson Crusoe assumptions underlying political economy is one influential earlier formulation – a specific individualization *thesis* is most closely associated with Simmel for whom individualism as an idea and social form emerged as a reaction to the corruption (in the sense of decay) of the institutions of European feudalism. It is worth quoting Simmel at some length here as the parallels to – and, more significantly, differences between – the arguments of second modernity and network theorists are striking:

> The ideal of freedom and equality, which animated the eighteenth century and which now appears to us as the fusion of two mutually exclusive

> demands, most accurately expressed the unavoidable reaction to the dominant constitution of society. It was a time when individual powers were experienced as in unbearable opposition to their social and historical bonds and form. The privileges of the upper classes such as the despotic control of trade and development [*Handel und Wandel*], the still powerful vestiges of guild constitutions as well as the intolerant coercion of the church, the unfree labour [*Fronpflichten* – i.e. *corvée*] of the peasant population, disenfranchisement in political life [*Staatsleben*], and the restrictions on municipal constitutions appeared as obsolete and decayed; as slave chains that constricted one's very breath. Out of the oppression of such institutions – which had lost all inner legitimacy – grew the ideal of the pure freedom of the individual: if only those bonds that coerce the powers of personality into their unnatural courses would break, then all inner and outer values for which the energy is present but which are politically, religiously, and economically paralyzed would unfold, and society would be led out of the epoch of historical unreason into that of natural reason.
>
> (Simmel 1995a [1904]: 273–74)[18]

The breaking down of old structures presents actors with similar dilemmas to those now more usually associated with their present-day counterparts. Weber, for example, notes that rural workers are inclined to opt for the freedoms promised by wage labour despite the loss of security this entails: 'the rural worker forsakes positions that are often more favourable, always more secure, in a search for personal freedom' (Weber 1989a [1884]: 172). This theme is picked up in Polanyi's account of the Speenhamland System (see Chapter 1), which offered security but at the price of sustaining squirearchy, supressing wages, and binding the poor to the parish (Polanyi 2001 [1944]: 127). In all these arguments the characteristics ascribed to a second modernity appear immanent within the first, undermining claims either to novelty or an epochal break. Instead, what we see looks like a normal aspect of modern market society from its inception, albeit one thrown into higher relief during every new extension of the market and of market logic.

As noted earlier, theorists of the second modernity point to specific, selective conjectural trends viewing them as evidence of an underlying – and inescapable – social, economic, and political transformation that both breaks from that which preceded it and represents a coherent, unilinear, irreversible, and long-term shift. Contrast that view with this:

> The currents of modern culture flow in two apparently opposite directions: on the one side, towards levelling out [*Nivellierung*], equalization, the production of ever more inclusive social circles via the subsumption of the most remote elements under the same conditions; on the other side towards bringing out individual traits, the independence of the

> personality, and the autonomy of its formation. Both directions are borne by the money economy.
>
> (Simmel 1983 [1886]: 83)

Here modern culture is not characterized via the simple projection of selected and one-sided trends into the future, but is presented as a combination of apparently opposite, but in fact complementary, tendencies. No individualization without the application of common rules and standards to ever-wider circles of social life. No loosening of the grip of institutions without a simultaneous tightening elsewhere. In Simmel this argument takes a philosophical-anthropological turn: life must deposit itself in form and is only fleetingly free. Individualization for Simmel is thus accompanied by the increasing power of 'objective culture' (above all, but not only, money) and the growing '*Übermacht der Gesellschaft*' (Simmel 1995b [1903]), domination of society. This is not a contradiction in any Marxian sense, or even a paradox. Rather, modernization necessarily entails a complementary duality: more freedom *and* more control; more differentiation *and* more standardization, more individualism *and* the growing domination of society. Institutions may have changed their mode of control, but they have by no means lost their grip.[19]

In sum, the account of individualism we find in the arguments of modernist social theorists is more nuanced, less selective and unilineal, and couched neither in the language of lament nor of celebration. For these reasons, it captures better the double-edged and ambivalent forces to which we continue to be subject, and it is in this modernist spirit that we shall develop our argument and analysis.

2.5 Conclusion

In this chapter we have sought to locate the arguments of this volume in opposition to the influential – weakly postmodernist – theories that have shaped much social-scientific debate over roughly the last quarter of a century, and which continue to impact on current analysis. This has entailed a critique of the basic assumptions underlying these approaches and questioning their claim to have advanced beyond the point reached by classical – modernist – social theory. The next chapter, and what follows, have a more constructive aim: to develop a modernist counternarrative. Chapter 3 will set out a sociological sketch of the approach and themes that will be refined and developed in Part II. The world we seek to capture is very different from the Panglossian 'empowering of subjects' and from Stark's heterarchy. It is one that is still recognizably modern and in which hierarchy and its instruments have been refined rather than displaced. It is also a world that is, we suggest, closer to that typically experienced by more people, one in which new forms of control have been layered over old and orders of worth are not pluralistically negotiated and evaluated but strategically and instrumentally deployed.

Notes

1 The difference between a weak and a strong postmodernism echoes Bauman's (1992) distinction between a postmodern sociology and a sociology of postmodernism. The irony here being that in the latter postmodernism itself becomes the new 'grand narrative'. The distinction between weak and strong postmodernism is sometimes fluid with writers moving from the former to the latter position. For example, Roderick Rhodes– weakly postmodernist in our sense – has given way to a stronger form of constructivist postmodernism in his more recent work with Mark Bevir. See Bevir and Rhodes (2010).
2 In the meantime the term 'high modernity' has become associated with work of James C. Scott (1998) who has something narrower – and arguably more precise – in mind, namely the state in its phase as holistic planner. See Chapter 3.
3 The phrase is Beck's (1994: 25).
4 Beck seeks to distance himself from such epochalism: 'This kind of periodization is, of course, only a heuristic device. The goal of it is *not* to introduce a problematic new evolutionary periodization according to which one era comes abruptly to an end and a new one begins' (2001: 267). But the argument is rarely couched in such modest and tentative terms.
5 An interesting and influential possible explanation of this affinity has been proposed by Boltanski and Chiapello (2005 [1999]) for whom the arguments – such as those of the liberation management movement – that contributed to the renewal of capitalism drew selectively on the radical critique of capitalism of the 1960s and 70s.
6 Perhaps the widely noted influence of Giddens on 'Third Way' politics comes closest to Gramsci's working for a 'programme.'
7 Schultze (1992): the experience/adventure society.
8 It is thus necessary to distinguish between these broad-brush labels and those that seek to identify specific practices or institutional logics that have broader impact (e.g. Power's 'audit society', 1997), or the organizing principles around which (much of) society is being (re)formed – 'capitalist', 'market', society, etc.
9 Of the three theorists we are considering here, Scott Lash comes closest to acknowledging this danger.
10 Durkheim's intentionally counterintuitive inversion of mechanical and organic (solidarity) is something of an exception.
11 For some pointed observations on Bauman's sometimes over-egged use of metaphor, see Turner (2010: 100–103).
12 Bauman's focus since the mid-1990s on the fragmentation of the self and social relations (Bauman 1995) can be traced to his earlier – more conventionally 'sociological' – analysis in *Memories of Class* (1982). That work offered an early version of the argument that the forms of discipline associated with industrial capitalism were giving way to new, but not yet fully developed, instruments of control appropriate to a context in which the 'producer role' was being displaced by consumption. With this decline of the significance of class (its transformation into memory) comes a decline of faith in state (or what Bauman calls 'corporatist') planning: 'the attempt of the corporatist, or any other, state, to introduce planned order into the intrinsically chaotic, corporations-dominated market, with the purpose of setting the capitalist economy on a steady course, are bound to remain fidgety and half-hearted' (ibid: 150).
13 As Charles Turner (2010: 173) has observed, Bauman's rejection of planned progress is neither liberal nor postmodern, but the outcome of 'a long and painful coming to terms with his own previous commitments.' The result is the substitution of an ethical for an 'active' socialism. Bauman has little alternative but to take an ethical – or even theological – turn. If one retains faith in the ends but abandons hope in the means, what other option is there but to take a moral stance and

lament the state of the world? So this is Bauman's basic dilemma: what is someone to do who retains ethical commitment to the Marxism of their earlier years but who no longer believes that there is an agent (the working class) to bring a post-capitalist society about nor an instrument (the state as holistic planner) to implement it?

14 There are clear similarities here with David Stark's (2009) notion of 'search' discussed in §2.3.2 below.

15 This vacillation is evident too in Thrift's more political writings – in collaboration with another distinguished social geographer, Ash Amin (Amin and Thrift 2013) – which are designed to stimulate new thinking on the Left. As one careful, but clearly exasperated, reviewer notes, they offer a political vision 'premised on a systematic account of how whole fields of action, practice, technology, institutionalisation, accumulation, control, and programming hang perfectly together' and reserve the task of redefining the political 'for selected philosophical traditions and favoured fields of contemporary business, consultancy and design practice' (Barnett 2013: 32 and 33). These writings also display a cavalier disregard for the vast and sophisticated literature on social movements within political science and political sociology.

16 For a critique of the effects of this normative agenda and its incorporation of a 'normative, even ideological approach where we need analysis' in the British governance literature, see Crouch 2005: 21.

17 The term is taken from 1940s' neurology (see Stark 2009: 28).

18 This discussion and the quotations used here draw on Scott (2013).

19 This last point brings us back to Polanyi's argument (see Chapter 1) that the extension of markets is made possible by more rather than less regulation, at least of specific (artificial) goods (land, money, and labour). While there is an affinity between Simmel's broad – quasi philosophical – view of modernity and Polanyi's more historical and focused analysis of the rise of market society, there is also a sense in which Simmel's position might also help us address a problem in Polanyi. There is a tension in the latter's work between his opposition to all forms of teleology – to the idea that history has an end – and his own account of the double movement which implied an inevitability: the re-embedding of the market via the introduction of regulatory measures designed to lessen its socially destructive effects – i.e. embedded liberalism. The failure to sustain this supposedly inevitable development – of which the New Deal was thought by Polanyi to be a nascent form – and the reinstallation of the pre-war market order immediately after the Second World War thus came both as a surprise and disappointment to Polanyi even as he tried to hold on to the view that such an order was 'obsolete' (1947). Expressed in Polanyian terms, what Simmel posits is not a double but a multiple movement; a continuing oscillation between the poles of control and letting go, dis- and re-embedding. This frees us both from the before-and-after model of the second modernity thesis and from vestiges of teleology in the Polanyian critique of political economy.

3 A modernist counternarrative

3.1 Introduction

In Chapter 2 we discussed influential social theories of a putative 'second' or 'reflexive' modernity. Our claim was not that all contemporary analysis has been directly influenced by theories of the second modernity – though much has – but rather that this approach is indicative of a pervasive style of analysis; one that is highly dichotomous and asserts an epochal break. In this sense theorists of the second modernity articulated at a high level of abstraction the, sometimes implicit, assumptions of much contemporary social-scientific analysis. Our aim in this chapter is to offer a counternarrative to that proposed by the weak postmodernist programme. Specifically, we offer an account that challenges two key, and complementary, claims to the effect that: (i) state capacities are in decline; (ii) there is a loosening of the hold of institutions generally and a decentralization of power within formal organizations in particular. At the first level a partial decline of command-and-control and its increasing displacement by 'soft law', 'light-touch' regulation, partnership governance, and negotiated, consensual agreement is commonly asserted; all captured in the phrase 'from government to governance'. At the second – meso, organizational – level analogous claims are made by emphasizing quasi-voluntary compliance (in place of obedience), flatter hierarchy, decentralized decision-making, and the increasing diffusion of responsibility; all captured in terms such as 'heterarchy' and 'post-bureaucracy'. Claims at both levels rely heavily on the network metaphor discussed in the previous chapter (e.g. 'policy network' 'organizational network'), and are weakly postmodernist in our sense. The aim of this chapter is to show that these claims are unwarranted; that what we see is a further concentration of power in which new instruments (e.g. soft law, flexible regulation) refine and supplement, but do not displace, command-and-control. In other words, complementary changes in the nature of state and organizational hierarchy follow a modernist logic of increasing rationalization and instrumentalization.

Fortunately, in offering this counternarrative we can draw on both classical (modernist) social theory and recent social and political analysis in its spirit. Our concern here is less with the state than with the lessons that can be drawn from analysis of the struggle between 'club rule' and regulation at state level for understanding its equivalent – guild power – at the meso level of the organization. That these two levels closely interact – indeed, are not so easily separated – will be a theme that we shall take up in Part II of this volume.

3.2 The myth of the declining state

Weber offered a definition of the state that has long remained standard in political science and political sociology as 'that human community which (successfully) lays claim to the monopoly of legitimate physical violence within a certain territory' (1994 [1919]: 310). On this view, the state is what Giddens (1985: 120) famously labelled 'a bordered power-container'. It is this equation of the state with a territorially bounded monopoly of legitimate violence that is at stake when it is claimed that the (nation-) state is being, or has been, 'hollowed out' – i.e. that government has shrunk and sovereignty 'pooled' (cf. Rhodes 1994) – in the face of globalization, privatization, and deregulation.

But this claim shares the economic-liberal assumption that more market means less state; that there is a zero-sum relationship between states and markets. This is not an uncontroversial claim and has been challenged by empirically informed analysis of the relationship between markets and state regulation. Stephen Vogel's (1996) work on regulatory reform in Japan and the UK and Michael Moran's (2003) on the British 'regulatory state' are among the best-researched and most convincing examples of such analysis. We shall draw upon their arguments to reassert the centrality of the state.

Taking telecommunications and financial services as his cases, Vogel argues that 'deregulation' misdescribes the politics of privatization that has been rigorously pursued since the era of Reagan and Thatcher. These policies are, he argues, better understood as a combination of two complementary elements: liberalization plus reregulation. Whereas deregulation implies an absolute decline in state capacities (state retreat), reregulation implies a reordering of those capacities; a 'reorganization of control' (Vogel 1996: 196). Far from seeing a decline in the state's active role in regulating market relations, this reordering of control saw the market's self-regulation being replaced by what Vogel calls 'juridical reregulation', namely juridification ('putting informal rules into legal form'); codification ('putting tacit rules into written form'); and 'improved procedures to ensure accountability' (Vogel 1996: 17). This reorganization of state capacities was a way, under changing circumstances, of pursuing familiar state aims: 'finding ways of raising government revenue and designing new mechanisms of policy implementation' (Vogel 1996: 19).

Moran's analysis complements that offered by Vogel, but he is, if anything, more explicit in arguing that the 'regulatory state' does not represent the kind of break with 'command-and-control' that theorists of governance and network governance assert: 'the British experience is hard to reconcile with these images of a world that has renounced command, turned to the management of networks, and embraced Madisonian government' (Moran 2003: 20). Indeed, Moran sees the rise of the regulatory state in Britain as a response to the crisis in what he – following David Marquand – calls 'club regulation', the 'club model', or 'club rule' that characterized Victorian Britain, and well outlived it into the 'first six or seven decades of the twentieth century' (Moran 2003: 64). The struggle against club rule requires new and more formalized forms of regulation and leads to an increase in the state's active role as – to use Polanyian terms – market maker and modifier. Regulation is no longer left to self-regulation by 'professionals and gentlemen' but increasingly institutionalized, codified, and juridified (Moran 2003: 68). While much political discourse adopted the language of 'light touch regulation', in which regulatory authority and responsibility moved 'away from public officials and agencies, towards actors and institutions in markets themselves' (Moran 2003: 70), this represented not an absolute increase in self-regulation but its 'constitutionalization' into forms of control that are sensitive to the distinct logics of the systems that are to be regulated (Moran here deploys Luhmann's notion of 'autopoiesis'). This is a move 'away from either command regulation or regulation through market alone' (Moran 2003: 72) and – as for Vogel – is evidence not of an absolute decline in state capacity but of its reordering, formalization, and strengthening.

Both Vogel and Moran view privatization as compatible with regulation; indeed as requiring more, and more sophisticated forms of, regulation. Thus, for Moran, privatization stimulates 'hyper-innovation' in systems of regulation. This last point is generalized in the literature on so-called 'regulatory capitalism' in which privatization is seen as part of 'a new division of labor between state and society' accompanied by 'a proliferation of new technologies of regulation, formalization on interinstitutional and intrainstitutional relations, and the proliferation of the mechanisms of self-regulation in the shadow of the state' (Levi-Faur, 2005: 13). Here 'regulation is both a constitutive element of capitalism [...] and the tool that moderates and socializes it' (Levi-Faur, 2005: 14). This echoes Moran who argues that hyper-innovation leads to 'hyper-politicization' in which the metropolitan elite 'has intervened increasingly in the micro-management of the system' even with respect to largely operational issues (Moran 2003: 141). For all these writers, privatization represents not so much a breakdown of the institutional pillarization between state and market to the advantage of the latter, but a form of statecraft in which the state seeks to regulate more, rather than less, closely civil society and the conduct of life via the market. It is for these reasons that it has occasionally been counterintuitively argued that privatization strengthens rather than weakens the power of political elites (cf. Hibou 2004).

With its emphasis upon rule making and regulation, Vogel's analysis is implicitly modernist. Moran, on the other hand, is quite explicit on this point. He views the hyper-innovation that has accompanied privatization as an aspect of 'high modernity'. This term he adopts from James Scott's *Seeing Like a State* (1998). However, whereas Scott equates high modernity with the state in its phase as holistic planner, for Moran its successor – the regulatory state – is no less high modernist in its ambition to:

> make transparent what was occluded; to make explicit, and if at all possible measurable, what was implicit and judgemental; and, above all, to equip the state with the capacity to have a synoptic, standardized view of regulated domains and to use that synoptic view to pursue a wide range of projects of social control.
>
> (Moran 2003: 159)

The argument that the state remains a key actor enjoying considerable leeway and autonomy in how, and for which ends, it deploys what we shall call the 'NPM template' – even under conditions of EU 'multi-level governance' – will be developed and applied in Chapter 6. Rather than pursue these questions of state and governance further at this point, we wish to draw some conclusions from these arguments concerning the continued role of state and state regulation for a closely related – and in our view equally misguided – claim by weak-programme postmodernism, namely that institutions are of declining importance and power is becoming increasingly decentred within organizations. The analysis at the level of the state developed by commentators like Moran and Vogel applies, we will argue, to all institutions that operate 'in the shadow of hierarchy' (and of the state).[1]

3.3 The myth of declining institutions and centralized authority

As the first two case studies in Part II (Chapters 4 and 5) will demonstrate, these developments at the level of the nation state go all the way down, transmitted via what we shall call the New Public Management template. Before we move on to this analysis of these instruments and their dissemination, here we shall offer a preliminary sociological sketch of what is at stake for the key actors within what we shall later – and more formally – characterize as a 'three-level game' (see the Introduction to Part II).

We start by offering a sociologically thicker description of club rule and the struggles that ensue when the power of the club is challenged either by the state or by managerial power within an organization. Club rule at the level of the state has its equivalent at the meso level of organizations in 'guild power'; self-regulation by professions and professional associations. Most commentators on professional power – Moran included – view professions as successful examples of what Weber called social closure, the monopolization of specific skills and knowledge; control over the entry and the selection process; rule setting (the right to regulate members' conduct) and policing of the group's professional ethics. Any attempt to challenge such professional power will produce a reaction among those who, as Polanyi (2001 [1944]: 48) put it, see their 'social standing,' 'social claims,' and 'social assets' threatened by change and try to defend them. There ensues a struggle between those seeking to defend their social standing and those seeking to usurp it.

That such struggles at the level of individual professions are linked to the kinds of macro-level changes in styles of state rule described by Moran, Vogel, and others has long been apparent to sociologists of the professions according to whom the power (of self-determination and self-government) of professions lies in their degree of control over (i) associations; (ii) the workplace; (iii) the market, which in turn depends on; (iv) their influence over the state (Krause 1996). If they achieve a high degree of control in these areas, professions create a space that is relatively protected from the power of centralized forces and within which the professions themselves can exercise authority over their members. However, they can only do so with the tacit agreement of, or at least the absence of active opposition from, state and market actors.

The struggle between professions and those seeking to rein in their powers can be viewed as an attempt to access and control the enclosed and relatively autonomous spaces created by professional authority, or to resist that attempt. In Elliott Krause's analysis, since the professions form merely one corner of a triangle – the other corners of which being the state and capitalism – their practices of social closure can only work if opposition from the state and/or market actors is weak. The state – and indeed the market – can act as sponsors of the professions, but they can also act as their opponents since guild power over workplaces and markets limits state and/or market control over these areas and thus places constraints on the possibilities for commercializing, and thus drawing profits from, skills and services. Krause's argument is that, with national variations of degree and timing, since the 1930s, states, in conjunction with capitalist interests and in their role as market makers, have increasingly acted against the professions: 'guild power [...] is declining as state power and capitalist power encroach upon it' (Krause 1996: 22). This opening up of workplaces and markets requires the removal of, or at least reduction in, professional autonomy – i.e. bringing professionals under the forms of control to which employees are normally subject. In the terminology of the German political sociologist Heinrich Popitz (1992), institutionalization, centralization, and stabilization of power are associated with its increasing *scope* or *reach*; its degree of *validity* (i.e. the likelihood of compliance), and an intensification of its *effectiveness* (i.e. its ability to achieve aims and to innovate). In the case of professions, the aim of such an institutionalization of power is to facilitate the further commercialization of the professional field, whether law, medicine, or education. Our argument in Part II will be that New Public Management supplies this longer-term (and ultimately state-led) challenge to the powers and autonomy of professions with new and powerful instruments, and thus accelerates the longer-term historical trend that Krause, and before him C. Wright Mills (see Chapter 7), trace back into the 1930s. Here, however, we want to continue examining the institutionalization of centralizing power and the concomitant decline in professional autonomy in sociological terms.

The struggle between groups who enjoyed a relatively high degree of professional authority and autonomy within formal organizations – particularly in the public sector – frequently takes the form of competition over non-material goods: (i) conceptions of the nature of work, the workplace/organization and its associated values and ethics; (ii) what counts as legitimate knowledge, who judges, and by which criteria. Since, viewed sociologically, this is also a struggle between status groups, while the contentious issues appear non-material – or even symbolic or ritualistic – the stakes are anything but; they concern power and access to and disposal over organizational resources. Before we examine these struggles, we wish to introduce one modification to Krause's analysis the significance of which will become clearer in Part II. It is not all professions that are subject to such measures, but those that pose a potential threat to the preferences of their principals. What we are currently witnessing is less a generalized 'death of the guilds' than a selective effort to reduce the autonomy of specific professions where that autonomy represents a barrier to reform and/or a limit to the potential of commercialization and further enclosure of the commons (see Chapter 7).

3.3.1 The struggle over ethics and organizational understanding

It has been argued that moves against professional autonomy, power, and monopoly result in a clash between the expectations of would-be reformers (managers or politicians) and professionals' vocational ethic and ethic of office. In the case, for example, of the British civil service, du Gay (2008) chronicles the tensions that, under New Labour governments, emerged between political will and procedure; between politicians' demands for results ('just do it!') and the procedural logic of civil servants' ethic of office (see also Chapter 4). From the former's perspective, such vocational ethics are viewed as barriers to flexibility and transparency rooted in a self-serving ideology; for the latter the demand for quick solutions is potentially corrosive of traditional practices that have emerged historically for good reason.[2]

But there is more at stake here than a clash of values. The struggle between professions and centralized powers (whether state or managerial) is also a struggle between two world views; between two conceptions of what a workplace and work are, and what their proper ordering and aims should be. This point can be illustrated with reference to universities and higher education, which will be the subject of more detailed analysis in Chapter 5.

While both academics and university managers view the university as a means to an end, they differ radically in their understanding of what that end is. These differences can be set out ideal-typically as follows.

> *The academic's tale.*[3] For academics, the university is an organization that facilitates the pursuit of knowledge/truth, whether through research or scholarship, and its transmission via publication and teaching. Any other benefits – including those career benefits that accrue to academics

themselves – are incidental. On this view, the university is more than an organization containing 'expert humans', it is an 'expert organization' (Mueller and Dyerson 1999); that is to say, one in which internal organization has to be aligned with the logic of those knowledge- and innovation-producing practices upon which its success depends. One aspect of this logic in the case of universities is that the pursuit of truth takes place within disciplines that define their own object, determine their own methods of investigation, and are self-reproducing. Disciplines and the walls between them are necessary because they protect the 'deep specialization' upon which not merely the success of universities is dependent, but also historically that of the societies in which they are located (see Lohmann 2004). It follows that disciplines must constitute the basic unit around which the university's organizational structure is built. The traditional department led by a Chair (US), Head of Department (UK), *Lehrstuhlinhabe* (Germany), or *direttore* (Italy) is the practical expression of this organizational imperative. Furthermore, the defence of knowledge production within disciplines demands, as a further organizational imperative, a high degree of autonomy for both individual scientists and scholars and for the disciplines within which they work. Neither academics' work nor the purposes of the university itself should be subordinate to demands that are determined, or agendas set, from outside. While they may fulfil such requirements, these must remain incidental to their core business: the production and dissemination of knowledge; the search for truth. A further and broader organizational imperative follows from this: the necessity of a high degree of institutional pillarization between the university (and the HE system) and other social institutions, including those institutions that have, at various times and to varying degrees, funded them: the church, philanthropy, private corporations, the state. Like disciplines, universities have institutional walls that must be respected if they are to perform their knowledge production and dissemination functions effectively.

The manager's tale. Things look somewhat different from the perspective of managers charged with the preservation of the university as an organization, which, like any other, must be concerned with resource acquisition and mobilization. From such a perspective, it is not the organizational structures that should follow academic practices; rather the latter must be aligned (or realigned) with the university's aims as set out in business plans, strategy documents, and mission statements. Here the academic ethic characterized above, and the practices associated with it, can appear as obstacles: inflexible, narrowly focused, self-indulgent. The attention of those who have, to borrow Weber's metaphor (1989b [1919]), found in the vocation of science[4] the daemon who holds the threads of their lives is not easily redirected towards the requirement of the contemporary 'multiversity' with its proliferating missions and stakeholders. In the university case, one managerial response has been the attempt to break down

> disciplinary walls ('silos') by encouraging inter- or trans-disciplinarity and/or by downgrading departments into 'sectors' or (in a nice irony) 'disciplines' and their chairs into 'conveners', lest they get an inflated sense of their own importance. The powers previously held by departmental chairs have, in such cases, been transferred to their academic/managerial line managers in an effort to avoid, or at least disrupt, the self-reproducing logic of academic practices. These, and many similar, measures are thought necessary because the logic that the internal organization has to follow is increasingly a business one in which organizational imperatives flow from the need to maximise – or at least maintain – resources in an increasingly competitive environment and in the face of declining levels of state support. Managers are caught between pressures from above (from the state) and bottom-up demands (in this case from students and their parents) for greater regulation and transparency. Survival in such an environment demands flexibility, innovation, and speed of response (adaptation) to changing external conditions – i.e. the precise opposite virtues to those associated with knowledge production and dissemination within disciplines.

In brief, for both parties (organizational) form should follow function. What is contested is the function. This struggle to define the appropriate nature and aims of the organizations in which professionals still work can be found, with variations, across other sectors, from hospitals to corporate law firms.

3.3.2 The struggle over the monopoly of legitimate knowledge

The struggle between the guild power of professionals and political and managerial efforts to constrain and control it can also be framed as a tussle around the monopoly of legitimate knowledge. A useful starting point is an ideal-typical distinction that Weber (1972 [1922]: 128–29) drew between two forms of knowledge within a bureaucracy: expertise (specialist and trained knowledge of a particular field – *Fachwissen*) and an insider's knowledge of the – informal as well as formal – workings of a specific organization (*Dienstwissen*).[5] Both the distinction itself, and the differences between the context in which Weber applied it and contemporary organizational forms are instructive. One way of interpreting the change from a bureaucratic to a putative post-bureaucratic organizational form is to view it as a shift in the relative weight of these two types of organizational knowledge.

Weber insists that knowledge is a key source of power and authority within a (bureaucratic) organization. It follows that the possession of knowledge is a key power resource for actors. Since, in Weber's view, office holders typically possess both expertise and operational knowledge, these form complementary power resources. In the classical bureaucracy, expertise is learnt but operational knowledge is largely amateur; picking up how a specific organization works 'on the job' and gaining insight into its (official and unofficial) secrets. Weber's view was that office holders' possession of both kinds of knowledge enhanced their ability to impose their will, and/or to resist the will of superiors. But there is an alternative way to interpret the relationship between these kinds of knowledge. Firstly, since operational knowledge has a distinct source and object it is in principle capable of being formalized, codified, and translated into technical knowledge, and thus can become a specialized field in its own right over which a knowledge monopoly can be exercised. Secondly, where this is the case, the two knowledge types can become oppositional rather than – as Weber believed – complementary. There is then the – at least theoretical – possibility that competing status groups can develop closure strategies by claiming a monopoly of one or other of these kinds of knowledge. Our argument is that this is indeed what has been happening. The shift from the bureaucratic to a 'post-bureaucratic' organizational form can be understood in terms of the struggle between these two knowledge types, or better between the status groups who consolidate their practices of social closure around a monopoly of these respective sources of organizational power.

Those with specialist expertise within a bureaucracy (e.g. civil servants in a ministry) have this in common with professionals: in both cases it is primarily their specialist knowledge (and associated skills) that is the source of their authority. It is this specialized knowledge, and the authority flowing from it, Weber argued, that offers a degree of immunity to the power of hierarchical command. In some cases the parallel is stronger: some professionals in Krause's sense – i.e. members of guild-like associations – are also employees – e.g. doctors working in public or private health care, academics working as employees of public or private universities. There is thus a tension between their status as professionals and as salaried employees; and it is around this tension that a struggle emerges.[6] The challenge for organizations seeking to reduce the free spaces that actors have acquired via their claim to a monopoly of expertise and bring those actors under the systems of control and supervision that normally apply to employees is to create an institutional framework in which operational knowledge trumps expertise. The rise of managerialism can be viewed through this lens.

Our concern here is not with the history of management ideas, which has been well documented elsewhere (see, for example, Wren 2005), but with the institutionalization of operational knowledge as a form of specialized, technical knowledge, and with the consolidation of a class of cadres around it.[7]

The period (from the 1930s) in which Krause traces the absorption of the older professions (law, medicine, the academic profession, and engineering) into the 'powers and orders'[8] of private and public corporations saw the emergence of a new profession: management. In his recent and comprehensive account of the emergence of the management profession in the United States, Rakesh Khurana (2007) argues that management as a profession found its legitimacy not in law (as is the case for the medical and legal professions) nor in public opinion (as is the case for social work and journalism) but in a new institution: the American business school, which was the invention of forward-looking institutional entrepreneurs and members of the business community in the late nineteenth century.[9] The initial aim was idealist: to set management on a professional footing in which managers were to represent the wider public interest (on the model of traditional professions) rather than the narrower interests of business. Khurana traces the subsequent decline of this ideal and its displacement 'first by a managerialist logic that emphasized professional knowledge rather than professional ideals, and ultimately by a market logic that, taken to its logical conclusion, subverts the logic of professionalism altogether' (2007: 7). In the course of this development, the mission of business school education itself has been transformed from socializing managers into a culture of professionalism – a 'calling' in Weber's sense – into providing a set of technical tools that, in our own times, is increasingly at the service of shareholder value. This process was assisted both by internal developments, notably the growing dominance of neoclassical economics, and more specifically agency theory, as a technical discipline within business schools and by external developments such as the growing pressures emerging from business school rankings, which have, for example, led schools to attract potential students via promises of higher lifetime earnings rather than a calling.

We cannot do justice here to the richness of Khuran's analysis, but we simply want to draw a selective conclusion from it, namely that managerial control has taken an increasingly technocratic turn. In the spirit of one of the founders of management thought, Henri Fayol, management has once again become a form of engineering.[10] Khuran's story – read through Weber's distinction between *Fach-* and *Dienstwissen* – is one of the translation of operational knowledge into a specialist field and a technology around which a new profession was able to coalesce. It is a classic example of what the British neo-Weberian sociologist Frank Parkin (1979) called 'usurpationary closure', a form of closure that challenges that of a more powerful status group.[11] It is to some of the features of this specialized knowledge and technology and the new powers it offers that we now turn.

Formalized and codified operational knowledge can be seen as a power resource insofar as it offers (i) a way of knowing and a synoptic view over an organization; (ii) a set of technical instruments. The latter will be discussed in §3.3.3. Here we shall confine ourselves to examining how organizational knowledge, once it has been established as a form of expertise in its own right, can generate organizational knowledge and legitimize one form of such knowledge over its rivals.

We saw above that Moran locates his analysis of the regulatory state in terms of what James Scott (1998) calls 'high modernism'. Scott's analysis also provides a useful source for our argument. Scott and his colleagues (Scott et al 2002) argue that early-modern states faced a problem that had to be resolved before the governance of society was possible. The practices of local populations – 'vernacular communities' – were illegible to would-be rulers. Local practices must first be rendered legible and their patois intelligible before these populations can be ruled. Standardization – e.g. of road names or (Scott *et al*'s main example) permanent family surnames – was a necessary condition for rendering society legible (to rulers), and thus governable:

> central to the institutional hegemony of the nation-state has been the project of synoptic legibility. Its hard-won achievement against dogged resistance – an achievement requiring massive institutional investments in creating records and the personnel to manage them – represents the armature of state knowledge. Without this synoptic grasp, without the field of vision it affords officials, most of the activities of the modern state [...] would be inconceivable.
>
> (Scott *et al* 2002: 33)

Such 'synoptic legibility' is necessary because states can only govern complex material by translating it into simplified schemata, for which Scott draws an analogy with the cadastral map via which 'the same objective standards can be applied throughout the nation' and whose completeness depends 'on its abstract sketchiness, its lack of detail – its thinness' (Scott 1998: 44). The much discussed 'audit society' (Power 1997) might thus be said to have deep historical roots.

But such 'cadastral rule' is not the province of states alone.[12] Those who seek to govern organizations in which there is a high degree of autonomy enjoyed by those who possess both expertise and operational knowledge face a similar problem to early-modern states: how to translate arcane knowledge and practices into a legible and intelligible form. To a greater or lesser degree professionals and specialists set the conditions of their own work (Krause's 'control over the workplace') and determine the criteria by which the quality of that work is to be assessed on the grounds that only they are in a position to judge; only peers can review. Challenging this claim requires the translation of the knowledge on which such judgements can be based into a less arcane language, one more intelligible to outsiders, notably managers.[13] Such a project can be presented as – and indeed often is – a response to a democratizing demand and to bottom-up calls for transparency. The responses that organizations have adopted to address this challenge are likewise similar to those adopted by early-modern states: standardization and then, on that basis, the collation of aggregate data, and, more recently, the refinement of matrices and algorithms for evaluating that data (see Chapter 5).

The means of supervision available within Weber's bureaucracy – essentially the memo, record-keeping, and the filing cabinet – were limited, and this in turn limited the means of control; of knowing whether orders issued from above and passed downwards through a chain of offices were being implemented. Compare this to the plethora of means available to the contemporary organization to ensure synoptic legibility. An incomplete list would include

Total Quality Management (TQM), knowledge repositories, bibliometrics (in the case of research output), risk matrices, annual assessment, self- and team-assessment, 360° feedback, customer satisfaction surveys, corporate-intelligence-generated data, and league tables. Such means also require 'massive institutional investments' in human resource departments and corporate intelligence units. These measures enable organizations to recode information in a way that can be deployed in strategic decision-making. Scott *et al*'s observation about the early- modern state applies no less to the contemporary corporation, whether in the private or public sector: 'both vernacular systems and state systems of, say, naming and measurement, are codes. The question is who holds the key to the code, who can break it' (2002: 33). It is this recoding of information, now aided by technology in the stricter sense (see Kallinikos *et al* 2013), that renders illegible practices legible and lends codified information a greater legitimacy – and objectivity – than professional judgement. Holding the code facilitates 'management by numbers' (Hood 2007). The transformation of managerial thought from a calling into a technology analysed by Khurana is a necessary condition for this development.

Synoptic legibility on its own is not, however, sufficient. There have to be instruments and tools available to deploy that knowledge in the service of government or, in our case, organizational governance and steering.

3.3.3 Instruments and tools

The distinction drawn above between the means by which the vernacular practices of professionals are recodified into a language intelligible to non-specialists – or specialists in another (managerial) field – and technical instruments of steering and control is somewhat artificial. These are better seen as two aspects of the use of technical instruments, and we have drawn the distinction more for organizational than for analytical reasons. It is to the latter aspect that we now turn.

Many discussions of technologies of supervision and control start (and often end) with Foucault, but here we wish to take a different route. While it would be churlish to deny that Foucauldian scholars have made a major contribution to our understanding of technological aspects of power – indeed whole fields of analysis would be unthinkable without Foucault's work – his conception of power is perhaps too defused and all-pervasive for the (more mundane?) purpose we have in mind.[14] In line with the modernist perspective adopted in this volume, our account will take a more conventionally socio-logical turn building on Weber and, in the conclusion (§3.4), on the – in the Anglophone world at least – less familiar arguments of the German sociologist Heinrich Popitz.[15]

Recent neo-institutionalist literature offers a very useful criterion of funda-mental change as ensuing 'when a multitude of actors switch from one logic of action to another' (Streeck and Thelen 2005: 18). Such a reorientation of action requires the disruption of habitual patterns of behaviour. Weber provides what, in our view, is a still useful insight into the mechanisms via which such a fundamental reorientation of the logic of action takes place. In principle there are two ideal-typical alternative paths: via conversion or via adaptation and selection. The former Weber characterizes as a 'charismatic' and the latter as a 'bureaucratic' 'revolution'.[16] Charisma seeks to 'revolutionize people "from the inside" [*von innen heraus*]' and to 'shape facts and rules according to its own revolutionary will' (Weber 1972 [1922]: 658). As the term 'revolutionary will' implies, while an effective (and instantaneous) means of altering agents' '*Gesinnung*' (their basic convictions and orientation to the world), the charismatic revolution is highly unpredictable and what Weber calls '*wirtschftsfremd*' (indifferent to criteria of efficiency and economy) (Weber 1972 [1922]d: 142). It is therefore not a suitable means of bringing about the kind of change that is compatible with rational capitalism and the legal-rational state. In contrast, the bureaucratic revolution:

> revolutionizes by *technical* means (as does every reordering of the economy), in principle 'from the outside' [*von außen her*]: first facts and rules [*Dinge und Ordnungen*] then, on that basis, people; the latter in the sense of altering the conditions to which they adapt and perhaps by increasing their opportunities to adapt to the outside world by a rational setting of ends and means.
>
> (Weber 1972 [1922]: 657–58)[17]

As Wilhelm Hennis has noted, Weber's central concern here lies with the emergence of a rational conduct of life (*Lebensführung*) and its corresponding ethos; with creating a '"soul" fit for capitalism, the soul of the *Berufsmensch*' (Hennis 2000: 71). Hennis makes the point with reference to education, which 'can only be said to have been successful if it has fostered a definite *ethos* (*Gesinnung*) [...] a particular "ethic" in the pupil' (Hennis 2000: 71). The alteration of facts and rules referred to in the above quotation can likewise be seen as an educational measure. Rules are instruments of (re)education, but ones that work not directly on the subject but via their behaviour as they – slowly – bring their beliefs into line with their action and as responses based upon emotion, passion, and prejudice are displaced by ones based upon calculation, interest, and formal rationality[18]. The mechanism here is *adaptation*, the means methodological, and the time-scale is extended – actually extended indefinitely as the level of rationality can always be increased and the techniques for ensuring it infinitely refined.

Weber's account of the bureaucratic revolution only mentions adaptation as the mechanism of altering 'the logic of action'. But if adaptation were the only mechanism there would be a problem: resistance, rule takers' refusal to adapt to externally imposed rules. Christopher Hood has given us an influential and elegant account of the power of such resistance and 'functional disruption' to extract concessions from would-be reformers and of how such 'placation' can lead to 'reverse effects', the 'very opposite of the desired effect'

(Hood 1998: 210). But, as Hennis again notes, Weber offers a second mechanism to explain changes in the logic of action, one potentially able to circumvent such a response, namely selection (*Auslese*). The selection in question is not a social Darwinian natural selection but what Breiner (2004) has called 'unnatural selection': the ways 'powers and orders' are able to select the kinds of subjects most likely to be amenable to methodical training and acquire an ethic of rational conduct. For Weber, this enables large-scale industry to select the 'kind of man' *[Mensch]* according to its 'immanent characteristics' and to 'fashion' that subject according to its needs (Weber 1924 [1908]: 37). It is this combination of adaptation and selection, and their mutually reinforcing effects, that enable any organization (not simply the large-scale industry that Weber had in mind) to anticipate and evade functional disruption in ways that Hood's analysis does not anticipate. Those who can adapt will be selected; those who cannot – or will not – adapt can be selected out or, where this is not possible, will be eventually removed through generational displacement.

3.3.4 Selection, reward, sanction

There is an extensive and influential literature on how 'quasi markets',[19] audit, performance targets, and league tables alter 'facts and rules' and how this new bureaucratic revolution affects behaviour and alters conduct. It is not necessary to rehearse those arguments again here. Instead we shall focus on a less discussed aspect following up on the theme of selection, which is in turn part of a broader question of rewards and sanctions.

One aspect of the struggle between professionals and managers is the contestation over selection: who decides and by what criteria? Organizations in which specialists and professionals (even where they are salaried employees) continue to exercise authority permit the latter to have (or at least tolerate them having) a high degree of autonomy in recruitment (Krause's 'control over the association'). One aspect of the self-reproducing logic of professional practices is the selection of those who ally themselves with the values and ethics of the profession. In practice this can mean that selection occurs according to 'homophily' criteria.[20] In this way self-recruitment encourages path dependency and criteria of selection can be decoupled from considerations of performance, or even competence, because in a selection mechanism that works in this way conformity can trump ability (see Gambetta 1998).[21] This in turn can contribute to what neo-institutionalists call 'drift' (Streeck and Thelen 2005).

Both organizational steering and the consolidation of organizational power requires the disruption of these recruitment practices (and, more broadly, systems of reward and sanction), and contemporary organizations have developed a range of measures to disrupt these potentially self-reproducing patterns: the representation of line and/or senior managers on appointment committees; the latter's right to sign off on appointments; the formalization of appointment criteria, often with extensive lists of essential and desirable skills and experience; the standardization of interview questions (sometimes justified in terms of the equal treatment of candidates); the increasing use of performance indicators that are used to assess current employees as criteria for new appointments, etc. These attempts to wrest the selection mechanism from the grasp of professionals at the point of entry are continued once initial selection has taken place. Promotion based upon performance criteria, but also performance-related pay, provide leverage over actors' behaviour in ways that automatic salary advance and promotion based upon length of service (which was typical in the kinds of bureaucracy that Weber had in mind, and which rewarded loyalty and reliability) or based on peer-review (which rewards quality as understood by peers) simply cannot.

Performance-based sanctions and incentives represent powerful tools for steering behaviour by seeking to reward not loyalty but working to target. To take just one example: many of those the American political scientist Benjamin Ginsberg (2011) dubs 'deanlets' (middle-level academic managers) are appointed on temporary contracts and given clear (but often secret) key performance indicators (KPIs) – e.g. improving the publication and grant record within their school or department. Their pay bonuses and their chances of reappointment are dependent upon fulfilling their KPIs. Thus, both rewards and sanctions are in place to ensure that deanlets align their behaviour and identify with the aims of senior managers and avoid the danger of 'going native' by misunderstanding their role as one of representing their faculty. Their success is in turn dependent upon getting those working under their line management to perform in ways that are consistent with these targets (and with their own KPIs). To assist them in this they have at their disposal other (if weaker) tools, for example workload distribution (across teaching, administration, and research), their willingness (or refusal) to support a candidate's promotion application, etc.

The control over instruments of selection, reward, and sanction do not, and cannot, work in isolation but only in conjunction with other instruments. For example, defining what performance *is* requires not merely the 'synoptic legibility' and the associated investment in information gathering and processing discussed above, but other technical innovations required for the assessment (which frequently means measurement) of the information garnered. The institutional design required for this information to be of use entails breaking down an organization into separate cost (or profit) centres for purposes of budgeting and management accounting, while the tools needed to incentivise efficiency and monitor performance range from the simple – the spreadsheet – to the highly technical – e.g. the balanced scorecard. All this too has been the subject of much debate and analysis, which we need not reprise again here.[22] Here we want to focus on aspects of these developments other than the institutional framework and its associated instruments, namely on what Vogel (1996) calls 'rule proliferation' and, more especially, on rule innovation, or hyper-innovation in Moran's terms.

3.3.5 From rule proliferation to rule innovation

Just as we noted above that the means of supervision in Weber's ideal-typical bureaucracy were limited, so too were its means of control; limited largely (or at least formally) to the rule and the command. This leads Weber to analyse bureaucratic power via binary couples, notably the order or command and its execution, and to translate the question of power into one of obedience (*Gehorsam*).[23] That the term 'obedience' has largely been replaced by 'compliance' in contemporary social science is not evidence that social scientists have become more mealy-mouthed, it represents a genuine shift in the way organizations are steered. The command and the rule present actors with alternatives: commands can be obeyed or disobeyed; rules respected, broken, or circumvented. For Weber problems of possible disobedience and rule breaking are addressed via 'rational discipline': the 'planned, trained and precise execution of a received command in which all critique is excluded' (Weber 1972 [1922]: 681). But this sounds more like the Prussian bureaucracy (or army) than it does contemporary organizations that demand both less than obedience (compliance) and sometimes more (personal – or even passionate – identification with and engagement in the organization's mission). Nevertheless, the contemporary organization, like Weber's bureaucracy, must still find a means to ensure a stable and calculable environment. What has changed is not the ends but the means.

Such new means entail not only the rule *proliferation* discussed by Vogel (1996) or Le Galès and Scott (2010), but also rule *innovation*: the introduction of new *kinds* of rules that are innovative in the sense that they do not work on the simple binary – toggle-switch – logic of obey/disobey, but engage agents in actively monitoring their own compliance.[24] Like 'light touch regulation' and 'soft law' at the level of the state, codes of (good) governance (which work on the principle of 'comply-or-explain')[25] and 'soft' (i.e. underspecified and/or voluntary) rules are, within bounds, negotiable; they do not demand obedience, or even necessarily compliance. And, just as with light touch regulation and soft law at the state level, such soft rules and non-coercive, negotiable agreements are sometimes taken as evidence of the end, or decline, of hierarchal command-and-control and its replacement by flatter hierarchy, greater delegation of power, and the emergence of post-bureaucratic, network organizational forms in which, as in partnership governance, command has been replaced by dialogue and informed consent (see, for example, Johnson *et al* 2009). An alternative interpretation – the one we would support – is to view this new regulatory regime as supplementing and refining, rather than replacing, command-and-control. For example, government agencies in which semi-voluntary codes of good governance have been introduced are still inspected by national audit bodies and remain within lines of hierarchy leading back to government.[26] What we have here is not rule replacement but *layering*; the layering of new over old rule regimes.

By layering 'soft' over 'hard' rules the simple option obey/disobey is to a degree circumvented. The French organizational sociologist David Courpasson, for example, notes that with what he calls the principle of 'reversibility' 'nothing is established any longer as a matter of fact, everyone has to prove, to demonstrate that they are more or less valuable than their colleagues or counterparts' (2000: 153). Such 'soft coercion' within the 'soft bureaucracy' contributes to 'the emergence of a political centralization of organization, in line with the development of decentralized ways of conducting their activities: jobs and responsibilities have become more decentralized, but political decisions more centralized' (Courpasson 2000: 155). Graeme Salaman makes a similar point with respect to managerial *competences* – i.e. discretion in place of the exact specification of what actions are to be taken under which circumstances:

> The competent manager, like the bureaucratic manager, is exposed to rules. It is true they are different sorts of rules: output not input, internal not external, post-action not pre-action; descriptive not prescriptive. But they remain rules nevertheless – rules which are clearly, precisely, and formally specified; rules which may be more insidious in that they hold the manager responsible for designing and managing her own behaviour in order to achieve outcomes consistent with the organization's purposes. [...] And in insisting on the key rule: that managers regulate themselves towards the achievement of defined standards – the new organization may not have superseded bureaucracy but have found its fullest expression.
>
> (Salaman 2005: 126)

The arguments made by Courpasson and Salaman – and others – describe a simultaneous loosening and tightening of control – the centralization of power and the devolution of responsibility – of the kind that Polanyi envisaged rather than the emergence of trust-, contractual-, and consent-based 'post-bureaucracy'. As Salaman suggests, these developments have led to more, and more perfected, rather than less 'bureaucracy'.[27] This is a view strikingly at odds with Stark's account of heterarchy discussed in the previous chapter. Here the layering of rules, and with them systems of evaluation, are not negotiated within a context in which the pluralism of 'orders of worth' is acknowledged and respected, but represent complex expectations that all are expected to meet, and via which all are assessed. Such a layered multiplicity of rules and criteria of evaluation also create new opportunities. The simultaneous availability of 'hard' (coercive and non-negotiable) and 'soft' (non-coercive, negotiable, and quasi-voluntary) instruments offers political principals the option of deploying one or the other type of instrument according to their suitability for particular purposes, contexts, and actors. This aspect will be more fully explored in Chapters 6 and 7.

3.4 Conclusion: the concentration of power or the diversification of its forms?

We characterized the account of organizational power proposed here as 'conventionally sociological'. But perhaps in (at least) one respect it is too conventional. We have presented the struggle between status groups as one over the monopoly of power resources, from legitimate knowledge to selection mechanisms. This leads – perhaps more-or-less automatically – to an emphasis upon the *concentration* of power. However, the above discussion of the layering of power regimes implies not simply a quantitative growth and concentration of power resources but also a shift in the *type* of power in question. By way of conclusion, we wish to follow this up with reference to Heinrich Popitz's ideal-type of distinct forms of power.

As we mentioned briefly above (§3.3), Popitz understands the institutionalization of power in terms of its increasing *scope* or *reach*; its degree of *validity* (i.e. the likelihood of compliance) and an intensification of its *effectiveness* (i.e. its ability to achieve aims and to innovate). Understanding this requires a disaggregation of power into distinct types rather than treating it as a homogenous category. To this end Popitz identifies four non-reducible basic forms:

1 The power of action (*Aktionsmacht*) grounded in our ability to injure and conversely our vulnerability to injury, whether physical or economic. The force of pure action-power (violence) lies in the fact that inflicting harm is experienced 'not as a partial but as vigorous and generalized subjugation' (Popitz 1992: 46). Nevertheless, action-power requires actions that are discrete, short-lived, and need to be repeated each time such power is exercised, and has a natural limit: the death of the subject (including self-inflicted death) upon whom injury is visited.
2 *Instrumental power* grounded in punishment and reward is more durable since the threat of punishment and the promise of reward can substitute for the acts themselves. Such power feeds off uncertainty concerning the future; our fears and hopes, which can be manipulated in such a way that we may become the 'tool of another's will' (Popitz 1992: 27). With instrumental power we are still at the level of individual will: who is able to impose their will even in the face of opposition and resistance (in this sense, instrumental power is close to Weber's definition of power as such).
3 *Authoritative power*: this is a form of 'internal power' that requires no direct action (or threat of action) but is grounded in the subordinate subject's willingness to follow; to pattern their conduct on the example or the exhortations of the powerful. With this form of power we find not only durability but also a form of dependence based upon *authority*.
4 The power to establish factual realities, somewhat in the sense of the colloquial phrase (or cliché) 'creating facts on the ground' (*Datensetzende Macht*). For Popitz, such fact-setting power is grounded in our technical

ability to use and to shape the natural world. He traces it to our productive intelligence and ability to create fixed (physical) boundaries to our, and others', spheres of action.

Popitz is fully aware that these forms of power are rarely, if ever, found in isolation, and that there are complex complementarities between them (Popitz 1992: 36). Nevertheless, there is a general progression from the least durable and stable form to forms that are depersonalized and more economic. The *sporadic power* of violence gives way to *standardizing power*[28] in which dependent subjects can be influenced across a range of behaviours ('an always-if-then obedience', Popitz 1992: 239) and to *positional power*,[29] the consolidation of standardizing power into institutions transcending the personal.

If we think back to the previous discussion, viewed through Popitz's schema, what we have been discussing is not merely competition over power resources, but the deployment of different and competing forms of power. Professional power comes close to Popitz's authoritative power, while managers deploy both instrumental (reward and sanctions) and fact-setting power. For Popitz the last is the most 'perfected' form:

> In altering the world of objects we create 'facts' [*Daten*] to which others are exposed. We exercise a kind of material power; a *fact-setting power*, in which the effect of the power-holder over those affected by it is conveyed by objects.
>
> (Popitz 1992: 167)[30]

The objects Popitz has in mind are physical ones that constrain (a glacis, a ditch, a wall, a fence) or both constrain and enable (a road, a rail track). To make use of this schema we would have to widen the notion of an object or fact to include 'non-physical objects'.[31] It would then be possible to extend Popitz's view that 'the perfection of technical means is in many areas assisted by the perfection of the enduring exercise of power' (Popitz 1992: 179) to include social technologies understood as rule or domination (*Herrschaft*) in his sense, that is (i) depersonalized; (ii) formalized – i.e. translated into binding rules, regulations, laws; (iii) integrated into a broader social order, and thus 'consolidated' (Popitz 1992: 234).

The discussion of the NPM template that follows is our attempt to analyse 'fact-setting power' in this extended sense; as a social technology that increases the scope, effectiveness, and validity of power and not merely its concentration and centralization.

Notes

1 The phrase 'in the shadow of hierarchy' entered the literature via Scharpf (1993).

2 Paul du Gay's argument builds on Weber, and professional ethics and the ethic of office (respectively, *Berufsethik* and *Amtsethik*) are Weberian terms.

3 We are presenting this in this polarized fashion for heuristic reasons. It has been, very plausibly, argued that universities are 'super complex' organizations in which it makes little sense to speak of an academic ethic in the singular (Barnett 2003). As we present it here, the academic's perspective is close to the 'traditional' view more strongly found in some disciplines (the humanities and parts of the social sciences) and among a generation of senior academics. This is the vision of the university defended by Ginsberg (2011). We also know from Fritz Ringer's classical account of the German university that the model most closely approximating Ginsberg's ideal – the so-called Humboldtian university – was riven by status rivalry between colleagues and across generations (Ringer 1969). The plurality of views among academics and the frustrations of many with 'traditional' academic practices is a resource that can be – and has often been – harnessed by reformers. See Chapter 5.

4 'Science' in German (*Wissenschaft*) includes both the natural sciences and the humanities; both research and scholarship.

5 The English translation (1978, volume one: 225) has 'technical knowledge' for *Fachwissen* and 'knowledge growing out of experience in service' for *Dienstwissen*. We have rendered *Fachwissen* more generically as 'expertise' and *Dienstwissen* as 'operational knowledge', understood as knowledge of the formal and informal workings and secrets of an organization. We have translated these terms in this way because our argument is that *Dienstwissen* can itself become a form of technical and expert knowledge in a way that Weber did not – or could not have – anticipated.

6 We shall take up this theme again in Chapter 7 as it is central to C. Wright Mill's analysis.

7 This was the subject of a significant sociological study of the French case by Luc Boltanski (1987).

8 The term is taken from Hennis (2000).

9 The first business school – the Wharton School – was founded at the University of Pennsylvania in the early 1880s.

10 The two pioneers of scientific management (Henri Fayol in France and Frederick Wilson Taylor in the US) were both engineers; an apt confirmation of Weber's characterization of bureaucracy as a 'living machine' (1994 [1918]: 158).

11 Parkin (1979) distinguished between the 'exclusory' practices of established status groups and the 'usurpationary' strategies of challengers.

12 Scott's brilliant polemic *Seeing Like a State* was aimed squarely at the 'high-modern' state and at the perverse effects of holistic state planning. This led some critics to interpret it as an attempt to rewrite Hayek's critique of the state. But Scott's critique owes more to anarchist political thought than to neoliberalism. Nonetheless, it leads him to largely miss the opportunity to apply his analysis to corporations, and not simply in their classical – high-modern – bureaucratic form.

13 Similar arguments can be found in Foucauldian analysis. For example, Nikolas Rose (1999: 152) notes that professionals' newly acquired budgetary responsibility 'requires them to calculate their action not in the esoteric languages of their own expertise but by translating them into costs and benefits that can be given an accounting value.'

14 Steven Lukes, for example, notes that Foucault's conception of power is caught between the strong claim that the subject is constituted through power – a view which 'conveys a one-sided, monolithic image of unidirectional control' (Lukes 2005: 93) – and, as a response to criticisms, a weaker version that makes too many concessions to a more conventional sociological account and thus deradicalizes his analysis. Despite his scepticism, even Lukes concedes that Foucault succeeded in creating a 'successful and progressive research programme' (Lukes 2005: 98).

15 Popitz's major work – *Phänomene der Macht* – has only recently appeared in an English translation by Gianfranco Poggi (2017). This was too late for us, and the

translations we shall use are our own, and may not correspond to what will be the standard translation.

16 This distinction has been discussed by Le Galès and Scott (2010), so we offer a brief reprise of the argument here.

17 These are the authors' translations. The significant difference to the standard translation (Weber 1978, volume 2: 1116) is that we have translated *Dinge und Ordnungen* as 'facts and rules' rather than as 'material and social orders/ conditions.'

18 There are similarities to Albert Hirschman's arguments in *The Passions and the Interests* (1997 [1977]), which we shall not pursue here.

19 The concept of 'quasi markets' was introduced by Julian le Grand (1991), and has been the subject of analysis – and critique – ever since. On audit, see Power (1997) and Strathern (ed.) 2000. On performance targets, see, for example, Hood and Dixon (2010). On the disciplining power of league tables and rankings, see Sanders and Espeland (2009).

20 Namely, selection – or, more broadly, liking – grounded in attraction towards similarity ('birds of a feather stick together'), or what in German is vividly called *Stallgeruch*, the smell of the stables in which you were reared. The notion of homophily (and its opposite, heterophily) is central to network and social capital theory. See, for example, Lin (2001).

21 We might note a potential irony of these changes in the selection and reward mechanisms. There were (and are) good reasons for avoiding homophily criteria and institutional drift, and for applying more meritocratic standards. But another potential problem emerges: the homophily mechanism returns, but now filled with a different content: harmonizing with the values of managers. That too may well be incompatible with selection (and reward) based upon ability.

22 Indeed, a whole field of research – Critical Management Studies (CMS) – has developed to analyse – and critique – these management practices and tools. In an irony not lost on the community, CMS has itself become institutionalized within (particularly UK) business schools. See Rowlinson and Hassard (2011).

23 That binary opposition is still not uncommon and still useful in social analysis is evident in the rule maker/rule taker distinction in neo-institutionalist literature: 'regimes involve rule makers and rule takers, the former setting and modifying, often in conflict and competition, the rules with which the latter are expected to comply' (Streeck and Thelen 2005: 13).

24 Or what Foucauldian scholars call 'responsiblization'. See Rose (1999).

25 Governance codes were developed within the financial sector (in stock markets) as a response to financial scandals and have since enjoyed – with national variation – worldwide dissemination. See Aguilera and Cuervo-Cazurra (2004); Enrione *et al* (2006); and Haxhi (2010).

26 One key feature of codes of governance is that they are intended to be applied flexibly through the recommendation of best practices. No organization is expected to comply to the letter, but to adapt the code to its own needs and operations. For Seidl, a governance code is just that, a code: 'observational distinctions that create a particular reality for the observers using them for observing the governance of corporations' (Seidl 2007: 708). The comply-or-explain principle that underlies them works most effectively where 'secondary schemas' of observation emerge in practice within the 'self-activating cycles of mutual observations between the focal companies and their external observers' (Seidl 2007: 721).

27 This point has been developed recently, in a highly polemical fashion, by David Graeber (2015) and, in more measured tones, by Béatrice Hibou (2015).

28 *Normierende Macht* does not mean normative, but normed – i.e. a set of common standards broadly applied.

29 *Positionalisierung von Macht* – the nomenclature appears to be Popitz's own.

30 There are clear similarities here to Weber's characterization of the bureaucratic revolution brought about by creating new facts and rules – see above.

31 The reduction of objects to physical objects follows from Popitz's philosophical anthropology. But the distinction between physical and social technologies is difficult to maintain. For example, are flight paths and shipping lanes natural or social objects?

Part II

Models and cases: the New Public Management template

Introduction. New Public Management as a fruit machine: explaining public service reform as a three-level game

In this second part we discuss three case studies dealing with the application of New Public Management (NPM) techniques to distinct fields of activity within the public sector. The first concerns the transformation of the British civil service, the second considers the changes taking place in British higher education (HE) and the third deals with the role played by EU integration policies in the diffusion of the NPM template across Europe. The two British case studies have been chosen because they are at the root of the development of the NPM template. EU integration policies in those same fields have been chosen because they are for us paradigmatic of the process of policy dissemination promoted by transnational authorities under the aegis of good governance programmes. Before introducing the case studies, we wish to spell out the nature of the more empirical endeavour carried out in this part. We start by explaining what we mean by the expression 'NPM template': what characterizes the disparate features which, according to us, make up the NPM programme of government, the threads which link together the various component parts making them an integrated whole, and the ways in which this whole can be used as a flexible template to be adapted in distinct policy areas and cultural contexts. We seek to show that NPM is more than a set of Chinese boxes containing each other in turn; it comes closer to resembling a fruit machine where the different policy options can be spun independently of each other, producing changeable combinations of the basic template.

Following this account of NPM, we then consider three alternative readings of NPM's related reform processes experienced first in Britain and then across Europe. The first is what we call the 'ideology thesis'; namely the power attributed to neoliberal ideas in politics, policy making, organizational and managerial issues, and as a postmodern cultural phenomenon at large. The second perspective to be considered is what we label the 'functional thesis'; a perspective that views political and institutional change as derived from systemic dynamics selecting the most efficient innovations. The third reading of NPM identified is the 'depoliticization thesis'; an account of change that stresses the role of statecraft and power politics in imposing change and dictating its direction and pace. In assessing the relative plausibility of these three alternative readings of NPM (and related accounts of change), our intention is to defend the 'modernist' rationalization proposed by the supporters of the depoliticization thesis against the postmodernist rationalizations advanced by the supporters of the ideology thesis on the one hand and the functional thesis on the other. Finally, we shall explain the structure of the three case studies developed in this part, highlighting the different aspects considered in each of them so as to avoid repetition and improve the understanding of complementary aspects of the overall reform process.

The NPM: from a set of Chinese boxes to a fruit machine

According to many policy analysts and practitioners, the impetus behind the development of NPM techniques (in the Anglo sphere first and worldwide afterwards) has been the introduction of market discipline into the public sector. Supporters and critics alike share this belief and employ the tenets of liberal political economy to show either the improvements or shortcomings yielded by such an attempt. In assessing the value of this hypothesis, our first step is to distinguish between three sets of policy tools comprising the NPM as a neoliberal policy template: privatization, liberalization, and marketization. We understand these terms as follows:

- Privatization refers to legislative changes directed at altering the ownership of assets, or the legal status of organizations and contractual arrangements, so as to move them from one normative framework (public law) to another (private law). Privatization has been carried out in three main areas: that of state industries (P1), that of public services (P2) and that of administrative agencies (P3). Although privatization is often associated with consumer choice and competition between independent suppliers, the two are conceptually distinct. What makes choice and competition possible is not a mere change in ownership and legal status, but the introduction of novel regulatory regimes aimed at fostering choice and competition.
- The term liberalization covers three main sets of action intending to introduce these novel regulatory regimes: (L1) withdrawal of regulatory power (deregulation), (L2) reaffirmation of regulatory power (regulation), and (L3) shift in the modes of regulation (re-regulation). In the first case, L1, state actors are barred from using authoritative powers in given realms and regulation is here established in informal ways, by social norms or corporate rules. In the second case, L2, previously autonomous realms of social and corporate activity are brought under the

authoritative supervision of state actors. L3 identifies forms of intervention via which state agents force societal and corporate actors to shift between modes of regulation (which can in turn be located along the continuum whose poles are statute law on the one side and self-regulation on the other).

- Marketization refers to the proactive creation of competitive dynamics in areas of activities where the ownership of assets and contractual practices remain under public legal status. This is achieved by introducing changes that establish a market-like system of incentives, evaluate individual performance through peer-review or independent systems of audit, and reward individual performance according to the results. The outcomes of these changes have been threefold: (M1) the imposition of compulsory competitive tendering (CCT) practices designed to externalize the production of in-house services whenever this could realize value for money; (M2) the creation of quasi-markets among the executive agencies which have been hived off from large departmental structures; (M3) the development of market-testing techniques aimed at the definition of competitive price systems.

From the outset, it is clear that we are dealing with policy sets resembling Chinese boxes, which obviously need to be first unpacked in order to be able to analyze their inner components. Once this is done, we discover that they contain each other: privatization contains elements of liberalization and marketization, liberalization contains elements of privatization and marketization, and marketization contains elements of privatization and liberalization. The next step requires understanding whether and how those policy sets are interconnected. If privatization does not lead to choice and competition *per se*, liberalization does not engender a free-market system of contractual exchanges either, nor does marketization bring about systems of incentives rewarding individual performance *by fiat*. This is why different combinations of the inner elements making up these distinct policy sets are used in diverse policy areas at a given time to bring about the desired type of change. In turn, these combinations of policy instruments tend to change over time because either policy designers need to take into account possible unintended side-effects or 'reverse effects' (Hood 1998), or else because they are part of sophisticated conditional strategies adopted to neutralize counter-reactions and free-riding behaviour. It is in this sense that NPM needs to be thought of as a template that can be customized to suit the distinct needs and requirements of those interested in adopting it across policy areas, organizational boundaries, and cultural contexts.

In order to make these patterns of political and institutional change that have emerged in the decades following Margaret Thatcher's election in 1979 more vivid; we draw an analogy between the way in which polity instruments have been deployed and a fruit-machine game. As in the original game, the policy space is composed of three independent alternative sets each of which is made up of three smaller building blocks reproducing

Figure II.1 An artist's impression of the NPM fruit machine (Daniel Scott, 2016)

combinations of similarly shaped policy sets which can be operationalized independently of each other and periodically revised and recombined (see Figure II.1).

The case studies brought together in this part will be analyzed from this game-like perspective. In doing so, we want to develop the following elements:

- a methodology for assessing the degree of plausibility of alternative accounts of the political and institutional change brought about by NPM reforms of the public sector;
- a heuristic framework for analyzing the interconnected nature of political and institutional change across distinct policy domains;
- a dynamic account of the process that has accompanied the birth, development, and diffusion of the NPM policy template across policy areas, levels of government, and countries.

NPM, and the array of reforms it has promoted in the public sectors of many countries over the years, has been the object of study and critical analysis since the beginning. We see the three case studies collected in this part as an opportunity to engage in a genealogical study and test the plausibility of the alternative accounts of change put forward to date. In order to make these tasks manageable, we start by distinguishing two main perspectives from which political and institutional change has been studied and then identify the principal working hypotheses employed therein. The most relevant perspectives adopted to rationalize the reform of public administration and higher education (HE) are discussed in the first part of the book: 'modernist' and 'postmodernist' approaches, which have come to dominate academic debates in the social sciences in the post-war period. In particular, there are two broad 'postmodernist' readings of political and institutional change we wish to describe and assess. These two readings are labelled the *ideology thesis* and the *functional thesis* respectively. They will be contrasted with an alternative 'modernist' reading of political and institutional change we label the *depoliticization thesis*. Our assessment of their plausibility will be carried out in two steps. First, we will clarify what makes them 'modernist' or 'postmodernist'. After that, we shall list the analytical elements underpinning their explanatory and justificatory frameworks and test their ability to take into consideration the multiple variables highlighted by our heuristic frame of reference – the three-level game discussed below.

In comparing these analytical frameworks, our concern will be to test their heuristic value in relation to the set of reforms carried out since the 1980s. We are not interested in developing a general, theoretical model of social change and thus not concerned with the role ideas play in public policy *per se*, or even with more abstract questions concerning the pros and cons of materialistic and non-materialistic explanations in human affairs. In the three cases discussed our intention is to stress the role that is played by political factors that cut across the more traditional debates that periodically flare up in the social sciences. It is because it appreciates these political factors that we attribute a higher plausibility to the *depoliticization thesis* when compared to its postmodern alternatives. Moreover, we are also keen to point out that the rationalizations of change proposed by modernists and postmodernists alike are performative enterprises committed not only to explain change, but also influence its direction and pace. In order to assess their plausibility, we need, therefore, to separate the explanatory and justificatory analytical aspects of each framework, even while we refuse to subscribe to positivist tenets wishing to impose a clear-cut separation between facts and values. Our attempt to keep these aspects separate is merely analytical and is done for heuristic reasons.

It must be evident by now that we are pretty dissatisfied with postmodernist developments in social and political theory. In Part I, we made clear that several attempts to move beyond classic social theory have in reality blunted the critical edge of current social theory *vis-à-vis* political economy. In particular, we lament the attempt to strip society of political content and turn it into a self-reproducing apolitical force. Here we want to show that the political and institutional changes brought about by the multiple and overlapping reforms of the public sector can be better understood by using a modernist frame of reference; that is, the revised reading of Polanyi's theory presented in Chapter One. In adopting this critical modernist perspective, our goal is twofold. In the first place, we want to 'unmask' the rhetorical elements used to justify the reform process and highlight instead the old-fashioned disciplinary motives underpinning NPM. For us, understanding even the tactics used to push the reform process forward against mounting opposition does not require a new (postmodernist) paradigm. Such tactics are, in fact, quite familiar aspects of state repertoires for bringing about change. They rest on the ability of state actors to build collusive partnerships with powerful societal actors while undermining the ability of fragmented oppositional forces to constitute themselves as an effective countermovement. That the array of 'divide-and-rule' tactics used to do so can now be relabelled in system-theoretic terms as 'collibration' strategies (Dunsire 1993) does not, we shall argue, make them postmodern.

Our second preoccupation is to derive some practical lessons from this cultural enterprise. If the spirit underpinning the whole reform process is eminently disciplinary (rather than emancipatory), what are the possibilities open to those at the receiving end? If the reform process is simply a novel instance of past attempts to commodify land, labour, and money described by Polanyi, does it tell us anything about the normative solutions devised earlier to stop what looks like a modernist Groundhog Day? In our opinion, the confidence Polanyi had in welfare policies is not only in clear contradiction with his analysis of the side effects of the Speenhamland system, but is also refuted by subsequent events – those that determined the parabola of the welfare state and allowed the revival of free-market ideas in the 1980s (cf. Crouch 2004). Once again, this means that social theorists need to reassess the role of the nation-state in an allegedly globalized world and the ability of social interaction to bring about effective policy solutions as a by-product of decentralized and uncoordinated attempts at problem solving.

The case studies presented here show that state institutions and actors are still formidable forces at national and transnational levels. They were at the root of the reform process and remain able to control its unfolding in self-serving ways thanks to the use of changeable combinations of market-based policies. In this sense, modernist calls for democratization are for us still compelling. The welfarist road taken in the post-war period proved to be too narrow and unsuitable to fully accomplish that task. However, within modernism there were progressive traditions of thought that suggested non-welfarist routes. As we see it, the task of a critical social and political theory is to rediscover those traditions and rethink them, rather than adopting contentious postmodern positions.

NPM as a three-level game: methodological issues and conceptual distinctions

The case studies presented here are primarily concerned with the sets of reforms designed to impose the discipline of the market within the public sector by using the strategies identified by our representation of NPM as a fruit machine. Our focus is, therefore, on (i) the construction of managerial strategies; (ii) their actual working and; (iii) their overall results. Privatization, liberalization, and marketization must be seen as part of a dynamic and self-sustaining whole generating cycles of reform in a periodic fashion. Viewed from this perspective, what *prima facie* may be thought to be unintended consequences or reverse effects can equally be interpreted as part of a recursive and multistage policy approach that needs to be considered in its totality. As Kenneth Baker, the Conservative minister responsible for the 1988 Education Reform Act, explained to *Guardian* journalist Nick Davies:

> I was not going to take on the comprehensive system head-on. I'd had the teachers' strike, the national curriculum, you can't take on yet another great fight. So I believed that if I set in train certain changes, they would have, er, a cumulative beneficial effect. [...] In order to make changes, you have to come from several points.
>
> (*The Guardian*, Tuesday 16 September, 1999)[1]

Hence the need to use longer time frames and adopt a more dynamic approach to policy analysis; namely, an approach open to the possibility of considering diverse policy initiatives as part of nonlinear sequences unfolding in an apparently haphazard fashion.

To understand the unfolding of this process of change and test its degree of randomness, we further distinguish between the heterogeneous players involved in it. This endeavour leads us to consider a three-level game describing the ongoing interaction taking place between: (i) political principals and those in charge of service delivery; (ii) the suppliers involved in the production line together with public service users; (iii) public sector and civil society. Since these forms of interaction involve internally differentiated collective agencies, at each level of analysis we also try to take into account their inner dynamic by identifying typologies of actor, classes of activity, and related utility functions. For instance, with respect to the civil service, we distinguish between (a) the permanent secretaries located in Whitehall; (b) the middle-rank managers working within departments and; (iii) the frontline officers occupied with service delivery – Lipsky's (1980) street-level bureaucrats. Such distinctions among actors at different levels are necessary not only because they may have distinct utility functions, but also to understand the ways in which reforms reshape their roles and the set of strategies open to them. Once this analytical work is done for each of the collective agencies involved, it is then possible to speculate about the sort of informal coalitions that could emerge between subsets of players located at different levels, and the role those multilevel networks play in the success or failure of given policy initiatives. Furthermore, the existence of informal networks supporting or opposing reforms allows us to analyze how different policy tools can be used to overcome opposition and/or gaming, to better understand the recursive and multistage nature of reforming patterns. This way of proceeding gives us the opportunity to simplify complex social dynamics without idealizing specific features of the games identified and to move beyond the simplistic assumptions of rational choice theory.

With respect to the utility functions of the various agents, we assume that these do not exclusively reflect a self-seeking attitude, but can also be shaped by a broader understanding of the public interest or the ethos attached to the role individual agents fulfil within complex public organizations. To this end the distribution of player-types within each level needs to be considered both synchronically and diachronically. Reforms produce institutional shocks that upset existing patterns of behaviour and generate counter reactions. This is especially the case when reforms entail deep structural transformations modifying the internal balance of power within the targeted institution. In order to neutralize counter reactions, reformers can deploy a range of actions for which Dunsire (1993) has coined the term 'collibration'; that is, soft policy instruments the aim of which is to expose fault lines within the opposition and exacerbate the collective action problems actors face when attempting to resist. These soft policy instruments can be further discerned in *ex ante* interventions aimed at preparing the ground for further structural changes, and in *ex post* interventions whose goal is to consolidate the ground after structural changes have been carried out. Successful *ex ante* collibration activities have the power to either drive unsuitable players from the field, or modify their behaviour in line with the new sets of incentives established. Thus, generations of players succeed each other with time and the distribution of types within the overall population changes until a new institutional steady state is reached. Successful *ex post* collibration activities instead keep the process of change periodically in motion, thus preventing new generations of players from gaming and introducing recursive stochastic shocks that push the system of interaction from one steady state to another.

To conclude our methodological discussion, we would like to point out that, in proposing this reading of the reform process inspired by NPM, we are combining notions belonging to distinct, if not incompatible, epistemic traditions. We wish to be fair to all of them by keeping an eclectic and healthy distance from both the systemic approach used by Dunsire and the deductive formal models used by game theorists. While we remain deeply sceptical about the role played by impersonal social forces exerting systemic pressure on the political, we do not seek to propose a formal deductive model of action, nor to arrive at a foundational account of real life phenomena. As noted, we are mainly trying to propose an analytical framework with which to assess the plausibility of contrasting interpretations. In using the notion of a three-level game, we are, firstly, trying to see whether the various interpretations under scrutiny give equal weight to the distinct institutional levels where interaction takes place, or whether their reading depends on an exclusive focus on one single level of analysis. Secondly, we are keen to understand whether and how the interpretations under scrutiny consider the interconnections between the distinct levels of interaction proposed, the variety of players involved, and the informal networks operating behind the scenes. Finally, we intend to test the ability of those interpretations to take into account the dynamic elements that connect what look like discrete and contradictory policy initiatives with changing political actors and new emerging generations of players. Ultimately, however, we should not forget that the three-level game identified and the strategic logic of action discussed have only a heuristic value.

Dovetailing the case studies

The empirical case studies in Part II deal with the building of the NPM template (British civil service reform), its development and refinement (reform of British HE), and its diffusion at continental level (EU integration policies). Since the case studies are concerned with the application of a single policy template to three distinct policy areas in a slightly modified form, the discussion has been structured in a way that allows us to avoid major repetition. Thus, each chapter tries to shed light or develop aspects of the reform process that are not spelled out fully in the others. For instance, in relation to the British civil service, we identify the three major theses influencing alternative rationalizations of the reform process and the features that make them modernist or postmodernist in spirit. The same discussion is not going to be repeated in relation to HE, even if here too these accounts have dominated the scientific literature produced to date in the field. Instead, in discussing the changes occurring at university level we have given rather more space to perspectives describing the experience of complying with the new regulatory environment from the inside. Also, in the first case study we concentrate our attention on the role of quasi-markets while in the second the focus is redirected towards the question of liberalization and the way this policy can be used strategically to periodically rewrite the rules of the game, creating an intricate web of constraints in a non-state sector that was largely self-regulating. On the other hand, while in these two case studies we piece together the process of vertical diffusion that has allowed the NPM policy template to penetrate the fabric of the British body politic, in discussing EU negative market integration policies we are more concerned with the process of horizontal diffusion that has allowed that same policy template to spread across national borders.

The case studies presented here give us the opportunity to analyze and discuss three types of governance brought about by the application of the NPM template. The first is the type of network governance amply studied by the 'Anglo-governance school'. The second deals with the attempt to impose a corporate structure and a system of corporate governance on semi-autonomous professional realms, which were characterized by a distinct public ethos shunning the profit motive. The third investigates the role of good governance programmes to induce policy dissemination across national borders and generate a diffuse form of transnational governance. Taken together, the case studies wish to substantiate the claim that the NPM template must be seen as a solution looking for a problem rather than, as prominently suggested by the Anglo-governance school, the other way round. In fact, far from overcoming the one-size-fits-all mentality attributed to past bureaucratic arrangements, the same organizational model is employed to solve problems affecting not only diverse policy areas, but also cultural contexts with different administrative and educational traditions. The common elements that characterize distinct reform processes pertain to the nature of the changes they precipitate in reality. In all our case studies the effects experienced are:

- deprofessionalization and disempowerment of the individuals and groups affected, together with increasing personal responsibilities and deteriorating work conditions and terms of employment – heightening competition within what resemble zero-sum games;
- replacement of traditional lines of accountability, modes of regulation, and forms of social interaction with alternatives that are actually increasing organizational complexity, dependency on managerial and technical expertise, and the standardization and juridification of social relations;
- dissatisfaction with the outcomes brought about by unwanted changes and a growing inability to act on this by using collective action or individual forms of exit, except for tiny privileged minorities that try to benefit and/or shield themselves from the turbulence affecting the rest.

The final issue we want to raise concerns the role of meta-regulation and meta-regulators within the reform process. Although many narratives of political and institutional change explain it as a reaction to the pressures exercised by impersonal social and economic forces, and despite the popularity acquired by managerial theories extolling the virtues of decentralization, our case studies show that reforms are not only initiated by specific state actors, but that those very state actors retain a tight control over the overall process as meta-regulators. The role of the latter is crucial in overcoming social opposition, establishing the environmental conditions most favourable to make it self-enforcing and in preserving/rescuing the process itself from governance failure. We also contend that the introduction of meta-regulators with their own sets of interests and motivations helps explain many contradictory aspects of both the NPM template and the reforms inspired by it. First, it makes it possible to explain the simultaneous processes of centralization and decentralization observed in many quarters as the outcome of an institutional strategy committed to centralize decision-making power while decentralizing managerial and administrative tasks and responsibilities. Second, it sheds light on the coexistence of two distinct logics, procedural and substantive, driving the multiple and overlapping systems devised to measure individual performance. Last but not least, it clarifies the rationale behind the diffusion of a policy template the actual achievements of which are still unclear, especially when measured against the more tangible social costs it tends to generate. When such an assumption is factored in the picture we derive is an unsettling one: the reform process looks like an elitist attempt to roll back the stunted process of democratization set in motion by liberal democracies in the post-war period by applying double standards and self-serving policy instruments.

4 New Public Management and the British civil service

Setting the template of a complex policy instrument

4.1 Introduction

While Weber put bureaucracy at the centre of his theory of modernity, many contemporary social theorists consider the transformation of national public administrations, which occurred at the turn of the twenty-first century, an indication of a momentous shift towards postmodernity (Rhodes 1997). As noted in Chapter 2, postmodernity stresses three distinctive sets of change: (i) the abandonment of hierarchical forms of organizations in favour of more horizontal and sleeker ones; (ii) the adoption of reflexive forms of rationality to replace the legal formal ones employed previously; (iii) the switch from input-oriented to output-oriented modes of assessment dictated by criteria of performance management. Following Weber, this shift is explained by looking at the efficiency gains brought about by the innovations introduced. However, unlike Weber much contemporary analysis ignores the existence of bureaucracy in the private sector and, by focusing exclusively on the apparatus of the state, implicitly equates bureaucracy with the state. Moreover, the alleged shift towards a postmodern organizational setup is associated with diverse attempts to introduce market discipline (and related private sector managerial practices) into the public domain via so-called New Public Management (NPM).

In proposing an outline of the reform process that has beset the British civil service since the 1980s, our goal is to challenge the postmodern readings proposed to date on all three counts and show that the whole reform process can be accounted for within a modernist framework. To put it bluntly, we claim that, far from promoting post-bureaucratic organizational forms, NPM can be seen as a policy template the goal of which is to (i) re-establish hierarchical lines of control; (ii) embed instrumental rationality in alien domains; (iii) allow meta-regulators to switch between procedural and substantive logics at will. Moreover, to a large extent, even the modalities with which this process of rationalization unfolds follow a modernist script. In an uncanny Polanyian fashion, the reform process is not a spontaneous occurrence (due to the pressure of impersonal social forces), or the outcome of unintended consequences, but the result of state planning having genuinely modernist political aims. State intervention is, once again, supported by several non-state actors interested in 'enclosing' the tangible and intangible 'commons' recreated by welfare states in the second post-war period and in commodifying them. In short, we maintain that the pragmatic justifications (what works) and the performance-based language often used to legitimate these interventions work only at a rhetorical level. In practice, the reform process ends up adding a new layer of market criteria on top of pre-existing procedural means of assessment. This allows meta-regulators to use both procedural and substantive criteria of evaluation, or switch between them at will; that is, in order to discipline the clerical workforce, de-professionalize middle managers, and strengthen top-down governability.

The reconstruction of this case study will be accomplished in three steps. In the first section, the various types and waves of reforms that have transformed the British civil service are presented. In the second section, we assess the relative plausibility of alternative readings of this process proposed to date. We do so by means of a three-level game that allows us to distinguish: (i) the actors involved in the overall process at different institutional levels; (ii) the rationale underpinning the strategic moves of the agents involved, and; (iii) how the different institutional levels interrelate. The chapter closes by suggesting that, to the extent that reforms in other realms of the public sector follow the same political logic and use similar techniques to undermine dissent and gaming, evaluations of the NPM template based on the limitations of output-oriented modes of assessment tend to miss the point. Similarly deceptive are the claims calling for outcome-performance measures to replace output measures. Given the political logic driving the reform process, any managerial innovation can potentially be exploited by political principals in order to foster their positional power, regardless of the resulting loss of social efficiency.

4.2 Pimping the Rolls-Royce of public administration: origins and development of the NPM template

The pre-Thatcherite civil service is conventionally described as 'Weberian'. Indeed, the long process of consolidation started by the 1854 *Northcote-Trevelyan Report* tried to reshape the plurality of existing administrative offices and practices into a single organization run according to, and inspired by, the set of managerial values later outlined by Weber in his theory of modern bureaucracy. The elements composing the latter to which the British civil service tried to, anachronistically speaking, conform were as follows: (i) hierarchical organization structure; (ii) division of administrative roles and functions; (iii) a legal-rational approach to policy (selection of the best means to achieve given ends); and (iv) mechanisms of appointment and progression based on competence, merit and impartiality. Combining both the utilitarian suggestions of J. S. Mill and the idealist ethos of T. H. Green, the British civil service aspired to be a highly efficient and professional administrative organization shielded from political interference and able to serve the government of the day regardless of its complexion. Those aspirations are fully spelled out in

A.V. Dicey's (1915) constitutional theory (the so-called Westminster system of government), which were to influence the 1918 *Haldane Report*, from which the civil service reforms carried out in the interwar period were derived. In the course of the second post-war period, textbooks in politics and administration restated the principles underpinning this form of government *ad nauseam*, on each occasion pointing out the inevitable gap between the 'dignified' and 'material' aspects of the British Constitution (to use Walter Bagehot's vocabulary). Following government growth brought about by the development of the welfare state, that gap increased to the extent that not merely the effectiveness of its constitutional framework, but the validity of the Westminster system as an accurate representation of British politics started to be seriously questioned (Rhodes 2007).

The problems raised in public debates during the post-war period can be easily classified under three labels: responsiveness, accountability, and efficiency. Moreover, these include, in equal measure, the role of the civil service within the British political system *and* its internal mechanisms of regulation. All over the Western world, the post-war settlement ended up attributing remarkable policy-making powers to public bureaucracies by granting them a dominant role in policy implementation. This reinforced their constitutional relevance *vis-à-vis* other state actors (namely, legislative and executive branches). In the British context, we find three additional factors that reinforced this general trend. First, there was the role played by Whitehall in managing the war effort and in reconstructing the country afterwards, definitively described by Hennessy (1990). Second, we have the responsibilities attributed to the civil service for developing the welfare state, as outlined in the *Beveridge Report* of 1942. Finally, we must also note the contribution of the administrative apparatus to the smooth handover of imperial powers to the new Western hegemon – the USA – as required by the 1944 Bretton Woods accords (see §6.2). If these roles contributed to building the reputation of the civil service as a highly reliable and effective institution – the Rolls-Royce of Western public administrations – its policy capability soon came to be perceived as limiting the possibility of political and institutional change open to the country. In other words, it was felt that the civil service represented a conservative force preserving privileges that were in marked contrast to the progressive democratic values at the core of the welfare state itself. This perception was shared both by (part of) the political establishment depending on the support of top civil servants to accomplish its political programme, and by large sectors of the expanding middle classes for whom careers in the public sector provided an opportunity for social mobility (Savage *et al* 1992).

The question of responsiveness, which appears in public debates during the 1960s, needs to be understood as a manifestation of growing dissatisfaction within these two distinct constituencies. On the one hand, the political establishment felt constrained by a tight-knit Whitehall village assuming an informal constitutional right to express the public interest of the country and imposing 'departmental points of view' on the ministers of Her Majesty's

Government – the only institution entitled to represent public interest within the Westminster system. On the other hand, the expanding number of middle-rank civil servants resented the power enjoyed by a caste of top civil servants able to reproduce themselves by acting as gatekeepers. To a large extent, the issue of responsiveness overlapped with the question of representativeness (political and descriptive) of top civil servants. This was to become apparent in the landmark 1968 *Fulton Report* commissioned by the then Labour prime minister Harold Wilson. The report noted that the civil service was dominated by a class of Oxbridge generalists lacking specific professional skills. As a result, it advocated managerial solutions aimed at redressing this state of affairs by promoting professional training and professional figures within the top ranks. Moreover, the report's emphasis on professionalism went hand in hand with the defence of the traditional public service ethos, in effect a restatement of principles of anonymity and impartiality that should characterize the civil service and a reaffirmation of the constitutional supremacy of Parliament (through Her Majesty's Government). The failure of the incomes policies launched by Conservative and Labour governments in the 1970s and their inability to professionalize the civil service made evident to the political establishment the existence of a subtle trade-off between responsiveness and accountability that would eventually shift the terms of public debate. Thus, the question of responsiveness was suddenly superseded by one concerned with top-down governability (King 1975). Within the Westminster system, this meant restating the supremacy of central government over the sprawling institutions of the welfare state, and reaffirming the vertical conventions of accountability linking civil servants to their ministers against calls for a full-blown democratization of the administrative branch of government.[2]

A bird's eye view of the waves of reform carried out in the last three decades reveals three things (see Appendix 1). First, the overwhelming majority of policy initiatives listed result from external political interventions directed at changing either the machinery of government or the managerial practices employed within departments. Moreover, even the few ambiguous instances of reform that can be classified as 'internal' have a reactive character, their aim being to anticipate changes that the government of the day was keen to make. This casts some doubt on rational choice readings of public bureaucracy proposed to date. The reform process cannot be directly linked to some budget-maximizing strategy of public officers, as suggested by Niskanen (1971), nor to the bureau-shaping logic proposed by Dunleavy (1991) as a refinement of Niskanen, nor even to the veto-power model employed more recently by Tsebelis (2001). A final judgement on the validity of these deductive models of political and institutional change can only be acquired indirectly by assessing the plausibility of the rationalizations derived from them. Another element highlighted by the list of policy initiatives is that the main instigator of these reforms is central government rather than Parliament. This in itself is not surprising given the fact that the civil service has lacked a statutory legal basis for more than 150 years. It is worth noting, however, that central government has ignored almost all the substantive suggestions made by Parliament in this same time frame – including the passing of the Constitutional and Government Act 2010, pushed through by Gordon Brown at the end of his short premiership (2007–2010). The activism of parliamentary sub-committees dealing with the issue over the years served mostly to supply a platform to those dissatisfied with either the direction or pace of change imposed by central government. By and large, their actual policy-making power proved irrelevant.

The second consideration concerns the cyclicity with which distinct policy tools have been employed. On the one hand, it emerges that privatization, liberalization, and marketization are not seen by central government as alternative forms of intervention, but as complementary in key respects. Thus, if the creation of quasi-markets was initially perceived as an implicit acknowledgement of the limitations of neoliberal attempts to 'roll back the frontiers of the state', and the consequent need to preserve the public nature of core government institutions, successive reviews and market testing exercises showed that marketization could simply represent an intermediate step towards new rounds of privatization. Similarly considerations were at work in the case of liberalization, a policy instrument often used to re-regulate fields of activities or change the mode in which they were regulated, rather than simply deregulate. On the other hand, structural interventions on government machinery and soft changes in managerial practice have followed each other constantly, keeping the reform movement permanently in motion. For instance, measures to boost efficiency introduced by the Rayner Scrutinies within a hierarchical departmental structure were followed by attempts to dismantle that structure through the 'Next Steps' agency model. This was succeeded by new reforms of managerial practices aimed at improving efficiency by involving consumers, followed in turn by structural measures directed at either reducing the civil service or reconsolidating departmental organizations through the Join-Up Government initiative, and so on. This cyclicity casts doubts on many periodizations of the reform process proposed by governance theorists, and their alleged links to changes in the complexion of government forces caused by the electoral cycle. From this we draw the conclusion that the rationalizations advanced by what Marinetto (2007) calls the 'Anglo-governance school' are no less controversial than those made by rational choice theorists.

The third and final consideration concerns the assessment of the results brought about by the waves of reform and the sets of policy instruments used. Over the years, policy analysts and practitioners have been at pains to identify the outcomes produced by these changes. New policy initiatives have in effect superseded old ones before the changes set in motion could be observed and analyzed. These initiatives were often carried out by distinct institutional agents with different degrees of conviction and priorities in mind. Rebranding old initiatives and reassessing previously established policy goals has made it difficult to understand the cumulative or contradictory nature of these processes of change and their magnitude. Persistent policy activism has thus combined with political and administrative reform fatigue producing in the process sufficient heat and dust to make the overall picture very hazy indeed. This haziness makes it impossible to carry out a straightforward empirical assessment and thus generates the wide range of middle-level rationalizations influenced by alternative epistemic and methodological traditions, such as the two mentioned so far: rational choice theory and the Anglo-governance school. At this middle level of analysis, the importance of both the role and relevance of the collective actors responsible for setting the reform process in motion can be questioned by introducing deeper causal variables or structural explanatory elements. Moreover, the rationalizations arrived at do not need to depend at all on the intentions, interests, and beliefs of those initiating them, but can be accounted for as the outcome of unintended consequences or reverse effects. Having no linguistic capacity, facts cannot speak for themselves and leave room for more complex theoretical interpretations.

We shall now discuss the three intermediate interpretations mentioned in the introduction to Part II: the ideological, the functional, and the depoliticization thesis.

4.3 'Rolling back the frontiers of the state': the ideology thesis

If for Daniel Bell (1973) the hallmark of post-industrial society was the death of ideologies, postmodern accounts of political and institutional change tend to re-establish their role as explanatory variables. The set of changes experienced since the 1980s by the British civil service is attributed to the working of an ideological movement, neoliberalism, that is re-writing the social and political history of the world after its ultimate victory over socialism, the last remnant of modernism (Harvey 2005; Prasad 2006; Turner 2008). Neoliberalism is described by advocates and critics alike as an ideological force that is committed to 'roll back the frontiers of the state' in order to make room for the market. The nation-state and the free market are thus presented as engaged in something resembling a zero-sum game, where the ground gained by one of the contending parties is always equal to that yielded by the other (see Chapter 3). As we shall see, what distinguishes different postmodernist accounts of change is the rationale underpinning such a game. Those supporting the ideology thesis insist in attributing an overwhelming weight to the power of ideas in shaping change – a power that assumes the form of a particularly heroic heuristic element in some sympathetic authors (Currie *et al* 2008), or can end up supporting critical narratives verging on the conspiracy theory genre (Mirowski 2013).

In the case of the British reform process, Margaret Thatcher is attributed the role of a Trojan Horse able to surreptitiously introduce neoliberal ideas into the Conservative Party first, into her programme of government later on, and finally into the set of reforms targeting the civil service (Denham and Garnett 1998; Reitan 2003; Jackson and Saunders 2012). Her ideological conviction and commitment to the neoliberal cause has been repeated many times, by friends and foes alike, using, by-and-large, the same anecdotal evidence. Each restatement of the story has stimulated countless rebuttals, questioning either the validity of the evidence used or the soundness of the inferences made. Our take on these debates is twofold: first, they tend to focus on narrow time frames that cut the overall reform process into discrete sequences – an operation that makes it very difficult to understand continuity and discontinuity between sequences; secondly, this subdivision is often based on elements related to only one of the many levels at which the reforms operate, giving some specific sets of events a privileged (but often unmerited) explanatory power.

Moreover, in relation to the civil service, the managerial reforms carried out in her first two terms looked like an attempt to accomplish the suggestion made by Fulton, rather than marketize it. Her first interventions were directed at introducing a unified grading 'down to and including the rank of Principal and corresponding Professional and Scientific Grades' (Fry 2008: 151). That is, to accomplish the Open Structure introduced in 1972 by including the very top levels and 'give better opportunities to those in specialist grades to get to the very top of the Service' (Fry 2008). This meant making the salary scale more uniform while rejecting calls for performance related pay schemes on the grounds that they were unworkable.

Far from providing an insight into the way in which government initiatives can tackle complex political issues and hostile public reactions, at this juncture the culturalist interpretations divide into two opposing camps. Those subscribing individualist methodological tenets end up supporting heroic visions of leadership harking back to Weberian and Schumpeterian notions of 'leadership democracy'. On the other hand, those who subscribe to systemic methodological tenets end up attributing causal power to mysterious impersonal social forces capable of exercising irresistible pressure for individual compliance – namely, globalization. The latter renders the power of the neoliberal ideology invariant across electoral cycles and institutional levels, while the former attributes unspecified thaumaturgic powers to selected individuals.

A second appealing, but extremely problematic, aspect of the ideology thesis, in its postmodern incarnation, pertains to its critical attitude towards instrumental notions of rationality. In this context, the power of ideas is set against both formal cost–benefit analyses and the proceduralism characterizing more positivist approaches. In the case of the British civil service, this critical attitude appeals to those unable to appreciate the rationale behind the permanent revolution set in motion by multiple and overlapping waves of reform and those dissatisfied with the explanatory power of the Westminster model of government. To the former it is evident that the so-called Reform Policy Syndrome (that is, initial enthusiastic policy activism followed by sudden disinterest in outcomes) makes it impossible to understand either the result of single managerial innovations, or the cumulative effects produced by the whole process of reform. To the latter, the haphazard way in which the process of reform is carried out and the messy outcomes it yields is evidence of the inability of the Westminster model (and received political wisdom) to reflect what is going on in the real world. Once again, the upshot is twofold. On the one hand, there is a very postmodern celebration of the irrationality of the political process; on the other, there are restless attempts to spot epochal changes and the inevitable logical breaks entailed by the passage from one epoch to another. We shall come back to this latter position when discussing the functional thesis (§4.4). We would like to close the discussion on the ideology thesis by highlighting some shortcomings affecting those approaches that see politics and the political as a domain of activity dominated by irrational and contradictory drives.

In our view, these postmodern attitudes end up using the ideology thesis as an argument of last resort; as a *deus ex machina* used to get out of any methodological impasse in which policy analysts and practitioners find themselves. Such theoretical impasses could be the result of more mundane reasons related to the fragmentary nature of our knowledge (the outcome of the proliferation of academic sub-disciplinary fields) and the resulting need to restrict the field of vision of a progressively more specialized academic personnel.[3] In other words, they can be related to the set of policy initiatives seeking to redefine the division of academic labour and the academic profession – another instance of the application of NPM ideas in need of sound explanation (which we will sketch in Chapter 5). Alternatively, they can be due to the exclusive focus on only one of the institutional levels where interaction takes place. To us, the reading offered by the ideology thesis is a case in point, for it is concerned with the relationship between ministers and mandarins (Page 2015), while disregarding both the ones unfolding within the civil service and the one between the latter and civil society; that is, the other two of our three levels considered here.

Deep and lasting changes in the apparatus of the British state required the neutralization of possible oppositional forces; namely those which in the 1970s managed to stall the implementation of the *Fulton Report*. This meant dividing the opposition by exposing internal fault lines and exerting pressures on them by using subtle policy instruments, what Dunsire (1993) calls 'collibration' strategies. The first step in this direction was made by Thatcher with the abolition of the Priestly pay system (established in 1955 to settle pay disputes involving public officers). Thatcher accomplished this by using the 1982 *Megaw Report* in a very self-serving way (after having rejected the earlier *Scott Report* on indexing pensions), and thus managed to undermine the 'formula under which, in principle, Civil Service salary levels were decided on the basis of "fair comparisons" with outside pay' (Fry 2008: 140). This, in turn, led to the abolition of the managerial autonomy of the civil service with respect to the determination of salary levels, and of the Pay Research Unit charged to uphold it. As a reward for going along with this (and helping the government quash an industrial action that lasted 21 weeks) the top echelons of the civil service received not only a distinct system of salary determination from the rest of the work force, but also a salary increase, further alienating the rank-and-file.[4] Similar divisive effects will be achieved by means of the Rayner's Scrutinies, as we shall explain below. By neglecting to consider these internal dynamics properly, advocates of the ideology thesis miss crucial elements with noteworthy significant explanatory power. The same can be said about the other side of Dunsire's collibration coin, the policies directed at building social consensus through the creation of specific policy networks and dedicated PPPs.

4.4 'Realizing public value': the functional thesis

The functional thesis tries to address the shortcomings of postmodern readings based on the ideology thesis by focusing on the intra- and inter-organizational aspects of the reform process that are neglected in culturalist readings. Analytically, this leads various authors to employ binary oppositions in which the 'state' and the 'market' are identified as having distinctive features (reflecting the disciplinary interests of the authors themselves), which are then qualified as either modern or postmodern. For our purposes, the finest example of this way of approaching the question of political and institutional change can be found in Hooghe and Marks (2003), who identify two types of governance systems currently competing against each other in the political and administrative domains. One, identified as Type I, defines the salient characters of the ideal type of hierarchical government brought about by modernity. The other, identified as Type II, is an outline of the horizontal postmodern regulatory regimes that are allegedly in the process of gradually replacing the former. Distinct understandings of the institutional setup and of the logic underpinning its actual working are employed to explain the rising of postmodern political and administrative practices.

At an institutional level, the main emphasis is placed on the conceptual distinction between hierarchical and heterarchical modes of organization (see Chapter 2). If in modernist accounts hierarchical forms of organization are used to formalize a twin process of vertical integration and functional differentiation, postmodern theorists wish to identify heterarchical mechanisms where functional differentiation is achieved without vertical integration (Hummel 2007; Miller and Fox 2007; Stark 2009). Markets and networks are such kinds of heterarchies, which, according to this line of analysis, contrast markedly with hierarchies, to show their ability to assure coordination via decentralized systems of enforcement and voluntary forms of compliance. Once the working of those heterarchical mechanisms is fully understood, a proper comparative assessment of their relative degree of efficiency can then be carried out and political and institutional change explained as the outcome of social gains. Within this analytical frame of reference, it is also possible to observe two intriguing bifurcations: one between political economists and economic sociologists on epistemic questions, and the other between neo-liberal advocates and their opponents on questions of value. Do we have to understand heterarchical forms of organization as combinations of markets and hierarchies, as suggested by neo-institutional economists like Williamson (2000), or should we consider them as a distinct ideal-type mode of organization, as suggested by network theorists like Powell (1990)? Is our comparative assessment to be limited to test the relative efficiency of hierarchies and heterarchies or should it go a step further and also analyze the relative efficiency of markets and networks? Are we to consider the creation of quasi-markets within the civil service as a distinctive policy tool for boosting public value or should we consider them as temporary measures preparing the ground for new rounds of privatization?

A second distinctive feature concerns the notion of rationality employed to explain the inner working of post-bureaucratic organizations. In an emphatic postmodern style, facts and values, explanatory and justificatory elements are combined seamlessly, making the various ideal types identified 'performative' analytical frameworks quite unlike the 'value free' ones sought by Weber (Burger 1976: Ch. 4). Thus, the approaches influenced by liberal political economy tend to adopt substantive notions of rationality, which connect questions of institutional efficiency with output-oriented modes of legitimacy (as opposed to the input-oriented modes employed in the past) (Bekkers *et al* 2007). Accordingly, political and institutional change is explained (and justified) by the degree of social satisfaction it is able to produce; something that in this context requires the individual's ability to choose among the public goods and services supplied by a multiplicity of competing suppliers. By contrast, the approaches influenced by alternative sociological traditions of thought adopt the reflexive conceptions of rationality and connect these to notions of public value established through the dialogical engagement of all affected interests. Political and institutional change is here explained (and justified) as the result of bottom-up deliberative practices aiming at supplying 'a functional compensation for the low global legitimacy of electoral democracy by generating legitimacy "locally" – issue by issue, policy by policy, and constituency by constituency' (Warren 2009: 8).

How these two performative analytical approaches operate in the context of the British administrative reforms can be more fully appreciated in relation to the issue by examining quasi-markets. What explains the shift from large-scale privatization policies to more managerial attempts to make the civil service work according to a market logic without changing its public legal status?

4.4.1 Economic analyses of the administrative process

The need to dismantle departmental structures organized hierarchically in order to turn them into more market-like sets of contractual relationships follows from the alleged failure of previous managerial attempts to improve the productive efficiency of public bureaucracies. According to this economic reading, the meagre gains achieved by the Rayner's Scrutinies (and various other initiatives to rationalize the activities of departments carried out in the first half of the 1980s) showed that public bureaucracies were simply irredeemable. A panoply of rational choice models was employed to explain the ability of civil servants (and in particular the mandarins) to thwart any government attempt to make them more professional (as suggested by Fulton) or entrepreneurial (as sought by Thatcher) (Dunleavy 1991; Dowding 1995; Le Grand 2003). However, given the fact that many of the bodies making up the civil service were engaged in the production of public goods and services that had no market alternative, their all-out privatization was not reputed to be a feasible course of action. Hence the attention given to the market socialist tradition and the attempt to introduce quasi-markets by (i) hiving off the operational branches of individual departments; (ii) giving the resulting administrative agencies a business-like managerial structure; and (iii) making those administrative agencies compete *as if* they were operating in a real market environment. The development of quasi-markets is therefore presented as the outcome of the electoral cycle – the traditional competition among political parties wishing to maximize their share of the electorate by promising efficiency gains. Quasi-markets are thus presented and defended as the 'other' invisible hand mechanism (Le Grand 2007); one able to develop virtuous social dynamics once a new structure of incentives is set up by newly imposed contractual arrangements, whereby the public disclosure of hidden information is enforced by auditors and the competitive pressures operated by consumers start to be felt.

Two things need to be noted about this economic reading. First, it is based on deductive models primarily concerned with the likely interaction between consumers and producers, under the assumption that (i) both act as self-regarding utility maximizers; (ii) the right sets of monetary incentives are in place; and (iii) information is universally available or easy to access. The very possibility of achieving and maintaining these conditions is seldom scrutinized properly, though. Often it is conveniently left out of the picture as part of other game-like aspects of political life conforming to the same underlying logic. Secondly, as it is possible to apprehend intuitively, this also is a highly normative approach to questions of social efficiency. Its goal is in fact more that of giving indications about possible courses of action worth following than that of explaining *why* a given course of action has been actually taken and *how* it works in practice. To answer those questions by using the same functional logic is very tricky indeed. On the one hand, it would commit political economists to follow the chain of interconnected game-like situations holding together the overarching explanatory approach. This is not only hard to manage due to its complexity, but it is also likely to produce indeterminacy since the outcomes of a given game-like contest are dependent on the outcomes of another game-like contest, and so on, creating a problematic series of interdependent strategic decisions. On the other hand, this incompleteness makes it possible for political economists to explain almost any empirical departure from the deductive models used by imputing that failure to the inherent incompleteness of the market architecture; something that requires ever more proactive intervention by the state to facilitate the market. The inability of actually existing quasi-markets in Britain to boost social efficiency and public confidence (the empirical evidence of which has painstakingly been collected by Hood and various collaborators over the years, the most recent instalment being Hood and Dixon 2015) can thus be routinely blamed on those who fail to comply with the consumer/producer role attributed to them (service users, students and teachers, patients and doctors, etc.).

Postmodern economic accounts of the administrative reform process therefore keep moving back and forth from calls, directed at politicians, for more market-like interventions to injunctions, directed at dissatisfied customers, unhappy workers and disgruntled citizens, to assume their responsibilities and behave in a proper market manner. Failure to boost social efficiency is never attributed to a failure of theory, but frequently to the lack of political resolve in installing the quasi-market mechanism or to the inability of public service users to exploit the choice and opportunities they have been given. In this way economic explanations have immunized themselves against counterevidence however carefully garnered, collated, and analyzed.

4.4.2 Sociological analyses of the administrative process

A blend of distinct epistemic and normative tenets lead sociologically oriented readings of the reform process to depart from the accounts supplied by political economists. First, the former reject the individualist perspective and notion of substantive rationality employed by rational choice theorists. As already mentioned, these are substituted by more holistic perspectives using a socially embedded model of agency and notions of reflexive rationality attributing to those embedded agents the dialogical ability to revise the preferences they have in common. Second, they reject neoliberal values concerning the notion of individual choice and the priority attributed to what Hirschman (1970) aptly calls mechanisms of 'exit' over channels of 'voice' in the public domain. Against the consumerist worldview inspiring neoliberal attempts to give the individual power of choice, sociological approaches aim to re-evaluate the value of participation. By contrast with neoliberal attempts to give people the ability to vote-with-their-feet, reforms of public bureaucracies are therefore seen as an opportunity for creating forms of active citizenship that give all affected interests the ability to influence policy making and be directly involved in the implementation of public policies (Stoker 2006). These differences (and ambitions) come to the fore when the readings of quasi-markets supplied by policy analysts and practitioners influenced by socio-centric perspectives are analyzed.

Attempting to clarify the difference between the hierarchical logic of the state, the contractual logic of the market, and the deliberative logic used by networks, economic and political sociologists advance a novel explanatory framework for understanding political and institutional change as the outcome of bottom-up attempts to tackle the side-effects created by neoliberal reforms of central government (Rhodes *et al* 2003). In adopting this explanatory framework, policy analysts and practitioners reject the very idea of quasi-markets. As Rhodes (1997: 195) explains, 'British government is searching for a new operating code to manage the shift from direct to indirect controls. Intergovernmental relations, now transmuted into intergovernmental management (IGM), are central to that search.' And again:

> market testing and contracting out, competition and quasi-markets monopolize attention in the study of the new service delivery systems created by British government. We now need studies of IGM in 'action'; of facilitating, accommodating, bargaining and strategic surveillance; the keys to effective network management.
>
> (Rhodes 1997: 196)

At a theoretical level this means (i) switching from a neo-institutionalist economic paradigm where all institutional forms are located along the logical continuum from markets to hierarchies to a bi-dimensional space having three ideal-typical poles of attraction – markets, hierarchies and networks, and (ii) identifying the distinctive logics of action that characterize these three ideal-types – command-and-control, maximization of expected individual utilities, and monitoring decentralized-learning.[5] By explaining the working of these three distinct logics of action in theory, and how they ended up shaping facts on the ground, we get the narratives outlining the epochal passage from 'government' to 'governance' and from a 'legal-formal' to a 'reflexive' administrative model advanced by the Anglo-governance school.

These readings of change shift the analytical focus of researchers onto the third level of interaction identified by our game: the one pertaining the strategic relations between the civil service and civil society. Whatever the role of state actors in initiating change and their reasons for doing so, in these accounts the policy initiatives launched by central government inevitably end up producing unintended consequences with negative side-effects on the governing process. What explains the ability of a fragmented political and administrative landscape to avoid systemic crises is the power of crucially located societal agents to devise policy solutions and steer the administrative process accordingly. By contrast with the explanations supplied by liberal political economists, it is not the search for personal economic advantage that leads policy innovation and political and institutional change, but rather the attempt to maximize public value; a notion dependent, in turn, not on the aggregation of taken for granted individual preferences, but on deliberative engagement and dialogical practices (Hajer and Wagenaar 2003). Dialogical practices account for the bottom-up production of the standards established to steer a polycentric and multilevel administrative process, and for the decentralized and horizontal systems of audit supervising their application. Public deliberations directed at problem-solving are instead at the root of the selection mechanisms that help diffuse best practices across organizational boundaries and policy areas. Working jointly, they supply ultimate political legitimacy to areas of the public realm where expertise and objective knowledge have lost their modernist authority (Fischer 2009).

The problem is that these claims often lack theoretical coherence and empirical backing. In fact, the evidence empirical data provides seems to contradict the main assumptions of the socio-centric approach. To start with, it is possible to observe a permanent policy activism of government actors intent on using reform initiatives as signature dishes. The only other thing that empirical analyses tells us can be summarised thus: (i) the frontiers of the state have not been rolled back, especially when we consider the percentage of GDP used to fund the production of public goods and services either directly or indirectly; (ii) efficiency, red tape and customer satisfaction are still the hot issues behind attempts at justifying new reforms; (iii) other combinations of the inner elements making up the same policy template are used by distinct government forces regardless of their ideological complexion, electoral manifestos, and massive evidence of an ongoing political dealignment rocking the political parties doing so (e.g. Mair 2013). In this context, any attempt to explain continuity and change by appealing to the vagaries of the electoral cycle or the personality of the leader in charge risks contradicting the whole explanatory enterprise and the systemic claims underlying it. According to the hollowing out of the state/globalization thesis, the Keynesian rescue of the financial services engulfed in the 2008 subprime crisis should not have happened. Even more out of sync with the alleged passage from government to governance is the set of austerity policies imposed across OECD countries since then, especially in Britain where they look like Thatcher Mark II.

Equally unconvincing is the role played by public value in directing the problem-solving activities of a networked and multi-level civil service. The desirability of the general political and institutional setup of the emerging British polity is rejected by its main peripheral constituencies; to the point that the very survival of the country as the United Kingdom is no longer certain. But even within its metropolitan centre, England, discontent is rife and exacerbating old and new fault lines; a clear sign that the strategy of functional compensation proposed by Warren is indeed defective, to say the least. Symptomatic for us is the growing preoccupation with the declining morale and ethos of the civil service that has accompanied the New Labour experience (Marquand 2004; O'Toole 2006; du Gay 2008). The soft, deliberative and dialogical approach to network management pursued during this period has not delivered what its advocates suggested it could. Large numbers of civil servants continued to be dissatisfied with their working conditions and were willing to mount counter-reactions. Indeed, generational changes show the existence of several internal polarizations reflecting the corporatization of administrative institutions and the routinization of clerical labour. Street-level bureaucrats became ever more frequently engaged in industrial actions against their top managers to defend themselves from deteriorating working conditions and pay, especially in those agencies that can always be privatized or lines of work that can be easily outsourced. Among the higher managerial levels, the traditional ethos of public service continued to be tarnished by an informal spoils system that is removing all socialization mechanisms used in the past and rewarding instead strategies of exit at odds with the public interest. Within the civil service, revolving door practices have become so diffuse that moral hazard and adverse selection seem to be endemic problems, making any reference to the public value old-fashioned (Draca 2014; Wilks 2015).

4.5 The market as statecraft: on the depolitization thesis

Can we explain the perplexing elements used to cast doubts on the plausibility of the ideology and functional theses by appealing to an alternative depoliticization thesis? There are many versions of the depoliticization thesis, and some of them fall within the postmodern camp.[6] The version we want to outline and assess here falls squarely in the modernist camp since it views the whole reform process as the outcome of statist attempts to impose centralized control on peripheral administrative activities that had somehow escaped from it (or social realms that were left untouched by previous expansive drives) by using market-based policies. Fuelling this new round of modernization is once again the twin logic of vertical integration and functional differentiation eminently suggested by Polanyi (2001 [1944]). Within the civil service, the various waves of reform carried out since the 1980s are said to pursue a double aim: the centralization of decision making powers together with the decongestion of administrative activities (Palumbo 2015). *Ex thesis*, this double objective allows some state actors – namely, central government – to strengthen its power over the administrative subsystem while escaping both responsibility for policy failure and the supervision of representative bodies called to enforce traditional lines of political accountability, namely, Parliament. Such a centralizing political effort uses the policy instruments made available by the NPM template as tools for redesigning the internal division of administrative labour so that: (i) senior civil servants progressively lose their traditional function of policy advisors/policy-makers to take up more managerial (and less political) functions; (ii) the administrative personnel working in more operative departments have their activities streamlined and routinized in ways that make them easy to monitor and replace; (iii) myriad of quangos and audit agencies (ultimately controlled by central government) assume accountability powers, which were previously exercised by Parliament, displacing its remaining monitoring functions. It follows that, in this context, what is being hollowed out by neoliberal reforms is not the state and its system of government, but the constitutional framework that established democratic side-constraints and mechanisms of supervision on government action. By the same token, what is being engendered is neither the market nor some ideals of performance management, but an intricate regulatory regime letting meta-regulators play the game of the rules, and choose between procedural and substantive criteria of evaluation freely; a politically subservient 'market on the leash'.

Before we consider the plausibility of the depoliticization thesis in relation to the three levels considered by our game, it should be pointed out that, like liberalization, depoliticization implies a mixture of three strategies – depoliticization, politicization and repoliticization – making it extremely arduous for analysts and practitioners to follow the various trajectories (Peters and Pierre 2004). Areas of activity that had public relevance in the past (and were, therefore, subjected to democratic decision-making procedures or even had a collegial nature) have been turned into matters of individual choice. In the other direction, activities that in the past did not have public relevance have been politicized by hard and soft regulatory means placing them under the authority of central government. Finally, contexts of choice that had a public nature but were politically autonomous, have been brought into the remit of central government. With this clarification in mind, we can continue our investigation by considering how the strategy of depoliticization operates at the first level of interaction, the one concerning ministers and civil servants.

Our starting point is the characterization of the interaction unfolding between ministers and civil servants before the onset of the Thatcherite reform movement. As seen above, the British civil service developed as a fairly autonomous public body able to define its own criteria of employment without major political interference. This managerial autonomy allowed it to develop socialization practices that not only preserved it from external influences, but also preserved its public ethos from being corrupted by the play of private interests. The Whitehall village life described by Heclo and Wildavsky (1974) was the outcome of this autonomy at the highest level – the one encompassing the class of senior civil servants represented by the First Division Association, its main corporate body. Permanence of service, exclusive access to administrative and policy records, and a crucial gate-keeping role between political, administrative, and public spheres made top civil servants particularly powerful and the object of various types of resentment. Commonly identified as untouchable 'mandarins', top civil servants entertained a fairly conflictual relationship with the government of the day. Incoming ministers had, in effect, scant policy expertize, limited access to information, and often transitory careers and were, therefore, highly dependent on their permanent secretaries in discharging their ministerial duties. The relations between ministers and mandarins was thus often described in principal-agent language and fuelled rational choice attempts to explain both the post-war growth of governmental activities and the repeated failure of British governments to keep this growth in check.

Contrary to the reading of these relations offered by rational choice theorists, there is plenty of evidence demonstrating that administrative power was not used to maximize personal wealth or even office size, but the social prestige offered by the honorary titles system. In relation to ministers and prime ministers, the crux of the matter was that mandarins acquired the informal right to express the public interest against the government of the day, and the fact that constitutional principles shielded them from any political responsibility. The goal of the NPM template, as devised by Thatcher, was in fact to turn the tables, making them responsible for government failures while giving back full policy-making power to central government. The reduction of the policy advisory role mandarins used to enjoy, the more operational tasks they are now called to do, and the mechanisms established to measure and reward their performance are, for us, evidence indicating how successful the introduction of the template has been to date. To understand how this ambitious goal was implemented we must turn our attention to the other two levels of interaction. Turning the tables has required a three-pronged action directed against the very sources of mandarin power: permanence of service, exclusive access to information, and gate-keeping functions.

Privatization and liberalization have obviously had (and continue to have) as their main target senior civil servants' ability to control access to the rooms where crucial policy decisions are taken. They have been no less important in undermining their grasp on the implementation process that is now fragmented in ways that escape the direct control of Whitehall, giving a veneer of plausibility to the hollowed-out state thesis. Managerial measures and the process of agencification have supported and completed the Thatcherite programme of depoliticization by removing from the hands of mandarins the regulatory authority they had over internal matters related to employment, career progression, and conditions of service and pay, thus reducing their permanence in service *vis-à-vis* that of their ministerial counterparts. In turn, this was made possible by using collibration strategies that exposed internal fault lines and increased antagonism between the senior civil servants based in Whitehall and the middle-ranking managers working in more operational departments. The existence of this internal fault line had already emerged with the 1968 *Fulton Report*, and was based on the resentment of this middle managerial level towards an Oxbridge elite with a tendency towards generalism, policy advice, and in-house apprenticeship that set strict limits on their career prospects. This resentment was artfully magnified and exposed by the attempts to rationalize and improve the efficiency of departmental activities carried out by Rayner and other external fixers in the early 1980s. Caught between this internal crossfire and a streak of electoral bad luck, the post-war generation of senior civil servants that was pivotal to the Whitehall village life eventually succumbed. Some retired from service, a few moved into other fields of activity, and others decided to put their expertize at the service of the new managerial order and join a flourishing quangocracy.

Quasi-markets, and the plethora of mechanisms and regulatory regimes created to assess and reward individual performance completed the original Thatcherite programme by establishing the means to govern the middle-rank managerial class at a distance through market discipline. This entailed engaging in four modernist governmental practices:

1 interventions on the supply side directed at instilling an entrepreneurial spirit in the bureaucrats in charge of service delivery;

2 the stimulation of a consumer culture among public services users to keep pressure on producers;
3 periodic *ad hoc* interventions to adjust the working of quasi-markets and make it consistent with the overall strategy of political centralization-cum-administrative decongestion;
4 cyclical changes of the rules of the quasi-market game to avoid 'gaming' by periodically spinning the wheels of the NPM slot machine.

Far from letting managers free to manage and deliver services responsive to its patrons, as often claimed by policy reform statements and their postmodern advocates, interventions on the supply side seem to have applied the conveyor belt logic of mass production advocated by the scientific management school in the late nineteenth and the early twentieth centuries to fields of activities that were thought to be beyond its reach (Head 2003: Ch. 6). In short, they are engendering what has been aptly described as 'digital Taylorism' (Brown *et al* 2011). Clerical, managerial and even intellectual work has been painstakingly divided in interconnected but discrete sets of activities, which are then subject to standardization, routinization, and digitalization (see Chapter 3 and Conclusion). Working in complex administrative organizations like the civil service nowadays means being permanently engaged in achieving targets imposed from without and whose rationale often escapes both producers and consumers (Scott 1996). On their part, public service users are the relentless object of government campaigns to make them more consumer-like, even when the lack of reliable information and absence of exit mechanisms render this simply impossible. However, in doing so political principals are in effect shifting public responsibilities (and blame) downwards onto individual agents who have no real power to change the structural conditions within which they are supposed to make professional and responsible rational choices.

Enlightening in this respect are the innovations introduced by New Labour governments from 1997 to 2010. During his first mandate, PM Tony Blair carried on with the plan to undermine the policy advisory role of top civil servants by introducing a three-fold typology of 'Advisory Non-Departmental Public Bodies'.[7] First, he created a greatly enlarged and powerful Prime Minister's Office run by politically appointed personnel that included: (i) the Strategic Communication Unit; (ii) a Prime Minister's Policy Unit; (iii) a new Social Inclusion Unit; (iv) a Minister without Portfolio to assure coordination in government policy. Secondly, he established a myriad of task forces charged with supplying independent advice on 'wicked' policy problems that could not be dealt with at the departmental level. Finally, he appointed a growing number of independent authorities to deal with various social emergencies (real or putative) in policy areas like drug control, crime, immigration, transport, access to cancer treatment, children's welfare, etc., headed by omnipotent 'tsars' answering directly to him. Once the policy advisory role of top civil servants was thus hollowed out, the PM's attention shifted, during Blair's second mandate, onto the inner working of the departments themselves, so as to extend the control of central government over the delivery process and related mechanisms of implementation.[8] In brief, not only do departments no longer have a relevant policy advice role, but the senior civil servants running them have also seen their managerial power curtailed. And among the losers we must include ministers too, for their political role has dramatically changed, turning them into mere enforcers of directives emanating from the inner core of central government. To quote Richards (2008: 110): 'Blair reinforced his policy steers through regular bilateral meetings with ministers to ensure that they agreed on policy objectives'.

This close bilateral relationship between the PM and ministers was meant to reduce the risk of the latter becoming ambassadors for the departments they were in charge of, an innovation that contributes to explaining the loss of political leverage experienced by mandarins. More to the point, it explains the decreasing power of the cabinet and the centralization process that the British system of government as a whole has been undergoing (Heffernan and Webb 2005). As in international relations, bilateralism is used as an alternative to multilateralism to avoid the rising of defensive coalitions that could offset the asymmetric power enjoyed by some actors (Stone 2011). Within the Westminster system of government this means the power of the inner core located in Downing Street against the other members of the cabinet. Unable to count on the likely concerted action of his or her cabinet colleagues, individual ministers need to tow the PM's line in order to avoid damaging their political career or being ousted from government altogether at the next reshuffle. Finally, at ministerial level performing and conforming have now become interchangeable terms.

The analysis of the interaction unfolding at the third level complements the sketch given above in two ways. Firstly, with the rhetoric of individual choice and productive efficiency used to sell this array of reforms to the British public, not only by the Conservative governments that dominated political life from 1979 to 1997, but also by their New Labour successors, who found the new state of affairs highly congenial. From this perspective, the market instruments embodied by the NPM template have neither a mere ideological value, nor the objective of improving the productive efficiency of public bureaucracy, nor even that of realizing public value. Viewed from Downing Street, they are meant to respond to democratic pressures for remedial actions within a Westminster system of government that attributes to the government of the day full responsibility for things it cannot effectively control. Rather than changing features of the British Constitution that could jeopardize its royal prerogatives and control of Parliament, central government finds in NPM a better tool for pushing responsibilities for policy failure away while reinforcing its policy making capacity. The array of private businesses and non-profit organizations that are taking up those public responsibilities through privatization, liberalization, and, above all, marketization are doing so in the hope of being able to access, enclose, and commodify areas of the public sector that previous regulatory regimes, socialization practices, and a public service ethos had, by and large, preserved from private appropriation. The 'market' turns out, therefore, to be a universal solution looking for specific public problems rather than the reverse; one that in addition allows a new class of enclosers to separate responsibility for services delivery from financial liability. Not only does the funding of privately-run public services remain overwhelmingly public, but it is the taxpayer who is ultimately called to bear the burden of market and quasi-market failure whenever it occurs. Social, economic, and financial crises call in fact for emergency measures which allow central government and its partners to by-pass democratic procedures and parliamentary supervision, thus starting a new cycle of reforms.

4.6 Conclusion

In this chapter we set ourselves a double task: that of outlining the various waves of reform that have beset the British civil service since the 1980s and that of evaluating different rationalizations of the reform process. The variety, overlapping, and contradictory aspects of the processes of political and institutional change set in motion over the years by the NPM template make it clear that a simple analysis of the empirical evidence available cannot reveal whether there is a rationale behind those reforms or what that rationale could be. These difficulties are at the root of the proliferation of readings based on more sophisticated analytical frameworks supported by distinct explanatory variables and adopting alternative methodological tenets. As performative enterprises, a great number of these rationalizations are influenced by a postmodern ethos and celebrate the arrival of a post-bureaucratic age. We have collected some of the more compelling accounts under two labels: the ideology thesis, attributing causal explanatory power to (neoliberal) ideas, and the functional thesis, explaining change as the outcome of social and political pressures to maximize either productive efficiency or public value, and we have assessed their degree of plausibility by comparing them to a modernist reading of change we have called the depoliticization thesis. According to this alternative reading, the political and institutional changes promoted by the reforms of the British civil service represent an act of statecraft: an attempt to reinforce governmental control on the apparatus of the state and on sectors of civil society that escaped it (either because of the growth of governing functions imposed by post-war welfare policies, or because of the ability of those sectors to retain their social and political autonomy). In relation to the civil service, this attempt has in effect (i) strengthened the policy-making role of central government; (ii) shifted responsibility for government failure downward to middle-rank managers and street-level bureaucrats bereft of any decision-making power; (iii) undermined the ability of Parliament to supervise the executive branch of government through the old mechanisms of accountability; and (iv) turned the cabinet system into a presidential complex unhindered by formal constitutional constraints.

In assessing the relative plausibility of modernist and postmodern accounts of political and institutional change we employed heuristic tools – derived, in an eclectic fashion, from games theory – which distinguish between three main levels of interaction: one concerning ministers and civil servants, another concerning the competing forces inside the civil service, and the third concerning civil society and the civil service. The upshot of our comparative analysis is as follows. Readings of the reform process influenced by the ideology thesis focus almost exclusively on the first level of interaction and fail to clarify how neoliberal ideas come to be accepted across the various levels of interaction and distinct generations of players. Functional analyses of the reform process switch the focus of their inquiries onto the third level and rely not only on a partial understating of the administrative phenomena under investigation, but also on explanatory frameworks unsupported by the available empirical evidence. The reading supported by the depoliticization thesis is, we have argued, the only one attempting to consider the interplay between the three levels of analysis and to explain the interconnected phenomena highlighted by the empirical evidence available. We therefore believe that this modernist approach is not only highly plausible, but that it also gives us a good heuristic basis for analyzing the process of diffusion of the NPM template across policy areas, within national contexts, and even transnationally. It is our opinion that what is driving this other process forward is a logic of political centralization and administrative decongestion wherein the market and performance management measures play only a token, rhetorical role. In this politically charged environment, current calls to replace 'output' managerial criteria with 'outcome' standards of evaluation seem to be both misplaced and counterproductive. At best, their adoption will add another bureaucratic layer to an already convoluted regulatory regime and give meta-regulators more opportunities to exploit the existence of multiple standards to foster their positional power and escape democratic accountability. Indeed, analyses of the impact measures recently introduced within British higher education – the switch from an output-based system like the Research Assessment Exercise (RAE) to an alternative outcome-based Research Excellence Framework (REF) – supply additional empirical evidence in support of the depoliticization thesis discussed here and represent a clear warning about the effectiveness of managerial fixes and those suggestions in particular. It is this policy area that we shall consider next.

Notes

1 'Political coup bred educational disaster', *The Guardian*, Tuesday, 16 September, 1999. Online: <https://www.theguardian.com/education/1999/sep/16/educationincrisis.uk4> (accessed 5 December 2016).

2 Page's (1985) work summarizes these problematics of government by comparing five Western countries: Britain, France, Germany, Holland and the US. In his words, 'the central problem posed by the development of bureaucracy as a form of social and political organization is that it limits the scope for policy initiatives to be made through the exercise of political authority of politicians who have gained their authority through the democratic struggle for power. Without the ability to exercise this authority, "democratic" forces, such as interest groups, parties and ministers,

may be *involved* in the process of governmental policy-making, but they cannot give it direction for which they can be held accountable' (Page 1985: 168, italics in original). Across the Atlantic, calls for a more representative bureaucracy brought about the formation of what Gruening (2001) calls the New Public Administration.

3 This point has been developed by Gruening (2001) in his discussion of NPM in American academia.

4 If Fry (2008: 152) is correct on this point, the government even managed to shift responsibility for the pay increase onto the devious mandarins, blamed for having classified 'the relevant documents in a way to ensure that the Prime Minister's Policy Unit did not see them officials ensured that the cabinet simply nodded through increases in Higher Civil Service salaries'. Similar strategies have along the years been used in higher education and the NHS, so the reading we are suggesting here of those events cannot be simply dismissed as a conspiracy theory.

5 The last expression is suggested by Sabel (1995) in relation to network form of production crossing the public–private divide and is more specific of the 'logic of appropriateness' suggested by March and Olsen (2006).

6 The thesis was first stated by Bulpitt (1986), taken up by Burnham (2001) and then developed by Buller and Flinders (2005) and Flinders and Buller (2006) – see also the exchange between these authors in the *British Journal of Politics & International Relations* (Burnham 2006 and Buller and Flinders 2006). More recently, a monographic issue of *Policy & Politics* (Flinders and Wood (eds) 2014) has been dedicated to this topic, which has also been taken up by Wood (2014), who proposes an interesting case study, and Diamond (2015). An analytical systematization of the thesis is to be found in Hay 2007.

7 According to cabinet office figures in 2006 there were 447 Advisory NDPBs in operation (Richards 2008: 113).

8 As Richards (2008: 120) explains, the newly established 'Delivery Unit has created a direct relationship between the centre and the multiple services deliverers which, in particular instances, is not mediated by government departments. There is an important change in resources with executive power shifting from departments to the Prime Minister's Office. The Delivery Unit created a direct line of responsibility between those in the field and Number Ten in a way that has not hitherto existed.'

5 Refining the template

NPM in British higher education

5.1 Introduction

James Vernon (2011), in a memorable phrase, argues that the UK has a good claim to be the 'canary in the coal mine' – i.e., at the forefront of a global experiment in the re-formation of higher education (HE). We believe him to be broadly correct and in this chapter hope to show why this is so. Our argument will be that it is in Britain that a revised version of the NPM template used earlier to modernize the civil service has been systematically applied since the early 1980s to make the university system more entrepreneurial. Furthermore, Britain has been the launch pad for the dissemination of this template across the European continent. In proposing our reading of the way in which the process of reform has unfolded decade upon decade, we shall add several qualifications to the arguments used by Vernon to justify his claim. First, as already explained in the previous chapter, many of the building blocks used to assemble the NPM template were not made in Britain, nor did they have a genuinely neoliberal pedigree. More than a decade earlier we find Marginson and Considine making a similar claim for a different part of the globe: 'it is almost as if public policies in Australia, New Zealand and similar nations have been fashioned as zones of neo-liberal experiment, testing economic outcomes and political reactions before the application of these policies to the global metropolises of the United States and Europe' (2000: 55). Britain has however been the country where the NPM fruit machine has been persistently spun until the right combinations of privatization, liberalization, and marketization were deployed and made operative. Moreover, Britain makes it evident that the ultimate objective has never been to create a free market in HE nor to engender neoliberal visions of market society, but rather to bring the HE sector under the control of central government. Finally, Britain has provided an example that other European countries have been eager to emulate, and one which bequeathed the NPM template to future generations by uploading it onto policy platforms tailored, as we shall show in the next chapter, to local context and available to all.

Studying the British case also gives us an insight into the way in which governments of changing political complexion have dealt with the mounting opposition generated by those reforms. Various affected social and institutional constituencies have mobilized against the reform movement imposing growing political costs on the parties supporting the neoliberal consensus. The dramatic decline of the Liberal Democratic Party in the 2015 general election is perhaps the most emblematic example. The U-turn on tuition fees during its spell in government with the Conservatives was, according to many observers, the main cause of the Liberals' electoral debacle. These tensions between forces of change ('reform') and stability, standardization, and differentiation, and between institutional layers are the main focus of this chapter. There is now a vast literature on the transformation of HE over the last 30 or so years, some of it analytical, some polemical, much both. Our aim here is to propose a framework for understanding these transformations that is consistent with the Polanyian outlook developed in this volume. This entails discussing three distinct levels of interaction: first, the relationship between HE and civil society at large; second, the internal organization of universities and how it has been affected by the introduction of corporate governance; finally, the relationship between HE suppliers and their political patrons. In stark contrast to both defenders and critics we want to use the three-level game to show that (i) the reforming movement has tapped into, and continues to exploit, a pre-existing and widespread dissatisfaction with the university system; (ii) the current sets of allegiances and incentives established at the turn of the century enable the reforming coalition to periodically regenerate itself and displace opposition forces; (iii) the reform process thus continues to unfold despite its contradictions and wider dysfunctional outcomes.

5.2 The development of the modern HE sector

Although the university system has its roots in the middle ages, in its modern incarnation its developmental path parallels that of public administrations (PAs) all over the Western world. The modern university is the outcome of political processes connected with the rise of the nation state (Dumont 1994; Kwiek 2008). Like any other pre-existing social institution, in the course of this process the old medieval universities were reshaped and given a new *raison d'être* (Rothblatt and Wittrock 1993; Shattock 2006; Scott and Pasqualoni 2016). A blend of economic reasons, ideological commitments, and cultural imperatives were used. This blend succeeded in making the university (like the church) at once a universal and a national institution (Dumont 1994; Nemec 2006). It is no coincidence that the criticisms levelled against this institution and the measures employed to reform it mirror those used in relation to PAs, irrespective of cultural, social, and economic differences. Unlike their continental counterparts, British universities were never part of the state apparatus, while their distinct milieu and charity status made them paragons of cultural prestige and organizational flexibility. Our task is then to understand how a field originally identified with 'organized anarchies' (Musselin 1996) and taken as an example of 'new modes of governance' (Peters 2002) could come to be likened to hierarchical bureaucratic forms operating according to a command-and-control logic and subsequently subjected to measures intended to introduce the discipline of the market.

What we call the university system is, in the British case more than elsewhere, an ensemble of variable institutional forms. Several attempts to arrive at a typology of those forms have been carried out to date, and there is a proliferation of labels used to identify the whole sector (Filippakou *et al* 2012). To keep things simple, we use the expression 'higher education' (HE) to identify the field of activities and HEIs for the institutions engaged in the business of further education, of which the traditional universities are merely a subset. The HE label covers the same semantic space of the expression 'tertiary education' also in circulation and strongly advocated by the OECD (Santiago *et al* 2008). Besides universities, there were two other institutional forms operating in the British HE sector worth recalling: the research laboratories engaged in research and development (R&D) and the polytechnics (Brennan and Williams 2008). Compared to those two alternative types, the university system has two notable characteristics: first, it was committed to unite research and teaching activities, rather than specializing in one or the other; second, the scientific and educational activities of any single university covered a large spectrum of fields and disciplines, stretching from the natural sciences to the humanities via the social sciences, and from the most theoretical to the most applied scientific approaches. Arguably, it has always been because of these commitments that other aspects, notably freedom of research and teaching, managerial collegiality, organizational autonomy, and non-instrumental academic values, were justified (Merton 1973 [1942]). By and large, the historical development of universities' legal status and their special relation with the modern state rested on multiple attempts to either foster or preserve those core values against external interference while retaining the universities' hegemonic position in the field of HE.[1] We shall argue that their relative success (or failure) in achieving those goals is at the root of widespread dissatisfaction with their *modus operandi* and the multiple attempts to reform the whole field.

Consequently, our premise is that an explanation of the reform movement started in the 1980s, and still in full swing, has to take into account both the reasons behind that dissatisfaction and the ability of key political and societal actors to exploit it. To this end, we need to briefly consider the role the university system played in the development of the welfare state in the post-war period and the nature of the relationship it established with the state in the process. We contend that it was the changes occurring in this historical phase that explain the formation of the fault-lines upon which the success of future developments depended.

The development of the welfare state brought about a major expansion of the education sector in response to the economic, social, and political needs of, first, reconstruction and, later, economic growth (Williams 2006). The 1960s witnessed not only a massive expansion of the university system, with the establishment of several new (plate-glass) university campuses, but also the creation of polytechnics engaged, largely, in vocational training.[2] This innovation caused a double process of differentiation. Polytechnics joined the universities in a HE sector in which the latter previously had a monopoly. Throughout their existence, polytechnics remained less prestigious institutions reserved for those lacking the economic means, or the right cultural background, or the required academic skills to go to university. As such, they mainly evolved as vocational teaching institutions formally excluded from public research funding. The newly established universities of the 1960s joined instead a multi-layered system occupied by other institutions – civic (redbrick) universities and the elitist Oxbridge establishments – which had a far superior reputation and exercised an overwhelming political and cultural hegemony. These distinctions, and the informal social hierarchy they supported, ensured that growing educational opportunities could promote a degree of social mobility without undermining the basis of the pre-existing economic, social, and academic order.[3] Concomitant reforms at lower levels left in place a parallel system of private education (public schools), which reinforced class distinctions and traditional relations of power (Turner 2015). Such a hierarchical order was replicated within the academic world, through disciplinary, professional, and gender divisions that remained seemingly untouched by the political and demographic changes occurring in the rest of British society (Ball 2003).

Towards the end of the 1960s, dissatisfaction with this state of affairs led to the unrest experienced by the academic world in many Western countries (Albert and Albert (eds) 1984; Marwick 1998; Klimke and Scharloth 2008). It has convincingly been argued that the 1970s legitimation crisis was indeed sparked by the student movements that rocked university life and managed to radicalize other sectors of society in their wake (Weiler 1983). In our opinion, three main cultural contradictions criss-crossed the academic world at the time and made students and a generation of young academics highly receptive to their political significance. Firstly, in contrast to the rhetoric, which often likened scientific enquiry to some sort of democratic activity, research was in fact dominated by undemocratic elites and used as a hegemonic tool by nation states engaged in the 'Cold War' (Amadae 2003; Edgerton 2006; Gilman 2003). Second, against the meritocratic rhetoric used to justify academic privileges, funds and career opportunities were very seldom distributed according to merit – a slippery notion very much dependent on the arbitrary results of natural and social lotteries (Ringer 1969; Halsey 1992). Third, against the public rhetoric celebrating the social and economic achievements of the welfare state, the growing ranks of HE students and teachers felt politically disenfranchised – an experience they shared with the workforce employed in the civil service (Judt 2005: Pt 2). Hence this period was characterized by disenchantment with the politics of the ballot-box and repeated calls to recast democracy, whether of the state or professions, from the bottom up (Gassert 2008).[4] Recalling these events is for us important for three reasons. First, they make clear that there existed a wide movement calling for an overhaul of the system. Second, they help explain the route taken and tactics used by those state actors and societal agents who started the reform process in the 1980s and have been at its forefront ever since. Third, they highlight the limitations of those critiques based on romantic visions of a prelapsarian golden age and the normative suggestions drawn from it.[5]

5.3 Reforming the British HE sector: a plotted history

In Appendix 2 we list all the main reform initiatives launched in the last three decades. Our aim here is not to discuss each one of them, but rather to detect patterns that can help us understand the overarching logic linking them. In proposing a bird's eye view of overlapping and recursive waves of reform, we distinguish between two interlinked aspects that characterize the whole process. The first concerns the sets of reasons used by policy makers, advisers, practitioners, and analysts alike to justify specific interventions and changes. These will be discussed under three main headings:

- *efficiency drives*: measures directed at improving the inner working of the university system while reducing its economic burden on public finances;
- *corporate governance*: measures aiming to rationalize and standardize the organizational structure of the entities operating in the HE sector to make them fully accountable;
- *growth machine*:[6] the role attributed to HE within the evolving social and economic context that characterized the world at the turn of the twenty-first century.

In discussing these aspects of the reform process, we also need to remember that even when they are used in isolation from each other interventions that fall under one heading end up having consequences for the others. In other words, measures seeking to boost the efficiency of universities entail changes in the meaning of their activities and vice versa, and both of them have further implications for the division and organization of intellectual labour. We insist on discussing them first, in order to classify the variety of policy instruments employed, and then to spell out what causal relation can be established between policy instruments and policy issues. This way of proceeding also gives us the opportunity to identify and analyze the reasons used to justify intervening in the field and mobilize public opinion makers accordingly.

The second aspect concerns the connection between policy instruments and fields of activity. Taken as variables, distinct policy instruments have sometimes been used to change the architectural structure of HE (and/or the organizational setup of the institutions working within this sector); at other times to change the managerial practices employed in that sector without touching its formal structure and organization. Similarly, we can distinguish measures directed mainly at the research side of universities' activities from those targeting mostly their teaching activities. Obviously, many reforms operate simultaneously at both structural and managerial levels, and affect both research and teaching. Nonetheless, these distinctions have an analytical and heuristic value we are keen to retain. We want to investigate the possibility that structural and managerial changes are parts of more complex strategies and that they are meant to operate in concert. In this sense, we express growing reservations about those readings that present the shift from one approach to another as a function of the electoral cycle; the result of unintended consequences or functional drives to realize public value. The available evidence does not make this organic reading of the reform process implausible. Far from it, we maintain that it can explain many of the alleged paradoxes, puzzles, and inconsistencies noted about the overall process.

5.3.1 Efficiency drives

As for the rest of the public sector, the arrival of Margaret Thatcher as Prime Minister in 1979 meant the introduction of serious cuts in the budget of universities. The refusal of the government to renegotiate those cuts in a neo-corporatist fashion and its ability to survive multiple political crises eventually made universities realize that some rationalization and cost-cutting needed to be undertaken. At this initial stage, the reforms introduced were mainly managerial in nature and left to the discretion of the university system itself. The institutional actor that acquired a leading role in promoting change was the Universities Grants Committee (UGC), which thereby acquired a more proactive planning role (Brown with Carasso 2013). Replicating the experience of the Rayner's Scrutinies discussed in the previous chapter, the criteria used by the UGC to distribute the burden of the cuts among universities were highly controversial and created considerable resentment.[7] However, compliance with the austerity measures imposed by the government failed to endear the UGC to their political principals, and in 1992 a second round of reforms brought to an end both the commission and the system of block grants with which the university system had been funded since the 1950s (Tapper and Salter 1995).[8]

This was the start of a pattern of government intervention similar to the one noted in the previous chapter that has been repeated throughout the intervening period, with managerial reforms being followed by structural reforms and vice versa in a recursive manner. The main differences between parallel reforms of the civil service were due to the fact that, thanks to their charters and charity status, universities retained formal independence from the government of the day, and thus direct, top-down enforcement was not an option. Over the years, this forced various governments to build an intricate regulatory system aimed at establishing growing legal constraints and mechanisms of audit that have reduced the autonomy of the university system and its self-regulating powers in an expanding number of domains, not only administration, but also teaching and research (Brenneis *et al* 2005; King

2007; Gregory 2009). For Burnes *et al* (2014: 911): 'the 1981 cuts, in effect, signalled the end of university independence. From then on, successive governments took an increasingly close regulatory interest in the running of universities'.

The next managerial innovation yielded by external financial pressures that was to have an enduring impact on academic life was the establishment of the Research Assessment Exercise (RAE), as a pilot project, in 1986 (Broadbent 2010; Goldfinch and Yamamoto 2012: Ch. 4; Brown with Carasso 2013: Ch. 4). Although the intellectual paternity of the RAE remains hotly disputed, it is widely acknowledged that it was a discretionary act of self-regulation suggested by the university system itself in order to assuage those dissatisfied with the way in which the UGC operated in relation to the 1981 cuts and to counter the popular public image of universities as ivory towers by presenting them as meritocratic work environments. The aim of the RAE was to reward scientific output with research funding in a transparent fashion. The output of each institution engaged in research was henceforth to be assessed and rewarded in relation to the quality of the research produced, as required by then fashionable performance management models. This meant: (i) establishing a common metric to measure the research output of a heterogeneous array of colleges and departments operating in many disciplinary fields; (ii) producing a national ranking for all public funded British universities and research centres; (iii) redistributing a growing part of the overall budget allocated by the government to research according to the results of the exercise.

We shall return to the effects of the introduction of the RAE within the university system later. For now, we would like to note that the efforts of the universities in this direction notwithstanding, governments of different hues have persisted in altering the parameters by using changeable combinations of structural and managerial policies (Bence and Oppenheim 2005). After a couple of decades dedicated to fine-tuning the mechanism, in 2010 the government announced a shift from the RAE to the REF (Research Excellence Framework) that in effect attributes to itself growing powers in assessing the impact of research, thus undermining the system of peer-review used up to that date to lend legitimacy to the whole enterprise (Sousa and Brennan 2014; Willmott 2003).

The introduction of research audit should be seen in a broader reform context: government-led structural changes introduced by the 1992 Education Reform Act (ERA). The act put an end to the binary system in place up to then and set the conditions for creating a unitary model of HE by integrating the polytechnics into the university system.[9] The innovations brought about by the 1992 ERA cannot easily be reconciled with the efficiency drives that had dominated the reform discourse up to that moment (Dearlove 1998: 116). In fact, the Act pursued an organizational type of rationalization that had no clear impact either on efficiency or on the reduction of burdens on public finance. We shall thus discuss it under a separate heading.

5.3.2 Corporate governance

The merits of a unitary model were considered three decades earlier by the Robbins Commission and found wanting. Thus, the final report published in 1962 suggested maintaining a binary HE sector, and the rationalization that followed it brought about the formation of some 33 polytechnics – HEIs which came to be presented in the public discourse of the time as the 'people's university' (Robinson 1968). This solution meant retaining not only two educational models within the sector, one more elitist, reserved for those with more academic interests and skills, and one reserved for those in need of shorter, vocational training courses to prepare them for the job market. It also meant keeping distinct organizational models and systems of governance, both of them largely independent from central government: an autonomous system of universities committed to carry on research and teaching across the board and a locally controlled system of polytechnics engaged in teaching activities in more restricted professional fields. About the latter, Dearlove notes that,

> because most colleges of higher education were local authority institutions, their staff were employed and buildings owned by local education authorities. Governance was characterised by local political regulation (later replaced by national and more professional regulation through the National Advisory Body and the Council for National Academic Awards) and this made for a lack of institutional and academic autonomy. [...] the reality was that governing bodies and principals/directors went largely unchallenged even though institutional management was itself weakly developed because many key functions remained the responsibility of local authorities.
>
> (Dearlove 1998: 113, references removed)

Thus, prior to 1992, the British HE sector was characterized by the kind of 'educational schism' that still exists, for example, in the German-speaking HE sector between vocational education and training (VET) on the one hand and the *Volluniversitäten* (public universities covering a wide range of disciplines and engaged in both teaching and research) on the other (Graf 2013). Crucially, both systems used to enjoy a significant degree of autonomy from the government of the day in academic matters.

With the passing of the 1992 ERA, central government wished instead to reverse this state of affairs and create a single HE sector with a homogeneous system of governance (Holligan 2010); an objective that runs counter to the principled opposition to big government and one-size-fits-all logic that purportedly inspires neoliberal reforms of the welfare state. In a similarly contradictory manner, the task of bringing about the unification of HE was to be attributed to policy tools and audit mechanisms the main goal of which was to promote student choice, institutional competition, and bring the discipline of the market into the public sector (Burnes *et al* 2014: 911). Applied to the organizational forms working within HE, the NPM template has been employed in order to import an informal corporate structure into a field previously reserved for entities having a contrasting legal status (charities), and to impose upon them a mode of corporate governance at odd with the rationale supporting that (not-for-profit) status (Cox 2013). The reason for doing so has been attributed to the alleged ability of the corporation and its system of governance to enforce better mechanisms of accountability and a superior responsiveness of service providers to their political principals and patrons (Bleiklie *et al* 2011). In Shattock's words:

> concerns about the transparency and accountability to shareholders in public companies and the potential economic impact of large private sector corporate failure have prompted the state, as higher education's largest stakeholder, to wish to import the mechanisms being put in place in the private sector to safeguard the state's interests in higher education.
> (Shattock 2006: 209)

Besides the fact that no past university failure (large or small) could be invoked to justify this form of state intervention, the process of corporatization of HE has depended on the establishment of a complex regulatory regime that, in contrast to the one used to regulate public companies and the newly privatized utilities, has (i) precipitated the passage from self-regulation to centrally imposed norms (Moran 2003); (ii) opposed the emergence of an American-style free-market in HE, viewed favourably by some HEIs, on the ground of equality of opportunities and inclusion.

The chronicle of HE corporatization supplied by Shattock (2006) identifies three main milestones:

1 the 1985 *Jarratt Report*, whose recommendations where part of the provisions laid down in the 1988 and 1992 ERA legislation;
2 the 1997 *Dearing Report*, designed to extend those pieces of legislation to the pre-1992 universities;
3 the 2003 *Lambert Review*, commissioned by the Chancellor of the Exchequer to look at business community-university system collaboration.

During the building of this regulatory regime, the autonomy of universities has been progressively eroded: first by the need to plainly differentiate management from governance, second by the attempt to shift the balance of power from the faculty to the top managerial layers and third by the setting of limits (numerical and professional) to collegial bodies like the traditional senates. The two main actors leading this process have been vice chancellors on one side, and central government on the other. They were in time joined by academic entrepreneurs and private corporations. Working in concert and supporting each other politically and financially, these actors have imposed on the sector a corporate structure committed to top-down governability yielding far-reaching results affecting both the working conditions of those operating within HEIs and the identity of academics themselves (Barnett and Di Napoli 2008). This process is summarized well by Alderman:

> Managerialism has [...] undermined (and not simply redefined) academic priorities: learning has been replaced by teaching; disinterested academic inquiry has been replaced by centrally directed research likely to impress assessment panels. [...] Other than within the narrow confines of the classroom and the lecture theatre, academics today have very little autonomy. The academic community has been replaced by the institutional workshop, the academy by the corporation.
>
> (Alderman 2010: 251)

Here we want to recall three examples of distortions produced by the centrally imposed regulatory regime noted from the start, and often anticipated during the planning stage. The first pertains to the balance between research and teaching that is taken as one of the distinctive features of the university *vis-à-vis* more specialized institutions (Fuller 2009). The introduction of the RAE and its impact on the distribution of research funds has pushed universities and academics to adopt competitive strategies that have led them to neglect teaching, especially at undergraduate level (Jenkins 2004; Zaman 2004; Baty 2005; Cummings 2009; Locke 2014). Since universities get little economic benefit from running standard undergraduate courses, there was no real motivation to commit resources and energies into improving teaching standards at that level, and preoccupations about their decline have been raised ever since – to date teaching quality assessments (TQAs) do not have any financial implications. Moreover, since academic careers have became heavily dependent on the individual's research output, teaching has come low in the priorities of an academic personnel hard pushed to 'publish or perish' (Bauerlein 2009). Furthermore, since the RAE discriminated against publications that did not appear in peer-reviewed journals of international standing or as research monograph, and were thus not viewed as proper research outputs, even the traditional commitments toward the writing of textbooks and other didactic aids started to suffer. Following the introduction of tuition fees in the 2000s, this emphasis upon research at the cost of teaching has led to a growing discontent among students and their families, thus giving central government additional excuses for interfering in HE governance to redress that problem. These efforts culminated in the Green Paper submitted for consultation at the end of 2015, and which has since become a White Paper, that sets the course for a new overhaul of the system (Collini 2016; Holmwood *et al* 2016).

The attempt to establish a corporate system of governance within the universities by turning students into consumers is at the root of systemic tensions between the various disciplinary areas and the methodological approaches coexisting within HE. On the research side, the development of an entrepreneurial approach has shifted the balance between theoretical and more applied (or technology-oriented) scientific engagements (Noble 1998). Pressures to use scientific discoveries, developments, and innovations in commercially rewarding ways have undermined both traditional commitments towards basic research and the disinterested attitude towards knowledge advocated by Robert Merton in the 1940s (see Radder 2010). On the teaching side, this shift towards entrepreneurialism has at once reduced the number of undergraduate students interested in basic research and theoretical subjects offering poor career prospects (as measured by expected future income). Consequently, the viability of undergraduate courses in those disciplinary fields has been undermined, especially when they also require sophisticated and expensive infrastructures. As Williams explains,

> STEM subjects [i.e. research and teaching in science, technology, engineering and mathematics] are intrinsically more expensive to teach. If they were not subsidised, either their fees would need to be very high, or some of the fees paid by non-STEM students would need to be used to cross-subsidise them. In either case there can be little doubt that without subsidy many STEM subjects would disappear from many universities. This is what a market solution would decree.
>
> (Williams 2011: 2–3)

Once again, in contradiction to official denials about the real existence of the problem, this has given central government the authority to tinker with the artificially created student market in order to shield STEM disciplines from its unintended side-effects. In doing so, government has given itself and the constellations of regulatory agencies surrounding it the freedom to use double standards whenever they see fit.

The problem created by this last distortion was once again brought to the attention of the general public by the introduction of tuition fees and the system of student loans devised to support it since the 1990s (Greenaway and Haynes 2003). This set of reforms represents an interesting case study in itself, for it exemplifies the inconsistencies between actual reforms and the rhetorical appeals made to justify them while also making it clear that those inconsistencies do not depend on the electoral cycle. The various attempts to stop universities from raising tuition fees to cover the full costs of teaching have been imposed by both Conservative and Labour governments in order to guarantee widespread access to HE. Since the abolition of the block grant system and the cuts imposed on local authorities' finances in the 1990s, fair access has been assured by a raft of regulatory measures that have shifted the financial and moral burden to universities and to students and their families. Universities have been pushed to cross-subsidize British students by developing the educational facilities reserved to overseas students, whereas students and their families have taken growing financial responsibilities by using the loan schemes introduced by the government. Given the capping and other types of limitations imposed each time, the reforms have in practice avoided setting the conditions for the development of the very market used to justify their existence – and this despite the request of the universities themselves for a full liberalization. At the same time, government policy has not helped the students' case; British students now find themselves paying the highest tuition fees in Europe and are trapped in a loan repayment scheme that the government of the day can change anytime at will.

5.3.3 Growth machine

In the process of changing the governance of universities to make them follow a more corporate logic, the reforms introduced to date are transforming their very *raison d'être*. Although there has always been a lively debate about what universities are for, in the post-war period a substantive agreement was reached that connected them to the democratic value-system subscribed to by Western countries.[10] The university system was attributed four main roles: (i) that of producing knowledge in a free and democratic manner; (ii) that of forming the democratic character needed to live according to liberal democratic principles; (iii) that of embodying *in nuce* the style of life and forms of organization required by a well-ordered democratic polity; and (iv) that of turning such a well-ordered polity into a universal value ripe for global dissemination. As a result, radical left-wing students blamed university authorities for failing to live up to the very values they upheld at the rhetorical level, while their more conservative counterparts attempted justify the inevitable gap between facts and values by stressing the challenges posed by totalitarian ideologies and regimes opposed to liberal democracy – challenges which during the Cold War promoted a lively philosophical debate about the limits of toleration (Wolf, Moore and Marcuse 1965; Rawls 1971, §35; Williams and Waldron 2008). In this period, universities prided themselves on being beacons of tolerance, preserving social pluralism, and fostering individuality, even while performing their patriotic duties like few other public institutions (Edgerton 2006). Because of the stated need to make them either more efficient or more accountable and responsive, three full decades of change have undermined the hegemonic role universities once enjoyed and are now advocating a novel conception of HE as a growth machine, one which is highly contested by a clear majority of all affected interests (Newfield 2008).

Disputing the HE field at present are two main camps. A coterie of policy advisers and policy makers, consultants and practitioners, private suppliers and think tanks tend to present to the public a picture of the newly emerging HE sector as a vibrant sector made up of self-reliant organizations operating in synergy as engines for economic growth, useful social innovations, and cutting-edge scientific research (Etzkowitz 1990; Gibbons *et al.* 1994; Shane 2004; Thorp and Goldstein 2010; Adams 2013). In this glossy picture, HE is also ascribed the task of supplying high quality but standardized academic titles that students can reliably spend on the job market to secure a good return on their investment (Walberg and Bast 2003; Wildavsky 2010). Committed to engender this ideal, central government finds itself entitled to: (i) compel suppliers to release hidden information; (ii) make that information intelligible to investors; (iii) establish clear-cut responsibilities and lines of accountability towards shareholders and customers; (iv) appoint the auditors and regulators needed to make the market mechanism working; (v) instil the right work ethics on all those upon whom its success depends (Bundy 2004; Shattock 2006). Thus, structural and managerial reforms follow each other seamlessly and recursively, partnerships are established with all societal agents willing to exploit the opportunity offered by the HE proxy-markets within and beyond national boundaries, and public moneys are used to bring about the most congenial set of social incentives. In the process, university status and degree awarding powers have been given to an array of specialized institutions operating in restricted disciplinary fields, free from any commitment to do research, and moved by the profit motive (sometimes in spite of their charity status).[11]

By way of contrast, a broad alliance of stakeholders directly affected by those changes insist on pointing out that, far from removing old privileges and stimulating innovation, the reforms are granting new privileges and exploitation rights to private actors who, unlike traditional universities, are not willing to assume broader social responsibilities (Schugurensky 2006). The introduction of the NPM template is blamed for having made universities lean and mean; engaged in relentless costs-cutting exercises that are betraying both professional standards and the logic of the good employer to which they were committed in the past (Rhoades 1998; Johnson *et al* 2003; Meek *et al* 2010). Moreover, ceaseless austerity measures are pushing them to commodify and commercially exploit all aspects of academic life (Willmott 1995; Noble 1998; Radder 2010; Foskett 2011). Above all, the proliferation of external rules and managerial constraints are perceived as suffocating intellectual freedoms and organizational autonomy, and are attributing to those operating on the front-line responsibilities they cannot realistically discharge (Donoghue 2015). In research, the shift towards technology-oriented developments has been accompanied by reduced inter-organizational cooperation due to the need to preserve secrecy and commercial advantage over potential competitors (Irzik 2007). In teaching, a badly paid and demotivated temporary personnel is now in charge of many undergraduate courses and shares with the rest of the faculty responsibility for promoting economic growth and employment even when their own career prospects are deeply uncertain (Gould 2006; Professor X 2011). Finally, students are asked to make complex and costly decisions concerning their future life prospects in turbulent environments where HE providers are competing for customers, the information they provide is highly unreliable, and the employment market can change unexpectedly any time (Brynin 2013; Landry and Neubauer 2016).

Subtle but profound are also the implications that this regulatory regime has for liberal-democratic values. The corporatization of universities entails attributing a privileged position to their shareholders *vis-à-vis* other stakeholders (Benneworth and Jongbloed 2010). This means giving growing powers to investors, which, in a HE sector dependent on public finance, means mainly central government. Accordingly, collegiality and internal forms of workplace democracy are replaced by new mechanisms of accountability exalting the role of financial sponsors and the mechanisms of audit controlled by the latter (Shore and Wright 1999; Tapper and Palfreyman 2010; Bleiklie 2012; Burnes *et al* 2014). Students and the academic workforce are left with a residual power of exit similar to the one accorded to consumers and workers in other sectors of the corporate economy (Teixeira *et al* 2004). As a result, the model of representative democracy developed during the post-war period is progressively being displaced, in theory and practice, by an alternative vision of democracy relying on 'exit' rather than 'voice', and concerned with giving everyone an alleged power to vote-with-their-feet (Palumbo 2015, Ch. 2). This is the case even though, in the end, that power of exit always remains a promise impossible to fulfil in practice because of the public nature of HE as an economic good (Turner 2011), and the tendency of the suppliers working in it to segment the market itself (Shin and Kehm 2013; Enders 2015). By combining a notion of the universities as a growth machine and pressures to assume the behavioural traits of the corporate world, the reforms raise the prospect that even the HE sector could, in the near future, be caught in the cyclical crises that have beset those of other consumer markets in recent times (McGettigan 2013) and reinforce the current drift towards post-democracy noticed in several OECD countries (Schostak and Goodson 2012).

5.4 From hegemony to heteronomy: explaining cultural and institutional change in HE

As in the case of the civil service discussed in the previous chapter, there is no possibility of adjudicating between these contending claims on empirical grounds alone; not least because the process is still unfolding. Nor is it possible to separate facts and values easily given that both advocates and critics base their claims on idealized pictures of the university that tend to emphasize past aspects and future achievements that remain deeply contested. To put it bluntly, if the prelapsarian research university was the intellectual and scientific environment most suitable for the development of disinterested knowledge and democratic learning (Fuller 2009), how is it possible to explain the ability of reformers to shake its very foundations with the crucial help of insiders fancying themselves as academic entrepreneurs? Conversely, if the reforms have succeeded in improving the efficiency and social relevance of the HE sector, as often claimed by supporters, why is there the need to engage in periodic institutional and managerial reshuffles that could jeopardize those very achievements (not to mention the continuous opposition of the very constituencies that are supposed to benefit from those social gains)? The more complex hypotheses advanced to date overlap with the theses discussed previously and show the same weaknesses noted there. A further discussion of the relative plausibility of those theses in relation to HE would merely lead us to repeat the same lines of reasoning.

Rather than revisit concerns and lines of argument already covered in the previous chapter, here we shall argue that the introduction of the NPM template into HE was not aimed at creating the type of free market advocated by neoliberal ideologues and their think tanks. Were this the intention of policy makers, it could have been realized in a much more direct and simple way. This is especially the case in Britain where the university system was not part of the apparatus of the state and its internal differentiation made that objective more viable than in other parts of the public sector (utilities, transport systems, postal services, etc.) where privatization has created highly segmented markets dominated by oligopolistic powers. The intricate and evolving regulatory regime brought about by the various reforms listed in Appendix 2 has in fact created a 'market on the leash' that political principals can control and use in a self-serving way. We also believe that, rather than responding to external systemic pressures – globalizing market forces (Zgaga *et al.* 2013) or post-modern cultural drives (Nealon 2012), it is more plausible to assume that the reasons underlying those changes have to do with the often noted dynamic of centralization promoted as a result.[12] In our view, the latter cannot be explained as the result of unintended consequences, but has been the main objective of policy makers throughout.

What remains intriguing and in need of proper explanation is the way in which this centralization of powers (and the parallel decentralization of administrative functions) has been achieved in a sector that once enjoyed a substantial degree of autonomy, social and cultural hegemony, and (unlike the civil service) professional prestige. This is the task that we now set ourselves. To this end, we employ the heuristic of the three-level game to clarify the tactical moves and countermoves that have allowed central government to exploit a number of pre-existing fault lines in order to undermine resistance and impose its political will on the whole sector. Reversing the order used in the previous chapter, here we start with an analysis of the third level (university–civil society relationship), then move up to the second level (relations within the HE sector), to finally arrive at the first level (HE suppliers and their political principals).

5.4.1 Playing the HE game at the third level: the quest for fairness and responsiveness

As we saw earlier, the post-war reconstruction and the development of the welfare state attributed to HE (and the university system in particular) a pivotal role in democratizing Western societies (Glaeser *et al* 2007). Although the 1960s expansion of the HE sector fitted quite well with the economic philosophy of Keynesian consensus politics, the democratic aspirations went unmet. Culturally dominated by an elitist Oxbridge model, the British process of expansion introduced within HE new institutional layers and a growing number of people unable to identify with that model. Towards the end of that decade, discontent was rife and led to the student protest movements that challenged the system by highlighting its internal contradictions.[13] Universities were blamed for being hierarchical and repressive institutions; supporting social distinctions, class divisions, and colonial attitudes; keeping and maintaining a detached and unresponsive stance towards civil society (Maher and Tetreault 2007). In short, we find here a blend of elements closely resembling the ones discussed in relation to the civil service, perhaps unsurprisingly given the obvious structural links between the two sectors.

The 1960s expansionist policies had the effect of magnifying pre-existing internal contradictions, adding new ones, and attributing to them a larger social and political relevance. Attempting to tackle those contradictions autonomously and creatively, universities developed experimental forms of governance antithetical to the bureaucratic one based on command-and-control. Notions like the 'garbage can model' and 'organized anarchies' are derived from those experimentations and sought to identify alternative conceptual approaches to competing statist and market-based managerial philosophies (Cohen, March and Olsen 1972). The key to understanding why HE has been subjected to the same medicine as other sectors of the state and reformed using a NPM template purportedly seeking to impose the discipline of the market is, we argue, related to political (as opposed to economic) factors that are worth investigating. Social dissatisfaction with the university system was due, first of all, to its seeming unresponsiveness to the needs of its main stakeholders. Failure to carry out a full democratization of the universities meant in effect absence of proper channels of voice allowing distinct societal agents to make themselves heard and influence academic policies concerning admission, curricula, and social mobility (Greenwood 2007). Collegiality in many settings reinforced donnish dominance rather than supporting a form of participatory democracy, and was the object of strong criticism by junior faculty members, administrators, and students (Halsey 1982). Moreover, the dominance of both a privately run system of 'public schools' outside HE and the Oxbridge model inside it meant that only some sectors of society and some skills received favourable treatment. The binary system in place up to the incorporation of the polytechnics in 1992 institutionalized class divisions, reproduced social privileges and represented, therefore, a source of stated and unstated dissatisfaction that left universities politically isolated in the face of plans of a determined government to unify the HE sector and impose upon it the same model of corporate governance.

Similarly, the question of fair and equal access to HE has systematically been exploited by varying governments of all stripes to impose a consumeristic logic opposed by students and faculty alike (Clarke *et al* 2007; Needham 2007). Consumerism is, from this perspective, a means to create a permanent divide between students and educators, the aim of which is to increase the costs of collective action faced by those opposing new rounds of reform: 'one effect of the introduction of student consumerism is that previously integrated relationships between academics and students are likely to become dis-aggregated with each party invested with distinct, if not opposing, interests' (Naidoo 2008: 60). At the same time, given the public nature of HE as a consumer good, and the inherent difficulty of developing a pure competitive market in this sector, consumerism also provides an opportunity to interfere with the functioning of supply and demand and justifies using double standards to do so (Tight 2013).

As already mentioned, the introduction of a corporate structure and form of governance has been unable to overcome the biases that caused public dissatisfaction with the university system. This is hardly surprising, for corporate governance is predicated on the primacy of shareholders and aims at increasing their control over management (Palumbo 2009). Within the HE sector, the introduction of corporate forms of governance has reinforced the accountability of universities to their more immediate paymasters; that is central government and the handful of private investors entering into this new business (Gregory 2009; Shore 2008). As consumers, HE students are given a very ineffective power of exit and left with growing debts (which will in the end require, no doubt, public bailout). Current worries about the inflating of a HE bubble that will eventually burst (like the 2008 subprime crisis) are far from fevered and capture some uncanny similarities between the evolutionary paths of HE and residential property markets (Altbach 2013: Ch. 9).[14] On the other hand, growing student debts and uncertain career prospects are powerful antidotes to widespread revolts 1968 style – an effective tool to depoliticize a troublesome constituency – and that explains the commitment to it by alternative governmental forces.

At this third level of interaction, the picture gets even gloomier when we consider the effects of the commodification of academic research. While still waiting for the supposed financial benefits that academic entrepreneurialism is supposed to bring, a string of negative side-effects have been noted and analyzed (Krimsky 2003; Jasanoff 2005; Radder 2010). The first concerns the detrimental effects entrepreneurialism is having on basic research and on those branches of human knowledge that do not have an evident technological or commercial value, a point to which we shall return. Misleadingly, current debates on the matter draw attention on the negative impact the market is having on the humanities (Donoghue 2008; Collini 2011; Hyslop-Margison and Leonard 2012). Thus, the defence of the public university is often linked to the preservation of a liberal education, to which is in turn attributed heroic democratic virtues (Nussbaum 2010; Brown 2015). As we shall argue, the concern is genuine, but the lower status acquired by the humanities is not due to the market *per se*, but to the set of rules imposed to shield the STEM subjects from the combined effects of academic entrepreneurialism and the introduction of tuition fees and student loans (Allen 2016).[15] If tuition fees are discouraging younger generations from enrolling in courses that do not assure profitable career paths, it is also clear that the former is redirecting academic research towards those fields that could have clear financial returns, some of which have debatable scientific credentials. It is for these reasons and in order to counter these perverse effects that the government has had to ring-fence the STEM subjects. Ironically, shielding STEM subjects from the market casts doubts on the economic rationale used to justify the overall reform programme. First, it implicitly acknowledges that the market can have serious detrimental effects on the so-called knowledge economy in the long term. Second, it also corroborates the concerns of those warning about the limited benefits private entrepreneurialism could bring to universities financially. To date, even the most successful (American) research universities find it impossible to cross-subsidize the pure sciences with the returns of their techno-scientific activities (Williams 2006), hence the need to protect them with specific policies and dedicated public funds.

A related controversial aspect of academic entrepreneurialism concerns its support for predatory commercial ventures. Public research centres are often found to be engaged in dubious activities: from biopiracy, to the privatization of vast areas of knowledge that were already in the public domain and/or were acquired by using public funds, to hidden lobbying activities in support of mega corporations (Noble 1998; Washburn 2001). In the life sciences, suspicions about the emergence of widespread collusive practices involving research institutions, corporate actors, and the publishing industry have been raised, exposing both the problematic nature of scientific knowledge and the deteriorating conditions of professional labour (Kassirer 2004; Brody 2007; Rudy *et al* 2007; Walters 2011). Lack of scientific certainty is used in a highly postmodern fashion to stop outlawing or even regulating technologies and practices, which may have devastating long-term side-effects on consumers, the environment, or even knowledge itself whenever those actions entail liabilities for corporate sponsors and private partners. In short, the commercialization and corporatization of science is skewed in favour of some powerful societal actors and could well be exploited by corporations to externalize their R&D activities in order to reduce their risks and liabilities. As a result, they are rightly perceived as responsible for undermining widely held scientific public values and penalizing vast sectors of society upon whom the entire HE sector still depends financially, i.e. the taxpayer. In Jasanoff's words

> Science–state–industry collaborations designed for the advancement of public welfare may have had the contrary effect of introducing new zones of non-accountability into the democratic management of knowledge production and use. Underlying these debates was a growing concern about the capacity of elected officials to discern the public interest and adequately represent it in dealings with science and industry. In building their alliances with science to foster wealth creation, had states lost sight of other values and needs of citizens in contemporary knowledge societies?
>
> (Jasanoff 2005: 227)

When viewed and analyzed from a strategic perspective, the relationship between universities and civil society looks like one where the latter is fairly disappointed by the former (as ivory tower) and is pushing for change. This relation is however mediated by a political elite that has progressively removed from the universities a large part of their freedom to respond autonomously and imposed instead reforms that have created a high degree of internal resentment without addressing the root causes of that social disappointment. While adopting market rhetoric, the policy makers at the forefront of the reform movement have assiduously avoided establishing a market structure connecting suppliers and consumers directly. Rather, they are engaged in the development of a very intricate regulatory regime that postpones the establishing of the market *sine die*. The relation is thus evolving into a topsy-turvy triangular interaction with incumbent governments feeding distrust into it to retain their positional power (Gambetta 1988). Consumers are thus induced to behave according to a competitive market logic even when they have no real power of exit, whereas private businesses are given the opportunity to commodify and exploit a HE sector that was built and remains highly dependent on public monies. The reason why no genuine market has emerged so far (and will probably never emerge) is due to the fact that it would undermine the mediating powers of central government, while attributing to it full political responsibility any time the HE market fails. In contrast, the multi-layered regulatory regime imposed (one that combines procedural and substantive criteria of evaluation) preserves its mediating powers while shifting responsibility for failure to both suppliers and consumers. To appreciate this strategic logic and the responses it sets in motion, we need to consider the two other levels of our game.

5.4.2 Playing the HE game at the second level: performing, complying and enduring

The second level concerns the strategic relations within the HE sector. The first step in analyzing those relationships consists in identifying the various actors operating in it and the potential conflicts dividing them. As already explained, consumerism aims at turning students from what in the past was considered an inner subset requiring ‘voice’ into an external set of patrons able to ‘exit’. Besides the students–educators divide, there remain three other main fault lines that have been repeatedly exploited to create divisions set to weaken the political agency of universities *vis-à-vis* central government. The first is the discipline-based structure underpinning scientific activities within the modern research university; the second concerns the hierarchical structure underpinning the division of intellectual labour; the third pertains to the traditional distinction between faculty and administration. In analyzing them we shall in turn highlight each time how the newly established regulatory regime heightens tensions in order to pursue the executive’s centralizing agenda. We shall also endeavour to explain the role the corporatization of HE is playing in establishing crucial strategic alliances between reformers and subsets of the academic world, a theme that will be fully explored when we turn our attention to the first level.

Of the many divides criss-crossing HE, the divisions within self-contained disciplines is perhaps the most intriguing (Abbott 2001; Becher and Trowler 2001). As we noted in Chapter 3, from the perspective of many academics, the pursuit of knowledge and its attendant benefits require 'walls' around both disciplines and universities, and an organizational structure that respects that autonomy, both internally and externally. Here we wish to consider how the various waves of reform have affected and exploited disciplinary divisions within HE. Following the creation of cost centres and the abolition of the block grant system of funding in the 1980s, competition within and between British HEIs has reinforced disciplinary boundaries and the power of institutional gate-keepers (Oleinik 2015). The development of the RAE, for instance, has had a twofold effect. On the one hand, it has led to the standardization of assessment criteria. The preference given to journal articles above other publication outlets has been followed by the definition of the impact factor for each academic journal and then by the establishment of strict editorial criteria that need to be met before the paper is deemed publishable. Researchers across a variety of fields have thus been progressively pushed to conform to standards reflecting established orthodoxies that are thought to have unimpeachable scientific credentials (Lee 2007; Lee *et al* 2013). Often those standards are borrowed from some specific disciplines (notably the natural sciences) and then imposed on other research fields having distinct epistemic strata (say social sciences or humanities, or even the arts), promoting a problematic proliferation of controversial approaches and attitudes: vulgar empiricism, overabundance of micro case studies, salami-slicing publishing, cut-and-paste techniques, etc. This has transformed the mechanisms of peer-review as well, making them increasingly disciplinarian and controversial (Jasanoff 1990, Ch. 4; Shatz 1996; Gould 2012; Oleinik 2015, Ch. 7). Since the start of the REF, the progressive undermining of peer-review in favour of more 'objective' and 'cheaper' bibliometrics is exacerbating tensions within and between disciplines, leaving meta-regulators even more powerful and less accountable (Bence and Oppenheim 2004; Musselin 2013a).

On the other hand, the RAE has also promoted and strengthened rather than – as some had hoped – challenged the informal hierarchies within and between HEIs (Elton 2000). Rather than contest the Oxbridge model, repeated rounds of research assessment have in effect formalized the predominance of the universities belonging to the Russell Group, relegated the former polytechnics (whose spokes-person is the think tank MillionPlus) to the bottom of the national table leagues, and assigned a buffer role to the new (plate glass) universities belonging to the 94 Group (Brown with Carasso 2013: 21). Given the fact that the funds allocated to research have contracted over the years, the RAE has thus assumed the function of justifying state support for a restricted number of elite institutions, rather than a tool for rewarding performance (Willmott 2003). A similar competitive dynamic has developed within each academic institution. Research centres, departments, and academics are now supposed to compete against each other either *ex ante* (to acquire dedicated research funds) or *ex post* (to retain their position within the system). Since the evaluation mechanisms used to do so are based on a shifting mixture of qualitative and quantitative elements highly dependent on contextual variables (which are beyond the control of those assessed) and procedural and substantive criteria of evaluation (which are controlled by meta-regulators), contestants are seldom rewarded when they manage to perform but are heavily penalized when they fail to conform. Furthermore, given the inner limits of the peer-review process itself, any *ex post* form of assessment can end up being as much a measure of the reputational/social capital upon which individuals and research centres can draw than of the real quality of their scientific activities (Burris 2004; Locke *et al* 2008).[16] The resulting widespread dissatisfaction explains the current drift towards bibliometric indicators (as more 'objective' and 'cheaper' evaluation mechanisms), and the inevitable clashes between their respective advocates, even when it is evident to all and sundry that none of the two can solve the measuring problem and ultimately reinforce the power of meta-regulators and their enablers.

Those clashes point to a second major internal divide within the sector, the one between 'insiders' and 'outsiders'. The self-image of academia as a democratic community notwithstanding, the division of intellectual labour within the university system relies on unmistakable hierarchical lines: senior and junior academics; those working in prestigious institutions and those located in peripheral institutions; well-connected and flamboyant personalities and those modest souls toiling in obscurity (Martin 1998: Ch. 3). Moreover, those hierarchies are predicated on social, ethnic, and gender distinctions that characterize society at large and that the system itself is either unable or unwilling to redress (Maher and Tetreault 2007; Clauset, Arbesman and Larremore 2015).[17] The various waves of reform have thus represented windows of opportunity for all those (individuals, academic tribes, and HEIs) who are able to exploit them to foster their career prospects and/or ranking position (Alderman 2010). In an institutional context where virtues like individuality and talent are of prime importance, any reshuffle is an opportunity to vent personal anger, settle old scores, and prove oneself by maximizing one's rewards. Policy makers looking for change are thus able to mobilize support by exploiting all those (individuals, academic tribes, and HEIs) easily moved by an enemy-of-my-enemy-is-my-friend logic; even if, in the end, the chances offered to outsiders by structural and managerial reforms are slim – sometimes even inferior to the likelihood of winning the national lottery. However, since mechanisms like RAE also reflect the self-image of an academic world committed to exalting individual talent and productivity, any faults tend to be overlooked by those (individuals, academic tribes, and HEIs) who manage to be successful and endured by those who are not. The first group finds it against their self-interest to denounce the system as such, while the complaints of the second group can always be dismissed as sour grapes.

In the UK case, there is also a specific institutional context, one of the most significant aspects of which was the unification of the two-tier HE sector – universities and polytechnics – in 1992. Prior to that date, the polytechnics were excluded from research assessment, reinforcing their second class status and, effectively, barring them from research monies. Clearly, from that perspective any, at least formally, open and equal assessment process was a significant gain over the fate-like confinement they had previously experienced (Fullbrook 1999: 124).

What was the case for the ex-polytechnics also applied to a lesser degree to what prior to 1992 had been called the 'new universities' (i.e. those located in the plate-glass campuses opened in the early 1960s), and even the 'red bricks', the civic universities of the late nineteenth and early twentieth centuries (Wythe 2015). To varying degrees, all of these institutions have an interest in anything that challenges the historic domination of Oxbridge or of the 'golden triangle' (Oxbridge plus the University of London). The Russell Group, which was formed in 1994, extends the range of the top end of the hierarchy to include many civic universities beyond the golden triangle, but among even its members there is only one 1960s university, Warwick. For those who have experienced the fate-like power of traditions self-reproducing hierarchy there is at least the possibility of participation in the competition, even if the ranking outcomes based on research performance assessment turn out to be little different from the received reputational hierarchy.[18]

For a small subset, the wager pays off; some non-traditionally prestigious institutions make the breakthrough. For example, in the final RAE two non-Russell Group universities, Essex and York (both 'new' universities founded in the early 1960s), made it into the top ten in terms of average research ranking. By this time, however, the distribution of research funds operated through the RAE was no longer financially relevant, pushing Essex University to revise its strategic goals and maximize the income brought in by tuition fees instead, as Marina Warner (2014, 2015) acrimoniously revealed in the pages of the *London Review of Books*. In this competitive setting, the game of the rules played by meta-regulators can be unmasked if, and only if, the most successful HEIs jointly decide to boycott government policy, thus undermining the credibility of mechanisms like the RAE/REF. However, such an action is inconsistent with their self-interest making any joint strategy highly unlikely; for distinct institutions find themselves caught in a prisoner's dilemma. This explains why the strong objections periodically moved against the RAE by the spokespersons for the Russell Group in the end resolve in mere calls for marginal measures directed at fine tuning its inner mechanisms rather than discontinuing the whole exercise. A similar argument can be made concerning the abolition of tenure (Dnes and Seaton 1998), which in the UK allowed the most successful professors to move across institutions and negotiate the terms of their employment individually and privately with the HEIs interested in poaching them – a change that has undermined the role of collective bargain mechanisms and the negotiating power of those middle and junior categories still relying on them.

The power of the audit and market logic also lies in their ability to disrupt the cycle of self-reproduction at its crucial moment: the selection of recruits. As we noted in Chapter 3, insisting on achievement outputs (notably publication) as a key criteria of selection, managers, including heads of department, make selection according to homophily criteria (the right connections, having had the right supervisor, etc.) more difficult, and facilitates selection based upon performance-related criteria. Appointment committees are thus under pressure to appoint according to a set of criteria that is narrower, but more precise and 'focused'. The obverse is that, in turn, those entering the profession receive clearer and stronger signals about what is expected of them at the point of recruitment, of the decision whether to make their position permanent, or at the point of promotion. At the other end of the career scale, speeding up the generational process by removing, earlier than would otherwise have been the case, those deemed under-performers according to output-oriented research criteria further interferes with quasi-natural processes of self-reproduction by altering the selection mechanism (see Chapter 3).

This leads us to the third major divide upon which the reform process has fed, the faculty/administration distinction (Del Favero and Bray 2010). Although not related to the British case under investigation here, perhaps the best-researched, and certainly one of the most engaging, accounts of this contestation is Ginsberg's *The Fall of the Faculty* (2011), but it is also indicative of the weakness of endogenous explanations blind to the multi-levelled nature of the game. Ginsberg turns the arguments usually levelled by proponents of NPM against bureaucratic hierarchy – bureaucratic sclerosis, ossification, inward-looking competition, individual self-aggrandizement, wastefulness – against the all-administrative university. It is not the modern research university that manifests these dysfunctions, but the new managerial university in which administrators and 'deanlets' (his coinage) have an incentive to maximize their budgets, status, and remuneration irrespective of outcome or performance. While this is a neat rhetorical move, echoing the work of Hood and collaborators on regulation inside government (Scott and Hood 2004; Hood and Dixon 2015), such an approach fails to clarify both the nature of the staff–administrator adversarial relation and the ways in which this inner fault line has been exploited to sustain the reform process.

The first of the problems affecting any endogenous explanation of change is the tendency to idealize both the modern research university and established disciplines. Such accounts of the historical, and increasingly entrenched contemporary, role of academics as overwhelmingly heroic is contradicted by the more historical/sociological account of the 'Humboldtian university' (Ringer 1969) and is vulnerable to Susanna Lohmann's (2006) argument that the disciplinary walls that protect deep specialization carry on protecting areas of activity that are exhausted and have lost their innovative potential, and thus contribute to drift and ossification. Secondly, any division of the university into academic staff and managers (with deanlets as an intermediary category) is far too simplistic. By no means are all academics working in areas of basic research or scholarship. The university – as Barnett (2003) has argued – increasingly approximates a 'super-complex' organization lacking a single unifying ethic or ideology. The same can be said of administrators, another heterogeneous group without a unifying identity or common set of interests. Given this heterogeneity, while corporatization may threaten what Polanyi (2001 [1944]: 46) identifies as 'social standing', 'social claims' and 'social assets' of some categories of actors, for others it offers new opportunities for enhancing their social standing. Those introducing change can count on opposition, but they can equally count on support from those with a weaker stake in and affiliation to the *status quo* and who believe that change may benefit them. By giving administrators a major strategic role in the definition of standards and benchmarks, and in the adoption of institutional visions and developmental plans, the reform process has relied on the crucial support of an expanding managerial layer willing to cut to size the egos – and privileges – of pompous academics. But they are neither the only ones nor the main driving force. Many middle-level and front-line administrators are also badly affected by those very same changes and tend to side with junior academics and temporary staff, something that any clear-cut division between academics and managers overlooks.

5.4.3 Playing the HE game at the first level: nudging, pulling, and collibrating

The regulatory regime established since the early 1980s has redefined the division of academic labour and the system of checks and balances established in the post-war period. In doing so, it has altered the balance of powers between the players who once dominated the academic game and were given some constitutional role in the definition of the public interest. Accordingly, the analysis of the interaction unfolding at this level is crucial for understanding three main elements: (i) the set of policy tools employed to accomplished this task, (ii) the coalitions of actors who have been at the forefront of the reform process and benefited from it, and (iii) the new constitutional balance of powers the reform process helps bring about. In relation to these three points, our claim is that the changes brought about are not the unintended consequences of neoliberal attempts to make the HE sector (and the university system with it) more efficient or market-like. Rather, they are the result of sustained governmental actions aimed at undermining the political role acquired during the post-war period by some corporate actors in defining the public interest. Corporate actors who did not have such political relevance have retained their regulatory autonomy and have often been invited to share the spoils by exploiting the opportunities offered by various forms of privatization (Theisens 2003). To this end, the strengthening of the lines of accountability connecting HE suppliers and political sponsors has gone hand in hand with the enclosure and commodification of the public domain in ways that have carefully avoided activating formal constitutional mechanisms that could have boosted the supervising powers of Parliament or empowered civil society properly.

As we have seen, the reform process has been carried out by a blend of formal/hard and informal/soft policy instruments, which under the market efficiency banner have revised not only the structure of the sector, but above all the very *raison d'etre* of HE. A stream of new education acts were passed by a tightly controlled Parliament without giving the latter the opportunity to have a public and democratic debate about the larger implications produced by each. The opposition of professional associations, student organizations, and broad sectors of civil society was neutralized each time by using collibration strategies that have divided and antagonized its many constituencies. The main levers pulled to do so have been financial and managerial – areas that were fully controllable by central government. Financially, the crucial move was originally the abolition of the block-grant system of funding in the early 1980s. Since then, the overall budget has been split into a myriad of dedicated funding streams allocated by a changing number of agencies according to growing and overlapping criteria of evaluation combining *ex ante* and *ex post* review processes; formal and substantive modes of assessment (Woodhall and Richards 2008; Foskett 2011; Ahmad *et al* 2013). The financial lever has in turn allowed central government (and the constellation of quangos used as enablers) to wrest away the autonomy enjoyed in the past by professional academic bodies and local authorities in educational matters. Once again, another crucial factor was the creation of a unitary HE sector. The integration of the former polytechnics into the university system, carried out in 1992, was a masterful strategic move that at once managed to exclude local government from HE altogether and increase the sources of antagonism within an already pluralistic academic environment (Theisens 2003; Naidoo 2008). By allowing the polytechnics to acquire the more prestigious status of universities, central government managed to tap into widespread anti-establishment feelings to overcome the opposition of professional corporations and local authorities. By allocating the funds reserved for research by a complex system of assessment such as the RAE, central government managed to legitimate its traditional financial support for elite institutions as meritocratic and performance-based (Brown with Carasso 2013: 158).

The dissatisfaction brought about by the various rounds of reform among the constituent parts of the HE sector have, in turn, been used to justify the permanent interference of central government in every aspect of academic life, leading to the top-down micro-management of research, teaching and administrative activities. Individuals, departments and universities are now told what constitutes proper research, what to write on, how to do it, and where to publish it, even when the financial benefits they derive from doing so are no longer evident and long-standing scientific values are compromised in the process (Schugurensky 2006). Likewise, academics and their institutions are now told who to teach, what to teach, and how to teach, even if the requirements imposed from above do not make any sense to (or are far beyond the ability of) those involved in classroom activities under deteriorating working conditions (Professor X 2011). On each occasion, the imposition of assessment criteria started with some form of self-regulation but soon evolved in the opposite direction, increasing the role of central government and its enablers. Thus, the RAE that used to rely on peer-review inevitably evolved into the REF: an assessment system shifting the balance towards bibliometric indicators and impact criteria attributing growing discretionary powers to central government (Lynch 2015). The share of funds distributed selectively has similarly been increased over time and will undoubtedly keep rising in the future. Moreover, the distortions caused by the introduction of those review systems on academic activities are now used by central government as an invitation to employ similar instruments to redress unwanted side-effects, such as the imbalance between research and teaching. Thus, the most recent White Paper released by Department for Business, Innovation and Skills is proposing the introduction of a revised TQA mechanism (which mirrors the logic of the RAE/REF) to redress the research bias induced by the latter and improve teaching standards on behalf of students, who, like their American counterparts (Collinge 2009), as consumers are now burdened with mortgage-like levels of debt while lacking any significant power of exit (Johnstone 2014).

As we observed in relation to the case of civil service reforms, subtle policies of collibration (blending the nudge and pull techniques suggested by managerial gurus like Thaler and Sunstein 2008 and Hagel *et al* 2010) are used together with more structural forms of intervention in a somewhat cyclical fashion. Soft managerial measures aimed at improving efficiency are used to 'prepare' the ground for further structural interventions the aim of which is to 'restructure' the field. These are then followed by other soft managerial measures the goal of which is to 'consolidate' the ground, until a new round of reforms is introduced seamlessly:

- political critique aimed at undermining the legitimacy of the HE sector is initiated/exploited;
- a response from the sector to address this critique via self-regulation, greater transparency, and audit (e.g. case of RAE) is then solicited;
- political capture of these self-regulatory practices (e.g. linking them to financial formula) is finally carried out, which goes hand in hand with
  - their increasing formalizations (e.g. from peer-review to bibliometric) justified as a response to (internal as well as external) criticisms of the measures/previous assessment rounds and justified as fine-tuning;
  - adjustment of the policy as a response to the perverse effect of previous stages and gaming; linked to a further round of critique (stage one).

This cyclical process produces accelerated generational changes that periodically reshape the population of the players involved in the three-level game. The introduction of a new generation of players obviously means reshuffling the cards in ways that give policy makers the opportunity to build partnerships supporting further changes while weakening oppositional forces. As indicated above, the introduction of the NPM template in HE has relocated students outside of the system via consumerism, and brought into the system a growing number of private businesses as alternative suppliers. The latter now have a powerful role to play at the first level as well, for they are involved in lobbying Parliament, and thus help sustain government policies among opposition parties and backbenchers. Likewise, the corporatization of universities has detached vice-chancellors and the more entrepreneurial professors from the rest of the academic profession (Breakwell 2006; Smith and Adams 2008). By giving them the power to negotiate their conditions of employment privately, and appropriating part of the income generated by PPPs, they have in effect been successfully co-opted as enablers who are copying their principals by creatively offloading newly acquired managerial responsibilities down the line and across institutional layers. Last but not least, the quangocracy in charge of the multiple assessment processes has become an irresistible pole of attraction for administrators and 'bilingual' academics, and can then be easily exploited by policy makers as both Trojan horses and scapegoats (Trowler 2010).

Starting with the UGC in the 1980s, the whole reform process has relied on a multitude of semi-public bodies that have carried out the dirty work on behalf of their political patrons in a quasi-juridical fashion. Even when they originally had some representative role, these bodies have with time lost it and became part of the informal spoils system brought about by the overall managerial revolution in British government (Flinders and Geddes 2014): fully appointed positions offering alternative career paths to those willing to leave the academic ranks and join the rising managerial elite. In acting as free-riding third-party enablers, the emerging HE quangocracy has diverted towards itself an increasing amount of public monies and almost all the discontent produced by structural and managerial changes among front-line personnel and customers. New rounds of reform thus start with a by now ritualistic bonfire of old quangos in the hope that this can have a cathartic effect (Hodgson *et al* 2011: Ch. 8). It is therefore not at all surprising to discover that the changes proposed by the latest White Paper (2015) presage the dismantling of the Higher Educational Funding Council for England (HEFCE), the funding body at the forefront of the reform process in the last decade in England (thanks to the devolution process Downing Street has shifted responsibilities for the Scottish and Welsh HEs to their respective assemblies). It is quite easy to predict that the body that will replace it will be even less representative of the academic world and/or less responsive to civil society than HEFCE was. It must be noted, however, that crucially the bonfire of HE quangos tends to leave unscathed their individual members. Their contractual arrangements very often include safe-exit clauses allowing them either to retire in comfort or take advantage of the revolving doors that connect the quangos to each other and to the private sector in a way that is reminiscent of C. Wright Mills' (1956) analysis of the US power elite (see Chapter 7). In this way the quangocracy reproduces itself regardless of the dysfunctionalities produced by the overall reform process, and this has a regenerative effect on the latter in return.

None of the individual measures we have described could have had the effects that we attribute to their combined workings. Together, they constitute a concatenation of measures analogous to Gambetta's (1998) 'concatenation of mechanisms'; their efficacy lies in their complex interactions, mutual reinforcement, and feedback. This interplay helps explain the resilience of the reform process and its ability to permeate the fabric of the body academic top down and sideways. Self-interest and strategic considerations make the regulatory regime self-enforcing even when those benefiting from the changes are a restricted minority; for the rest it is a wager on the unknowable, and perhaps increasingly uncertain, prospect of an improvement in their life chances (see Bukodi *et al* 2015). Given the fact that reforms are depoliticizing HE unremittingly (making any collective action extremely difficult to accomplish), the only alternative left to those who disagree with the direction of change turns out to be an individualistic one, making TINA (there is no alternative) a self-fulfilling prophesy. This is the case in spite of the claims advanced by many analysts and practitioners keen on extolling the deliberative democratic virtues of peer-review systems and other new modes of governance (see Chapter 6). Used to bypass (rather than complement) traditional forms of representation and collegiality, deliberative fora, national surveys and horizontal mechanisms of accountability turn out to be merely consultative exercises assigning mounting managerial responsibilities to those involved while leaving them with decreasing decision-making power (Anderson 1998). The latter flows instead upwards to those who retain meta-regulatory power and are able to play the game of the rules at will. New modes of governance in effect allow central government to interfere in areas of activity, which in the past were beyond its control, but at the same time they reduce the democratic supervision exercised by other representative bodies dependent on vertical mechanisms of accountability. Such interference is justified through rhetorical appeals to output-oriented modes of legitimacy even when in reality procedural and substantive criteria of evaluation keep on coexisting and are used interchangeably by those in charge in self-serving ways.

5.5 Conclusion: knowledge commodified, intellectual labour standardized

The question raised by the student movements that emerged in the 1960s was about *who* was entitled to assess the social contribution brought about by universities and *how* to give voice to those constituencies that had a marginal role in the running of those institutions. By and large, the solution proposed at the time to solve the many agency problems besetting the university system was a greater democratization and the inclusion of all stakeholders in its political and managerial processes (Gassert 2008). By giving voice to marginal constituencies, it was hoped that the biases of the peer-review process could be kept in check without introducing perverse external interference. In other words, the question raised then was: *who* is the university for? This contrasts sharply with the one proposed more recently: *what* is the university for? (Collini 2011). This clarification gives us a point of entry for assessing the outcomes of three full decades of change affecting all aspects of academic life. The British case is for us extremely important not only because here change has gone further than in any other comparable national context, but also for the influence this experience has had on the rest of the Western world – as we shall spell out in the next chapter. To carry this assessment forward, we started with an analysis of the structural changes imposed to date, highlighting their most important implications.

By creating a unitary HE sector, upon which has been imposed an identical and uniform model of corporate governance, the various rounds of reform have promoted a twin process of managerial homogenization and functional differentiation (Theisens 2003). Thanks to a complex regulatory regime imposed from above, HEIs tend now to conform to a market logic and adopt the same corporate structure, even when they remain formally charities and are supposed to operate on a not-for-profit basis. To cope with the novel competitive environment within which they are asked to operate, HEIs tend therefore to specialize and offer to their customers a narrower range of courses and teaching expertise. Competition between and within universities for funds is, in addition, forcing HEIs to commodify their intellectual and scientific labour and streamline the productive process to improve their market value. As a result, there is a noticeable rush to enclose parts of the public domain, set artificial limits to the information flow, and engage in dubious scientific practices (Irzik 2007). At the educational level, HEIs are pushed to commercialize their activities by offering more vocational degree courses and even better grades to all their customers. Moreover, they try to make the academic experience more appealing by improving extra curricula leisure facilities in order to entice larger numbers of full fee-paying overseas students to enrol. In this market-like context, old representative notions of democratic engagement are being displaced by a blend of deliberative practices, having mostly consultative value, and rhetorical appeals to the power of exit granted to customers; a power that remains in reality extremely limited (Anderson 1998).

These structural changes are transforming the working environment, reshaping the identity of the academic profession in the process (Park 2013). For the majority of those who choose it, an academic career has become shorter, more competitive, and subjected to much external interference. Selection now depends more than ever on different and/or additional kinds of social capital and networking ability of aspiring candidates. In a context dominated by RAE, those qualities were necessary for getting published in high impact peer-reviewed journals, whereas in a context more dependent on social impact publications need to be supplemented by substantial amounts of research funds acquired through *ex ante* forms of assessment. Those lacking both the social capital and networking skills required end up filling the ranks of temporary personnel hired on teaching contracts only; that is, until the goalposts are once again moved in the next round of central government reform or latest White Paper aiming to rebalance the current bias towards research. This competitive setup affects the rest of professional life as well, for career progression has been made highly dependent on a host of additional and periodically changing *ex post* forms of assessment. Although the latter have built-in mechanisms for improving quality standards progressively, these very assessment criteria are exposed to external shocks induced by meta-regulators to pre-empt gaming. This explains, in turn, the increase in early retirement of those wishing to step off the treadmill, the accelerating mobility of personnel from one institution to another to maximise individual career prospects, and the growing temptation to move sideways into more managerial positions to join a flourishing quangocracy.

The joint effect of these changes is the reaffirmation of the lines of authority linking academics to their institutions and HE suppliers to their political principals (Musselin 2013a and 2013b). Far from measuring the quality of their output, performance management techniques have led to the standardization of every aspect of academic activity, forcing individuals, research groups, and departments to conform to an intricate regulatory regime imposed from without. Even when standardization relies on some form of peer-review (the relevance of which is slowly declining), its logic remains unmistakably disciplinary (Willmott 2003), and follows that of the conveyor belt developed by turn of early twentieth-century scientific management in low-skill manufacturing industries, creating what Brown, Lauder and Ashton (2011: Ch. 5) aptly call 'digital Taylorism' (see Chapter 7). In the face of increasing workload, individual academics, research groups, and departments have thus lost their most prized freedoms: (i) the freedom to choose how to allocate time between research, teaching, and administration; (ii) the freedom to follow their personal vocation in research and teaching; (iii) the freedom to think critically and develop their own intellectual identity. As in other more traditional areas of mass production, the proletarianization of HE workers goes hand in hand with their increasing responsibilization for the structural conditions they find themselves in, and their depoliticization. Similar pressures are experienced by students and their families, given that the consumerist turn in HE is forcing them to invest more heavily in higher education to get decreasing returns for their investment on a globalized high skills labour market.

In the Polanyian spirit that inspires this whole work, we have argued that this state of affairs is not due to the need of the nation state (in this case the British state) to adapt to globalizing market forces, nor to the allegedly hegemonic role acquired by neoliberal ideas in public life. Rather, we have stressed two things: (i) the role of market makers played by crucial state actors (i.e. central government) and (ii) the fact that market policies are used primarily as a tool for redesigning by stealth the separation of powers and system of checks and balances established by the British constitution. Expanding on the Polanyian account of market creation, we have also been keen to explain how the strategic responses of the players involved in the three-level academic game could lead to (iii) the entrenchment and (iv) reproduction of dysfunctional arrangements. Tapping into various sources of internal dissatisfaction, central government has managed to impose a regulatory regime that has brought the institutions working within the HE sector under strict political control. A raft of legislative interventions has managed to reshape the field by excluding local government and bringing in a new breed of private providers aligned with the executive. Simultaneously, a host of soft-law instruments have imposed a corporate structure on universities and turned them into *de facto* for-profit organizations notwithstanding their charity status. Resistance against the NPM programs has been quashed by the use of collibration strategies aimed at (i) increasing the costs of collective action faced by the opposition front and (ii) giving supporters the opportunity to enclose, commodify, and commercially exploit parts of the HE sector. The upshot is the creation of a 'market on the leash' that leaves central government as a powerful meta-regulator able to play the game of the rules while shifting political responsibilities downwards and escaping traditional mechanisms of supervision and lines of accountability. It is this dynamic that, in our view, explains the political activism in the field of a succession of governments having different political orientation as well as the diffusion of the NPM template across cultural boundaries, as we show in the next chapter.

Notes

1 The implicit social contract was signed on the understanding that a liberal democratic polity would guarantee the university system and its scientific mission much better than the Church or private philanthropy could. Only within a liberal democratic public framework could the values Merton (1973 [1942]) attributed to science be engendered. History supplies ample evidence that such a hope was in vain. But this also meant that any failure to realize liberal democratic values made the state an untrustworthy entity as well. On the idea of social contract and its implication see Jasanoff 2005: Ch. 9.
2 They were never exclusively vocational even though that was the policy aim. In many ways, they were repeating the history of the 'red bricks', which were also set up by 'practical men' for vocational training, but developed into full universities (Barnes 1996). Pratt (1997: 11) labels this tendency 'academic drift'. On the differences between universities and polytechnics see also Lewis (1991). On the parallel history of the 'red bricks' see Wythe (2015).
3 Polytechnics were indeed seen as a social and institutional counter-balancing force to the more conservative university system dominated by the Oxbridge model (Robinson 1968, 1969).
4 On the point C. Wright Mills' 1960 letters to the New Left and to the Port Huron declaration issued in 1962 by the Students for a Democratic Society (SDS) are instructive. These are now reprinted in Albert and Albert (eds) (1984).
5 There are parallels here with the arguments of Boltanski and Chiapello (2005): the selective adoption of critique in the renewal of the legitimation of capitalism.

6 The term is from Logan and Molotch for whom universities, in contrast to local government and business, are 'auxiliary players' in urban 'growth coalitions' (1987: 75–76). That knowledge has joined land, labour, and money as a 'fictitious good' from which profit is derived within the 'knowledge economy' may require an adjustment of this evaluation. See Chapter 7.

7 The worst affected university was Salford, in a deprived part of Greater Manchester.

8 Pratt (1997: 10) describes the block grant principle as follows, 'whatever arguments individual universities had made for the level of the grant, the actual grant, when it came, was not earmarked for specific purposes. The object of all this was to establish the UGC as a "buffer" between the state and individual universities, thus preserving and enhancing their autonomy'.

9 The ground for this overhaul of the HE sector was however prepared by the 1988 Education Act. The 1992 ERA accomplished what was already a work in progress.

10 This democratic mission is acknowledged by the Anderson Committee established in 1960 to justify establishing the system of student maintenance grants: 'the nation should not depart from the ancient and sound traditions that young men and women go to the university to become all-round citizens' (quoted in Pratt 1997: 13).

11 Note that, unlike in the US, in Britain a for-profit company can acquire a not-for-profit organization with degree-granting powers and run it as a subsidiary without re-applying for accreditation (see Brown with Carasso 2013: 39).

12 There is here at work a double process of political centralization and administrative decentralization, as perceptively noted by Dearlove (1998: 117 and 118). On the political uses of decentralization see also Weiler (1993).

13 These protests were weaker in Britain than in Germany, France, and Italy, where the HE system was more centralized (Klimke and Scharloth 2008).

14 To this we must add that universities are heavily involved in the property market to boost their revenue. While some of the richest use their property portfolio to speculate on rising market prices, almost all other institutions are engaged in campus expansion to attract more (foreign) students. In some cases, campus expansion is funded by using very expensive PFI schemes. Thus, universities' finances are becoming closely tied to the financial and property markets.

15 The existence of a market for history books and TV series illustrates this. Beyond that is the economic relevance of the whole entertainment industry and the role humanities graduates play in it. If there is a sector of the British economy that has consistently been at the cutting edge since the 1960s and able to successfully rival the US it is without doubt the music industry. However, music schools and arts department seems to be the most likely candidates any time austerity policies force HEIs to carry out new rounds of rationalization. Economic considerations of this sort raise the question concerning 'which humanities are we talking about?' posed by Miller (2012); a question that underscores the existence of a problematic hierarchical order between the various disciplines gathered under that label, and the HEIs involved in reproducing them rather than the frequently invoked economic rationale.

16 The notion of social capital used here is derived from Bourdieu (1986), rather than Putnam (2000). On the differences between these two understandings, see Portes (2000).

17 The pressure to address gender inequalities is great. Institutions that do not really try have a legitimation problem and those that merely play lip service will be found out. However, the same pressures do not exist to the same degree for class and ethnicity, and there may be a zero-sum relation between these.

18 Here we might note that one of the main recommendations of the *Roberts Report* was to apply the full RAE to only those universities that were likely to benefit and use a lighter assessments strategy for institutions that were research weak. Although there would have been considerable cost and efficiency gains had the suggestion been adopted, this suggestion was not taken up and the following RAE (2008) remained inclusive.

6 Exporting the template

EU integration policies and the diffusion of the NPM template

6.1 Introduction

In the previous two chapters we discussed the ways in which the NPM template was first employed to reform the British civil service and then applied, in a revised form, to a different policy area: British higher education. In both cases, we presented the various features making up such a template, the dynamic elements that made it possible to customize that template to suit the specific needs of distinct policy areas, and the common political rationale driving the reform process. These two case studies were selected for their institutional peculiarities: the constitutional roles these institutions were attributed (even if informally) within the Westminster system of government and the challenges they posed to a political elite determined to tackle the governability crisis experienced in the 1970s from the top down. While defending the political reading of change proposed against alternative forms of explanation, we also suggested the need to view the process of diffusion of the NPM template at the national level as a ripple effect generated by the strategy of political centralization-cum-managerial decongestion pursued by central government. The public bodies upon whom the NPM template was offloaded acquired growing managerial responsibilities and responded to that challenge by adopting the same strategic logic, passing those responsibilities down along hierarchical chains. Hence, we stressed the existence of a double process of diffusion: a horizontal process that has led the NPM template to spread across interconnected policy areas and a vertical process responsible for the deepening of that same template across institutional levels.

We also suggested that this process of diffusion has not been fully endogenous, but was helped by the activities of exogenous forces lending support from without. Our objective in this chapter is to clarify the identity of those actors and the nature of their contribution to the spreading of the NPM template across national boundaries. We want to show that even when pressure to conform is exercised from without this cannot be imputed to the coercive power of supranational institutions alone (i.e., the US or the EU), or to the competitive pressures exerted by impersonal economic or cultural forces (i.e., globalization, neoliberal ideology, postmodern drives, etc.). At the centre of the process of diffusion it is always possible to identify specific state actors keen to follow the policy of political centralization-cum-managerial decongestion to strengthen their positional power *vis-à-vis* competing substate units. In our account, policy diffusion in the fields we are investigating is the result of complex attempts, carried out by national governmental forces, to exploit internationalizing drives in a self-serving way. To this end, the NPM template is imported into a national context and policy area if and when this suits the political needs of state actors able to customize it in ways which can reinforce their top down control in those domains.

Our argument is threefold. First, we maintain that even when national authorities subject their countries to exacting structural adjustment programmes, they are able to retain political autonomy and the relation to transnational non-state actors is only very seldom one of subordination (*state autonomy thesis*). Second, we point out that this political autonomy is frequently used to subscribe to international agreements that can precipitate controversial policy changes able to redefine the extant balance of power among subnational entities posing challenges to top down governability (*self-binding thesis*). Third, we try to show that the partnerships national governments establish with those non-state actors have an intrinsic competitive nature and are thus the object of periodic renegotiation (*collusive competition thesis*). In other words, we claim that national policies supporting internationalizing processes are not reactive adaptations to pressures exercised from without and that the political equilibria underpinning global regulatory regimes have a dynamic nature that make dysfunctional collusive arrangements self-regenerating. The political reading of change we support requires some conceptual clarification concerning the role played by non-state actors: transnational corporations, non-governmental organizations (NGOs), the Organization for Economic Cooperation and Development (OECD), the Bretton Woods 'unholy trinity' (Peet 2009) and EU institutions. Rather than considering these as the main 'enforcers' of market-based policy instruments, we suggest that it is better to view them as epistemic authorities national governments try to enrol as 'enablers'. As such, these non-state actors find themselves caught in an ongoing struggle to preserve their epistemic legitimacy while retaining their policy relevance (Stone 2011).

This chapter is organized as follows. In the next section (§6.2) we discuss the notion of 'good governance' and the contribution this has had for understanding the process of policy diffusion in the two areas under investigation: public administration (PA) and higher education (HE). Our aim is to explain how a development programme designed for developing (mainly African) countries in order to fight corruption and maladministration by introducing liberal democratic elements into their political systems has progressively been employed to reform the very liberal democracies that were initially used as benchmarks. In §6.3 we restrict our attention to the EU and the policy of economic and administrative integration developed here. It is through the single market policy programme that the NPM template has been exported across the continent and employed by the governments of several member states to reform their public sectors. Our aim in the following section (§6.4) is to identify and discuss the specific vehicles used as conduits for spreading the NPM template across national boundaries, policy areas, and institutional levels. Section 6.5 is concerned with how the rationale underpinning the creation of the European regulatory regimes re-emerged in those fields. Building on the notion of a new *raison d'etat* proposed originally by Wolf (1999a and 1999b), we try to show that in both PA and HE the diffusion of the NPM template supports the political reading of change proposed earlier against competing cultural and functional accounts. The chapter closes with a few considerations stressing the more general implications the changes investigated could have for the future development of the knowledge society and the role new modes of governance play in it.

6.2 The good governance agenda and policy diffusion

Born as an attempt to fight corruption and stop undemocratic ruling elites from appropriating aid funds to consolidate their power bases or enrich themselves, the good governance agenda can be identified as the source of the widespread diffusion of both the principle of conditionality (i.e. making loans conditional on compliance to specific economic policies and/or principles of good governance) and the NPM template worldwide. Under its aegis, growing amounts of funds reserved for economic development were made available on condition that the receiving countries committed themselves to political reforms designed to strengthen the rule of law, transparency, and democratic accountability. Since, according to Western-educated policy makers, these principles could only flourish within a mixed economy where constitutional guarantees preserved the role of markets and private ownership from the centralized temptations of public bureaucracies, the set of reforms indicated by the NPM template (privatization, liberalization, and marketization of public assets) became the preferred means for grafting liberal democratic values and institutions into alien/backward political and administrative contexts. As part and parcel of transnational efforts to engender good governance, the NPM template came to be seen and was thus sold to international public opinion as a tool for the modernization and democratization of authoritarian regimes, first in Africa and then worldwide.

The literature on policy transfer has tried to explicate the worldwide diffusion of market-based policy instruments championed by the good governance agenda in two ways. On the one hand, the scientific focus has been on the nature of the mechanisms responsible for cross-border, horizontal diffusion. In reviewing this body of literature, Dobbin *et al* (2007) identify and discuss four such distinct mechanisms: coercion, competition, learning, and emulation. On the other hand, alternative but complementary perspectives have shifted the attention of policy analysts and practitioners onto the types of policy areas touched by the process of diffusion. Analyzing both the problems arising in distinct policy areas and the nature of the administrative solutions proposed in each, Esty (2006) uses two main variables to explain the diffusion of administrative law at the supranational level in different policy fields: their degree of integration and their political relevance. While the first approach is concerned with locating the various hypotheses along the logical continuum the ideal poles of which are 'coercion' and 'voluntary' compliance, the second seems more interested in explaining the degree of uniformity and variety produced by the diffusion process itself.

Starting with the second of the two approaches, our representation of the NPM template as a fruit machine is meant to show how a single policy instrument can spread across policy areas, institutional levels, and national boundaries and generate, in the process, a number of variations which retain, nonetheless, a distinct family resemblance. Three sources of variety that, in our model, give those adopting it the opportunity to customize that template in ways that suit their specific needs: (i) the possibility of choosing the right combination of privatization policies, liberalization regimes, and marketizating mechanisms; (ii) inbuilt requirements imposing on public managers the periodical revision of quality standards and the adoption of best practices; (iii) stochastic changes devised by political principals to pre-empt gaming. Given this structural flexibility, the diffusion of the same policy template ends up producing the Thatcherite logic of TINA without yielding uniformity, replication, and convergence without the need of overtly coercive measures, top down governability while giving the impression of being responsive to customers and citizens. Thus, our model can account for the blend of homogeneity and variation that has characterized globalization processes to date.

Concerning the mechanisms of enforcement used by good governance, we have repeatedly expressed reservations about the coercive hypotheses advanced in globalization studies. In disagreement with those who view policy diffusion as a top down hegemonic project supported by the sole remaining superpower, or present globalization as a 'rat race' due to the competitive pressures produced by impersonal market forces, we have been at pains to stress the crucial role the nation-state still plays as both market maker and first mover. Far from being eroded by technological, social, cultural, demographic, or economic factors, we view the nation-state not only as a remarkably resilient political actor but also as a net beneficiary of the policy diffusion process. On their part, the array of public, semi-public and private actors engaged in upholding the various and overlapping transnational regulatory regimes built since the end of the Cold War are far too heterogeneous to attribute to them converging interests and collective agency (Yi-chong and Weller 2009). The 2008 financial crisis was the latest of a series of events that has exposed inner tensions and lack of coordination power among them; factors that have brought into play traditional intergovernmental arrangements previously side-lined (or perhaps merely overlooked by analysts), as we shall show later on in discussing the EU system of governance.

Strategic considerations driving learning and emulation in a global context resemble those indicated by Wolf's (1999a and 1999b) 'new *raison d'etat*' approach; work that for us captures the logic underpinning the model of policy diffusion that we wish to illustrate. This approach developed as an attempt to assess the plausibility of two contrasting hypotheses on globalization. The first hypothesis is the mainstream one according to which supranational authorities and regulatory regimes develop in order to compensate for the reduced problem-solving ability of nation states due to growing interdependence. This is what in Chapter 4 we referred to as the 'functional thesis'. For Wolf, the hallmark of this hypothesis is a socio-centric liberal conception of the nation-state devoid of autonomous interests. Since globalization reduces the ability of state actors to satisfy societal demands, functional pressures induce a reconfiguration of sovereignty promoting the formation of networked and multi-level types of governance moving across traditional boundaries: domestic/international, public/private, inside/outside, up/down, etc. The second hypothesis suggested by Wolf starts instead with the assumption that state actors have interests and goals of their own and react against any challenge (whether from below, above, or from the side) seeking to reduce their ability to pursue those goals autonomously. According to this state-centric perspective, changes in the structure of national sovereignty are due to attempts to revise the configuration of the state in order to preserve its autonomy:

> in the context of an emerging world society the state's sphere of autonomous action is endangered not only by other states, but increasingly by these societal and sub-state actors. Challenged by the emancipation of their societal and sub-state environments, governments develop a 'new *raison d'etat*' [...,] a common interest in instrumentalizing intergovernmental governance structures for the maintenance of their internal autonomy.
>
> (Wolf 1999b: 233)

The analytical structure of these two hypotheses is that of a two-level game connecting the strategic actions of state actors at the domestic level with those taking place at the international level and vice versa. However, those who subscribe to the first hypothesis propose a reading of the two-level game suggested originally by Putnam (1988), and thus conceive state actors as operating at the international level on behalf of their domestic constituencies, whose interests they seek to protect. Wolf proposes an alternative reading of the two-level game where state actors attempt to exploit their international connections and commitments to pass controversial policy changes that alter the domestic balance of power in their favour. Since intergovernmental cooperation is traditionally reserved for the executive branch, the development of global forms of governance is an opportunity the latter has for acquiring supremacy over the legislative branch and other representative institutions like PA, local government, trade unions, universities, etc. The conditionalities imposed by good governance programmes are, consequently, sought only in those policy areas where the executive does not have, for whatever historical reason, significant decision-making power; policy areas in which the executive exercises full control remain outside international influence. Moreover, by committing themselves to submit to externally imposed arrangements, responsibility for policy failure in the areas that are internationalized has shifted away from the executive and passed on either to the legislative (in case it fails to pass the required policy changes), or the administrative sub-system (in case it fails to implement the policy changes passed by Parliament), or else onto the supranational regulatory bodies that imposed those policy changes in the first place.

In the rest of this chapter we are concerned with testing the explanatory value of this second hypothesis in relation to the process of diffusion of the NPM template in the two fields covered by the previous chapters: PA and HE. In order to do so, our focus will be restricted to EU integration policies in those areas, rather than to developing countries. Given the higher degree of political stability and democratic life characterizing European countries, we believe that here it is possible to appreciate the non-coercive nature of the process of policy diffusion and the strategic logic underpinning it in a much better way.

6.3 The EU good governance agenda: analytical framework and policy platforms

Critics of globalization have consistently opposed the good governance agenda because of its colonial overtones (Williams and Young 1994). The various programmes contributing to that agenda are often presented as instruments for the Americanization or the Westernization of the developing world, a task that is shown to be at odds with the actual economic history of industrialized countries (Chang 2002). In doing so, critics tend to miss a deeply ironic aspect that has characterized the process of diffusion of neoliberal solutions worldwide; namely, that similar conditionality-based programmes have been systemically imposed on Western countries as well, condemning them to lengthy periods of austerity and spiralling social and regional inequalities that are shaking their foundations. Within the EU, conditionality has, for example, been amply employed as criteria for (i) integrating the member states' policies in many administrative, economic and social realms within a common space and (ii) expanding the union eastward. Even more ironic is the fact that, since the 2008 American subprime crisis and the subsequent Euro crisis, the rigour with which stabilization policies and structural adjustments are being pushed throughout by the European Commission (EC) and Central Bank (ECB) is alarming the IMF itself, engaged together with them in rescuing the economies of Greece, Spain, and Portugal as part of the so-called 'Troika'. As a result, in Europe too, integration policies are widely perceived as an attempt to Americanize the old continent and are held responsible for the rising of anti-European sentiments and populist movements that are challenging the integration project from the bottom up (Guérot 2016).[1] Since the EU has been described as a paragon of democratic experimentalism and multi-level governance to juxtapose to the nondemocratic forms of good governance imposed by the Bretton Woods 'unholy trinity' (Sabel and Zeitlin 2010), an evaluation of the EU governance agenda turns out to be particularly interesting for understanding the mechanisms of policy transfer used in this context and thus assessing the plausibility of Wolf's hypothesis.

To make this task easier, we start by proposing an analytical scheme that gives us a synoptic image of the way in which EU integration operates. The scheme is arrived at by connecting aspects of the integration process that are often discussed separately. Following Stone (2011), we distinguish between 'formal' and 'informal' regulatory practices to illustrate the governance modes used to push integration forwards. Borrowing from Scharpf (1996), we also distinguish between 'negative' and 'positive' integration policies in order to discuss the instruments used in distinct areas and at different institutional levels (Peters and Pierre 2009). Such an approach allows us to connect ontological questions about the nature of EU institutions with more mundane questions concerning policy making and implementation; a task abhorred by many political scientists working in the field of European Studies. Moreover, it gives us the opportunity to appreciate both the generation of contrasting scientific perspectives on European governance and the limitations affecting each of them. We maintain that far from having been settled once and for all (Hix 1998), ontological questions keep resurfacing every time analysts detect a shift in the mode of governance chosen to overcome a political impasse. Furthermore, we claim that European institutions operate through multiple governance modes and keep shifting between them in response to changeable political conditions. Thus, we argue that the momentous shifts noted by political analysts and practitioners have to do with the competitive logic unfolding between distinct research programmes touching on the discrete anatomical parts of Puchala's (1971) European elephant. As such, we cast doubts on many claims made about alleged epochal changes, and the far reaching significance contending schools of thought attribute to some EU institutions and practices.[2] By contrast, we propose a reading that views the EU as a multifaceted and dynamic entity that embodies and combines both aspects of the Regulatory State and of the Networked Polity theorized in EU literature (Palumbo 2015).

The synoptic representation proposed above (see Table 6.1) identifies four aspects of an integration process that are part of cyclical patterns the goal of which is to (i) upset existing equilibria; (ii) promote political and institutional changes; (iii) consolidate those changes (see Chapter 4). Moreover, we maintain that those patterns are part of sequences that follow nonlinear trajectories devised to move across an uneven political seascape full of obstacles to overcome. In this context, choosing the right combination of informal/formal modes of governance and negative/positive types of policy instruments is like finding the right combination of sails to use when navigating uncharted

Table 6.1 Synoptic representation of the European integration process

	Type of policy instruments		
Governance Mode		*Negative*	*Positive*
	Informal	Intergovernmental arrangements based on negotiated agreements within the Council of Europe	Negotiated interpretations of constitutional treatises between the Council and European Commission
	Formal	Creation of the single market and introduction of the NPM template within the public sectors of national state members	Legislative and regulatory activities of EU institutions, legalization practices of European Courts and monetary policies of the European Central Bank

and treacherous waters. Unlike regattas, the EU integration trajectory is not only open-ended, but gives those steering its course the possibility to modify structural aspects of the EU vessel as well, making the whole enterprise resemble the crew engaged in rebuilding the ship on the open sea. Within each of the four combinations supplied by our analytical scheme, the possibilities open to those in charge concern deciding on both the magnitude of the changes thought to be necessary and the level at which they are supposed to take place. As illustrated in the table reported below (see Table 6.2), changes can affect the constitutional setup of the polity, or the procedures regulating its political activities, or else the policy instruments employed. In each of these three instances, we can also distinguish between the more politically salient changes pertaining to decision making and those allegedly more technical aspects concerned with policy making and policy implementation.

These schemes give us a spectrum of strategic choices available to the main political actors involved in the integration process, above all Council and Commission. They also identify the variety of issues implicated in the overall process and the levels at which each issue is supposed to be discussed. Finally, they give us the opportunity to follow the way in which issues can be classified

Table 6.2 Political and institutional changes at European level

	Decision making	*Policy making*	*Policy implementation*
Polity	constitutionalization	multi-level arrangements	polycentric approach
Politics	legalization	subsidiarity principles	open method of coordination (OMC)
Policy	comitology	choice of policy instruments	peer-review systems

and reclassified and moved across levels. By contrast with other accounts of the diffusion process, our framework does not seek to identify ideal-typical mechanisms of policy transfer relying on pure forms of coercion, competition, learning, or emulation. From our perspective, each time we confront a blend of enforcement strategies the aim of which is to bypass political obstacles and social opposition; we also witness a shifting blend able to seamlessly modify the mix along the coercive–voluntary continuum. Since we are dealing with the interaction of a plurality of collective actors, what looks like top down imposition for a subset can easily be viewed as the outcome of a negotiated agreement for another subset, or even as the outcome of democratic deliberation. Although fairly complex, the analytical framework proposed here is no match for the variegated and multifarious aspects of the actual integration process. It has, however, heuristic value and will be used to understand how the NPM template managed to spread across the continent, and identify the actors and policy transfer mechanisms responsible for this. In §6.4, we will use this analytical framework first to account for the modernization of national PAs and then to follow the parallel process of harmonization of HE policies among EU member states.

6.4 Europeanization and the building of dedicated policy platforms

The spreading of NPM ideas and solutions across Europe is described in the literature as a clash between two ideal-typical forms of policy intervention: the first is hierarchical and procedural, the second horizontal and results-based (Gualmini 2008). Regardless of the rationales used to explain the passage from one ideal type to the other (the three theses discussed in Chapter 4), we side with those who attribute to EU institutions a leading role in tipping the balance in favour of neoliberal arrangements. Using the ICT jargon suggested by Börzel (2002), we liken the EU to a generator of dedicated 'policy platforms' that has allowed the NPM template to be 'uploaded' and made available to all member states willing to 'download' it making it possible to adapt a general policy template to distinct policy areas. Accordingly, the modalities that have allowed the dissemination of the NPM template across Europe are mostly indirect and based on non-coercive forms of enforcement. From our standpoint, this representation accounts for a commonly noted aspect of NPM: its ubiquity. By combining the fact that the EU has established a unique policy platform and that the NPM template seems to be the only option freely available on that platform, NPM has become what critics refer to as 'the only game in town'. The number of downloads is thus related to the exclusive position NPM enjoys in the administrative market of ideas: it was the first administrative package to be uploaded onto the EU policy platform and subsequently adopted by core member states (the E-15) and it remains, to date, the only one, despite revisions and more nuanced efforts that have created what Pal (2008) calls 'inversions without end'. A second aspect of the phenomenon this representation is able to explain quite easily is its variability. The introduction of NPM features within various public sectors has not been mechanical, but has yielded a number of distinctive hybrids combining neoliberal ideas and traditional policy solutions. This is so because to make it operative the NPM template had to be customized; and the customizing process is always a creative one. Current discussions on the shift towards post-NPM forms of administration (Drechsler 2009) fail to distinguish between variable setups and changing models. We shall dwell a little longer on the ICT metaphor and suggest a reading of the way the process unfolded in relation to PAs and HE systems. In doing this, each time we shall discuss qualifications that take into account the role played by more coercive means used in relation to prospective Eastern European members.

6.4.1 Administrative travels across Europe and beyond

In Western Europe, several attempts to reform national PAs along NPM lines were carried out in a more decentralized and fragmentary fashion in the course of the 1990s; that is, since the success of British efforts in the field became evident and the logic underpinning those efforts became clearer (see Chapter 4). What, however, gave consistency, continuity, and impetus to the whole process was the adoption of the British NPM template by the EC towards the end of that decade. This move was precipitated by the events surrounding the collapse of the Santer Commission in the Spring of 1999 and the need to recover the lost legitimacy felt by the incoming new administration led by Prodi (Craig 2000; Christiansen and Gray 2004; Kassim 2004). Prodi's leadership of the EC strongly supported the introduction of new modes of governance as an alternative to top down forms of government intervention and Weberian administrative solutions. New modes of governance were attributed a twofold task: (i) the modernization of the administrative arm of the Union (Brussels bureaucracy) and (ii) the promotion of the direct involvement of civil society organizations in the activities of the European executive (Topan 2002; Cini 2015). The first task was carried out by Neil Kinnock, a former leader of the British Labour Party whose credentials as a modernizer were boosted by Tony Blair's personal support. The second task was the objective of the more positive aspect of the European governance agenda as spelled out in the influential 2001 White Paper simply called *European Governance* (COM/2001/428). After prolonged negotiations involving the Council on one side and the Parliament on the other, Kinnock eventually proposed a White Paper that established the framework for reforming the administrative apparatus of the EU: *Reforming the Commission* (COM/2000/0200).

Since the administrative shortcomings of the EC had been attributed to a bureaucratic structure that combined the worst of the French and German models, the prospect of Anglicizing the Eurocrats was viewed sympathetically within a Council and a Parliament that at the time were dominated by social-democratic majorities in awe of Blair's recent electoral success. In the 2000 White Paper, any reference to NPM was studiously avoided, perhaps because of the mounting criticisms against such a neoliberal instrument from within Britain itself. However, textual analyses of the document make it clear that the philosophy inspiring Kinnock's reform project, the specific organizational arrangements proposed, and even the means of its subsequent implementation, followed those already tested in Britain (Schön-Quinlivan 2011: Chs 5 and 6). Its actual outcomes have been much discussed ever since (Bauer 2008; Ellinas and Suleiman 2008). The general thrust of those discussions tends, however, to corroborate the conclusions arrived at by Hood and his collaborators in relation to Britain (Lapsley 2009). Be that as it may, the administrative reform of the Commission marked at the same time the creation of a European administrative policy platform and the uploading of the template developed originally in Britain. Thus, against the view that the NPM reform movement was an attempt to Americanize the old continent, the spreading of the NPM template across the emerging European administrative space (EAS) can be described as an act of 'modern Anglicization'. We also maintain that the reformist drive of the EC and various other EU member states eager to follow suit was fuelled by the logic of political centralization-cum-administrative decongestion employed in Britain and, finally, that the modes of implementation used here share with their British counterparts identical strategic goals and tactical moves. The real objective of the reform process was in both cases to reduce the political reliance of continental countries on neo-corporatist arrangements dependent on the legitimizing force of labour and the technical skills of semi-autonomous PAs.

It is widely acknowledged that the process of diffusion has received an additional and more overt push by the negative integration programme; a mechanism of policy transfer that although indirect possesses some degree of coercive force and is backed up by more formal and structured means of enforcement. Since we are dealing with changes that are challenging traditional administrative structures and practices established, in some cases, in the course of more than a century, the exclusive availability of a freely downloadable template by itself cannot be thought of as the only or even the main mechanism of policy transfer. The authority acquired by the Weberian model (not to mention the sets of interests surrounding national public administrations) would have seen that challenge off quite easily were it not for additional pressures exercised from without. The delegation of sovereignty upwards and the pressures put by EU institutions to create a single market are thus compelling explanations of the diffusion of NPM at continental level. Negative integration policies directed at the creation of a single market in goods and services have influenced the diffusion process in two distinct ways. *Ex ante*, they have helped prepare the ground for the introduction of the NPM template by (i) forbidding direct state intervention in support of domestic producers through the liberalization of market activities; (ii) undermining the economic role of the public sector through a) the privatization of national industries and public utilities and b) the externalization of several administrative activities; (iii) cultivating pro-reform 'astroturfs' through a highly biased application of good governance principles directed at undermining the power base of the despised welfare coalition. *Ex post facto*, negative integration policies managed to consolidate the ground in newly subjugated realms by outlawing social and political attempts to reverse the course via inflexible legal protection guaranteed by the European Court of Justice to controversial property rights and contractual relations locking in future majorities. As in previous historical phases, the rule of law and the system of Europeanized courts and tribunals called to uphold it operated as a neoliberal bulwark without the need to centralize the whole juridical apparatus; a further lesson learnt from a common law country like Britain (Mattei and Nader 2008).

An even more overt coercive element driving the process of diffusion is detectable when we consider the progressive enlargement of the Union eastward. The concession of political membership to Central and Eastern European (CEE) countries has been made dependent on the subscription of a number of non-negotiable conditions. As part of this European good governance agenda, aspiring members of the Union were asked to adopt and conform to the *acquis communautaire*; that is, the common body of norms developed by the EU, as well as the common set of legal practices elaborated by European jurisprudence for interpreting and applying those norms. As such, the EU (through the supervision of the EC) has compelled CEE countries to restructure their PAs by using the NPM template thus generating the distinctive EAS mentioned above (Olsen 2007; Hofmann 2008; Heidbreder 2011; Trondal and Peters 2013).[3] In order to do so, the EC made available to those countries a range of intellectual and economic resources enabling them to download and setup the NPM template in their national contexts. To this end, crucial partnerships with other supranational authorities were established. Among them, the most active and prolific is the one with the OECD that begat SIGMA (Support for Improvement in Governance and Management), a joint initiative aimed at strengthening public governance systems and public administration capacities in CEE countries, which is nonetheless an integral part of the OECD older PUMA (Public Management Committee) project established in the 1990s and rebranded several times (Pal 2008). According to the organization's webpage (http://www.sigmaweb.org/), SIGMA has a team of around 20 experts who provide assistance in five key areas: civil service and public administration organisation and functioning, policy making, public finance and audit, public procurement, strategy, and reform. The task assigned to the team is twofold: (i) to assess governance systems and institutions, legal frameworks, reform strategies and action plans, and progress in reform implementation; (ii) to provide methodologies and tools to support reforms, recommendations on improving laws and administrative arrangements, advice on the design and implementation of reforms, opportunities to share good practice from a wide range of countries, policy papers, and multi-country studies. As proof of the organic nature of the European and global good governance agendas, SIGMA finally states that 'with the EC's Directorate General Development and Cooperation – EuropeAid, we currently work with Algeria, Armenia, Azerbaijan, Egypt, Georgia, Jordan, Lebanon, Moldova, Morocco, Tunisia, and Ukraine as EU Neighbourhood countries'.[4]

Our interest in the EU enlargement process and its implication for the diffusion of the NPM template eastwards has to do with the compelling nature of the conditionality system: was this so strong that it has to be understood as a compulsory mechanism of policy transfer, or can it be made compatible with our claims insisting on the overall non-compulsory nature of the process itself? This aspect of the European good governance agenda is far more challenging than the one related to the coercive effects of the negative integration programme. In fact, unlike the latter, good governance entails a much more positive and pro-active intervention of supranational institutions such as the EC in domestic affairs. Such an inquiry would also help us understand the limitations of contrasting accounts of European integration and the relationship between intergovernmental and supranational forces pushing it through. Obviously, the constructivist pro-activism of the EC militates against accounts that insist on portraying the EU as a Madisonian regulatory state operating according to an intergovernmental logic. By relying on strong and non-negotiable conditionality, the enlargement process also gives us an insight into a facet of the overall European governance agenda that cast serious doubts on the concurrent picture of the EU as a networked polity operating through deliberative supranational practices. At this stage we wish to point out that even when these more coercive elements are factored in, the nature of the relationship between supranational and domestic authorities remains affected by asymmetries leaving to the latter ample discretion and political leverage. Rather than being a top down imposition, the neoliberal elements characterizing the emerging EAS are the outcome of the strategic moves of domestic forces looking for conditionality to facilitate self-serving changes. Even when criteria of good governance are decided by external actors (the E-15), their implementation leaves the domestic authorities affected in a crucial position to determine the pace in which its done, and those who will, in the end, benefit from the reform process. To quote Stone (2011: 118): ‘it is consistent with the logic of informal governance that rules are enforced only when the powerful countries do not find them excessively inconvenient, and that executive powers are the easiest for powerful countries to suborn’. In this sense, the current E-27 is grounded in a version of the good governance agenda that resembles the one discussed in the earlier part of the chapter and can, therefore, be analyzed from the same standpoint. Here too, supranational authorities like the EC, OECD and their offspring operate as enablers and face the dilemmas noticed by Stone in relation to their Bretton Woods counterparts: to preserve their objectivity while retaining their policy relevance.

6.4.2 Bologna to Lisbon and back (via Dublin): searching for academic excellence and virtuosity

We reach a similar conclusion when the Europeanization of HE policies is considered. We shall discuss this case in some detail, first, to flesh out our abstract model; secondly, to illustrate the non-coercive aspects of the diffusion of the NPM template and the need to go beyond functionalist and systemic explanations. The Bologna Process and the Lisbon Strategy are the tools through which a European HE policy platform was politically constructed and a revised version of the NPM template made available to all member states interested in reforming their own HEIs. Working jointly, they are also a fairly successful story, as policy diffusion goes, for the spreading of neoliberal solutions at the transnational level. The official starting point of the Bologna Process is the 1999 *Bologna Declaration*, a document signed by 29 European HE ministers convened in that Italian city to commemorate the anniversary of the founding of Europe's oldest university. The Declaration formalizes and expands on the precedent Sorbonne Joint Declaration, signed a year earlier in Paris by the education ministers of the four largest European countries (French, British, Italian, and German) invited there to celebrate the 800th anniversary of that other prestigious institution. Since then, the Process has produced a significant number of documents that describe the action lines and policy tools required to bring about a common European Higher Education Area (EHEA), and the many supporting structures dedicated to achieving such a goal and now operating in some 45 countries. The proliferation of regulatory means and supporting organizations notwithstanding, the Process still remains a free-standing intergovernmental initiative formally independent of the EU and grounded in a non-binding normative framework. The action lines developed and the policy tools employed to engender a common EHEA are restricted to the teaching side of university activities and have aimed at: (i) creating a common three-cycle degree structure; (ii) improving the legibility and compatibility of degree titles and other professional qualifications; (iii) promoting the mobility of students and teaching personnel across the EHEA; (iv) establishing quality-monitoring and quality-boosting systems of assessment and accreditation. In the course of the intervening quarter of a century, the attempts to achieve those goals have set in motion deep processes of change within HE sectors across Europe and beyond but have failed to achieve uniformity. Also lacking is a general consensus about the impact of those changes in fulfilling the programme's ultimate objective – i.e., to strengthen the competitiveness and attractiveness of the European HE and to foster mobility and employability through the introduction of a system based on undergraduate and postgraduate studies with easily legible curricula and degrees.[5]

Implementing the changes necessary to bring about the EHEA by means of a non-binding intergovernmental policy framework has been a challenge tackled by adopting new modes of governance; a task that has led, in the process, to the creation of a myriad of functional and overlapping regulatory agencies of the type described by Hooghe and Marks (2003) already discussed in Chapter 4. Like the horizontal mechanisms of auditing established in European PAs, those regulatory agencies are attributed three main tasks. First, they are put in charge of the standard-setting and benchmarking of teaching activities carried out by HEIs across all member states involved in the Process. The mechanisms of evaluation produced pursue, in turn, a double goal: to establish common standards of assessment across disciplines, HEIs, and national cultural contexts, and to provide inbuilt devices for progressively raising those standards. Second, regulatory agencies are given the task of accrediting all organizations operating in, or willing to enter, the HE business in the emerging EHEA. This objective is likewise twofold in that it concerns both the accreditation of HEIs and that of the quality-monitoring entities that have been springing up within the EHEA at a fast rate ever since. Last but not least, a significant subset of the emerging regulatory archipelago is engaged in establishing and updating databases collecting the indicators, surveys, and statistical analyses carried out in order to accomplish those tasks in a reliable and objective fashion. Among them, special relevance is assumed by Eurydice, 'a network whose task is to explain how education systems are organised in Europe and how they work',[6] which is not only complementing the statistical activities of other international organizations operating in the field (i.e., OECD and UNESCO), but is able to compete with them as well. The emerging evaluatory seascape is being charted by a host of empirically minded studies to which those interested can be redirected; from our more theoretical standpoint, its interest resides in the nature of the evaluatory process and the objectives it is entrusted with.

According to those who adopt a governance perspective, the implementation stage follows a deliberative and bottom-up approach. Standard-setting, benchmarking, quality assessment and accreditation are all activities (i) involving a variety of stakeholders; (ii) relying on peer-review mechanisms; and (iii) carried out through forms of democratic deliberation. As such, it is hailed by policy analysts and practitioners as being able to avoid the pitfalls of traditional command-and-control techniques and for suggesting more innovative solutions to wicked policy problems. Moreover, the overall process involves a significant number of stakeholders committed to abiding by the 'unforced force of the better argument' rather than the neo-corporate bargaining practices that used to dominate the HE sector at domestic level. This is viewed as the best way to establish both an equitable playing field for HE suppliers and a fair system of protection for HE consumers. In this spirit, new modes of governance are presented as the right institutional complement to the open method of coordination (OMC) used by the Lisbon Strategy – the two genuinely European policy innovations that can generate novel forms of democratic legitimacy and boost the voluntary compliance of all those involved in the Process in the way described by Warren (2009) in the passage quoted in Chapter 4. The euphoria with which those policy innovations have been welcomed in the first decade of the new century by the scientific community has somehow cooled thanks to the more critical voices of educators worried about the 'facts' the Bologna Process is creating on the ground (Furlong 2005). From our standpoint, the worries expressed by those authors can be fully appreciated only when the Lisbon Strategy is brought into the picture, for the two programmes are meant to work in tandem. As Keeling explains,

> the Bologna Process is an intergovernmental commitment to restructuring higher education systems which extend far beyond the EU and the Lisbon Strategy as part of the Union's wider economic platform that extends beyond the higher education sector. In combination, however, these European-level actions are supporting and stabilising an emergent policy framework for the EU in higher education.
>
> (Keeling 2006: 203)

The interest of EU institutions such as the Council and the Commission in education policies precede those of the ministers of education who subscribed to the *Bologna Declaration*. The Lisbon Strategy launched in 2000 at an inter-ministerial meeting held in the Portuguese capital was only the latest of a series of interventions in the field of HE seeking to Europeanize it. As already mentioned, the Lisbon Strategy deals with research activities and pursues a very ambitious objective with clear neoliberal overtones:

> the Union has today set itself a new strategic goal for the next decade: to become the most competitive and dynamic knowledge-based economy in the world, capable of sustainable economic growth with more and better jobs and greater social cohesion. [...] Implementing this strategy will be achieved by improving the existing processes, introducing a new open method of coordination at all levels, coupled with a stronger guiding and coordinating role for the European Council to ensure more coherent strategic direction and effective monitoring of progress.
>
> (European Council 2000)[7]

Within this overall perspective, HE is mainly viewed in instrumental terms: as a productive sector that could actively contribute to economic growth by stimulating innovation, and as a training field for upgrading the technical skills of a flexible and highly mobile workforce. HEIs are called to fulfil those economic objectives by redirecting their research and educational activities accordingly. On the one hand, scientific research is steered towards applied and patentable scientific endeavours (Mode 2 science) and collaborations with the technology industry through dedicated European funding streams (framework programmes, the latest of which is Horizon 2020).[8] On the other hand, degrees and professional qualifications are required to reflect learning abilities and technical skills that can maximize the market opportunities of those investing time, energy, and financial resources into acquiring them. In both cases, the policy solution specified to achieve those outcomes is the development of competitive dynamics among suppliers and customers, and the acquisition of the right managerial techniques to help HEIs survive the challenges posed by a globalizing knowledge economy. Although the Lisbon documents also stress the relevance of social cohesion and sustainability, it is clear that social and environmental concerns are there as part of the rhetorical elements used to sell the policy package to a

European public increasingly sceptical about the EU and the market integration process.

Concerning the more technical aspects of the *Lisbon Strategy*, the salient features are related to the attempt to combine, at least initially, a binding normative framework 'upstream' with a decentralized mechanism of policy implementation 'downstream'. While decision making is carried out according to intergovernmental means, Council decisions do not attempt to modify European treaties but restrict themselves to expanding their current interpretation. If the instrumental and economistic reading of HE can be seen as a tribute to neoliberal ideas, no less relevant is the fact that this reading allows educational issues to be rescaled at EU-level in spite of the limited mandate attributed to EU institutions in that field by extant treaties (especially arts. 126 and 127 of the Maastricht Treaty). Those interpretations of European treatises attribute in fact an increasing proactive role to the EC at the policy making level and reinforce its supervision of the implementation process. Although the latter is carried out through the OMC, which leaves national authorities free to choose the means, the EC is left in charge of defining the targets to be achieved and can exercise various forms of external pressure by using progress reports based on traffic-light schemes and scorecards – a subtle strategy of 'naming-and-shaming' laggards. Moreover, the EC has the power to manipulate the OMC itself by choosing its degree of flexibility, as demonstrated by the more authoritative interventions witnessed since the inception of the Eurozone crisis in many policy areas. Since then the Lisbon Strategy has assumed the shape of an open-ended reform programme that can be relaunched every five years or so (its present iteration is the Europe 2020 strategy). Supranational bodies like the EC are, therefore, given the opportunity to learn, use, and revise conditional strategies that give them considerable political leverage in their interactions with state actors, especially those operating at the subnational level.

We wish to conclude this section by considering how this complex machinery of multi-level governance affects our hypothesis concerning the non-coercive nature of the diffusion process. Briefly, we maintain that even when the role and power of supranational institutions are factored in, the building of the EHEA must be considered the outcome of a non-coercive intergovernmental process: member states' association has remained voluntary and their active involvement in the decision making process reinforces this impression even on the few occasions in which qualified majority voting has been applied. The same can be said about the uploading and downloading of the policy template available on the EHEA platform. Countries like Britain, where that template was first elaborated and tested, were happy to upload it to reinforce its domestic legitimacy and exploit their familiarity with it. Countries that have downloaded it have done so because their national governments were eager to modernize their HE sector in the first place. In the process, they have contributed to the diffusion process by devising novel ways of setting up that template and uploading them on the platform. Once again, we reach the conclusion that the introduction of market elements within national HEs and of NPM techniques within domestic HEIs, overall, are acts of statecraft rather than external coercion or due to the pressures exercised by impersonal systemic forces. Understanding why national governments were eager to do so means investigating how the process has affected the internal distribution of power between subnational entities and who must actually foot the bill of modernizing the HE sectors. It is to this task that we now turn.

6.5 EU regulatory regimes as new *raison d'etat*?

To recap, we have proposed a representation of the diffusion process of the NPM template as due to the support received by the good governance agenda of supranational institutions. We maintained, however, that those institutions operated as enablers rather than enforcers, and that the whole process rests, by and large, on the voluntary association and compliance of state actors, rather than external coercion or the pressure exercised by systemic forces. This can be fully appreciated when the state is disaggregated and we consider the competitive dynamics between sub-state units and international organizations. Our aim in this section is to do this and thus clarify who copies what, from whom, and why. We want to show not only the crucial role that the diffusion of market solutions plays in hollowing out democratic values and institutions, but also the limitations of those worldviews and scientific approaches that see markets and states as contrasting forces and new modes of governance as superior postmodern alternatives. Our main claim is that, lurking behind the various attempts to modernize and Europeanize realms of the public sector, governments are attempting to copy the strategy of political centralization-cum-administrative decongestion that helped British authorities to achieve a top down form of governability. The creation of an EHEA is the most paradigmatic example.

Despite their being part of the state apparatus, continental universities used to enjoy an autonomy similar to that of their British counterparts, especially after the events of '68. As in Britain, all over the continent the HE sector was funded through block grant systems. As a result, central governments had limited powers – e.g. on deciding what increments to give that sector during the negotiations surrounding the determination of the annual budget. Organizational and managerial issues were either a matter for state legislation, and therefore controlled by the legislative branch, or left to the discretion of the universities themselves (either as individual entities or as a corporate body). Within past neo-corporatist arrangements, central government had little leverage on academic matters and universities regularly lobbied ministers or national parliaments directly, bypassing the respective ministries when they refused to act as ambassadors. However, public dissatisfaction with the way in which the HE sector was run affected ministries and central governments, for they were formally responsible for the sector to their own parliaments and public opinion. Europeanizing HE issues along the lines suggested by the

Bologna Process and the Lisbon Strategy gives national governments the opportunity to turn the tables, allowing them to acquire full policy-making power while shifting political responsibilities onto other entities located below, above, and to the sides. This is why, from our standpoint, they are always at the forefront of the reform movement, and why all the policy initiatives discussed so far are initiated and relaunched in intergovernmental settings.

Thus, to understand why domestic policy areas are internationalized the real question upon which we need to focus is whether that specific area was under the actual (as opposed to formal) control of central government or had, on the contrary, some degree of political autonomy. Our reading suggests that in the former case there would be no interest on the part of central government to join or to start an internationalization process, while in the latter case central government would be very keen to do so.[9] Neoliberal ideas and managerial solutions are economic means for achieving a genuinely political end, rather than a tribute paid to ideological worldviews. They are policy instruments that have been tested in practice and found highly reliable in freeing central governments from the iron cage of past neo-corporatist arrangements. New modes of governance are, in turn, sophisticated expedients through which central governments attempt to build consensus, undermine oppositional forces, displace other representative institutions and, last *and* least, deflect the attention of policy analysts and practitioners.

It is not our intention to supply a heroic picture of central government's strategic abilities. The top-down governability engendered by this form of statecraft has been possible thanks to the help of other powerful actors willing to play along out of their own self-interest. The nature of the relationship underpinning what are for us *collusive* partnerships is a permanent source of controversy among those studying these phenomena and occupies a great deal of space in the literature dedicated to them. First, disagreement is due to the existence of two alternative readings of the two-level game employed in international relations scholarship. This debate often overlaps with a second one concerned with the methodological perspective to adopt when studying the interaction between collective agencies such as states. Here disagreement occurs between those who tend to attribute to the state a unitary will and set of interests, and those who wish to disaggregate such an entity and peek inside what would otherwise remain a mysterious black box. Our position in relations to those debates is somewhat eclectic. We agree with those urging social scientists to disaggregate complex collective entities, but we also believe that the interaction between domestic and international levels needs to be analyzed through the lens of a three-level game of the type used in the previous chapters. Following Weiler's (1999: 271) suggestion, we maintain that at the EU level such a game has to take into account the interrelations between 'three modes of governance: international (or intergovernmental), supranational and infranational'. In order to do so, we first tried to identify the actors and the set of strategies used at each level and then understand the way in which those levels are interconnecting.

From this multi-dimensional perspective, the success of the strategic actions of central governments in exploiting transnational policy platforms where to upload and download templates that enhance their domestic leverage is related to their ability to (i) establish cooperative relationships with supranational institutions able to supply intellectual, logistical, and financial support; and (ii) mobilize the domestic forces dissatisfied with or excluded from traditional neo-corporate arrangements (those that would not pose any significant threat to their centralizing aspirations). The resulting partnerships rest ultimately on an economic calculus whose currency is wealth *and* power; their nature is therefore not only collusive, uninterested in the national or public interest as such, but also inherently competitive. Consequently, their members are led to renegotiate the terms of their agreements each time some sort of crisis (stochastic shocks) upset the *status quo*. The collusive nature of the partnerships established by state actors is underscored by the analysis of good governance carried out in the first section of this chapter, where it also emerged that collusion takes place at two distinct levels. The first level is the one considered by Stone (2011) and pertains to the use of the good governance agenda as a hegemonic tool favouring the US and her allies. Under the pretence of fighting corruption and autocratic regimes, the US and other major donor countries push for constitutional and economic reforms that inevitably expand the influence and reach of both Washington and Wall Street (Seabrooke 2001). In playing the art of paradigm maintenance (Wade 1996), supranational institutions assume the role of enablers required to supply objective evaluations and scientific assessments while retaining policy relevance. The second level concerns the selection process according to which developing countries choose to adopt the good governance programme even when there is scant evidence about its positive effects on growth. Vreeland (2003, 2007) skilfully shows that the decision to call in the IMF is taken by sub-national entities driven by domestic considerations that have nothing to do with the national interest, and that its success rests on the ability of local elites to shift the overall costs onto other domestic constituencies. By helping make the implementation process more or less flexible, supranational agencies legitimize the use of what are in reality predatory policies, stabilize the collusive partnerships between local, national, and international players, and try to retain their policy relevance when subjected to critique.

This basic pattern is repeated within the EU context, even if here the asymmetries of power between member states are not as great and all state actors engaged in playing the three-level game subscribe to liberal democratic values. As seen, the creation of both the EAS and the EHEA is the outcome of the interplay between an intergovernmental logic that initiates and refreshes, at given intervals, the process of Europeanization, and the activism of supranational institutions (EC and ECJ, mostly) supplying, once again, intelligence, logistics and resources to carry the process forward in the face of multiple forms of opposition.[10] The alleged conflicts between intergovernmental and supranational authorities, about which so much ink has been spilled in

European Studies, are a side-show. In our view, these conflicts are more reminiscent of the game of good cop/bad cop familiar from countless Hollywood movies: sometime national member states are responsible for the flaring up of crises that justify the intervention of Brussels; other times it is exactly the reverse; the end result of the role play is always to confuse public opinion and escape accountability (cf. Streeck 2014: 104).[11] To be sure, those conflicts are real, but they are mostly related to various attempts to renegotiate the terms of the collusive partnerships between the actors involved. That is why those who see them as political turning points are often disappointed when the partnership emerges phoenix like from its own ashes. The events following the 2005 constitutional crisis supply us with clear examples of this renegotiation process leading, eventually, to a new agreement and the consequential refreshing and relabelling of old policy initiatives. The same can be said about the one opened up by the 2008 financial crisis still underway.

Among the actors involved in those collusive partnerships are domestic forces that can benefit from the changes set in motion or can help carry the process of modernization forwards. The privatization and externalization of public services of any sort has, for instance, mobilized many private businesses willing to exploit the opening of markets from which they were in the past formally excluded. This explains why many professional organizations and associations of producers are supportive and willing to invest in PPPs and start-up ventures. Adopting the NPM template at state level offers them three main sets of opportunities: first, they can benefit directly from the enclosure and commodification of public assets; second, they can supply services and expertise to the newly deregulated sectors; third, they can benefit indirectly from the fact that the public sector is becoming leaner and meaner and is no longer willing to be the employer of last resort, let alone a good one.

Focusing on the interconnections between intergovernmental, supranational, and infra-national dynamics, we have the opportunity to analyze the overall integration process as an evolving metagame. The notion of metagame is important because it helps us understand more general aspects of the integration process without introducing systemic categories and functional explanations. To begin with, the notion of the metagame allows us to distinguish between (a) rule-makers and rule-takers, and (b) interactions unfolding within the 'rules of the game' on the one hand, and interactions pertaining to the 'game of the rules' on the other. Those distinct types of interaction take place at all three levels identified above but have decreasing scope and reach: (i) the intergovernmental level allows meta-regulators to define the environment within which supranational institutions are called to operate; within this set of constitutional side-constraints, (ii) supranational institutions define the environment in which infra-national actors are required to operate. Although the rules of the game established at higher levels are always susceptible to interpretation, the leeway available to those operating at the infra-national level is less ample than the one enjoyed by those operating at the supranational level, and the latter is, in turn, less ample than the one enjoyed by the actors operating at the intergovernmental level. This means that the interconnection between levels occurs along a chain of authority attributing ultimate control to those located at the highest level, even when heterarchical solutions are employed in some realms at the lower levels (cf. Chapter 3). In this sense, governance always operates in the shadow of hierarchy, even when no state actor is formally involved in the process. Moreover, the new modes of governance employed at the infra-national level have to contend with multiple meta-regulators operating independently of each other: (i) national governments, (ii) supranational institutions and (iii) intergovernmental bodies.

This complex architecture, relying on soft-law instruments and multiple systems of evaluation, assessment, and accountability mechanisms allows meta-regulators to adopt that which suits them best and shift the blame for policy failure upon whomever they like whenever they want. By contrast with the hardware/software metaphor used by Weiler (1999) to depict this *modus operandi*, we find it more illuminating to represent the structure of the EU three-level game as sets of nested games where the players try to avoid engaging in structural reforms that could activate formal ratification processes involving national parliaments and public opinion.

An additional feature of EU integration that the notion of the metagame is able to convey is related to the way in which conditional strategies are devised, employed, and revised by distinct generations of players interacting across levels. Each renegotiation of the collusive partnership represents an opportunity to revise the strategies used by the various players. Learning from previous mistakes explains both the various forms of integration unfolding within the EU framework and the varying fortune of EU programmes, methods, and institutions. Member states are given the freedom to join (or withdrawn from) several programmes of Europeanization involving subsets of the EU-27 (i.e. Schengen, Euro, diplomatic and military initiatives) or extending far beyond the EU-27 (Lisbon Strategy, EHEA, economic cooperation and development, migration policies). Intergovernmental meetings pertaining to those *à la carte* groupings can, in turn, decide to discontinue some programmes altogether or focus on some parts at the expense of others; they can relaunch initiatives that are evolving in unwanted directions or make the initiatives that are working well (for them) open ended. In doing so, meta-regulators have the power to change the policy environment in which other actors are supposed to operate, which could become more-or-less competitive. This is assured by the choice given to them to employ the right mode of governance among the various types available. Hence, the relevance acquired, for instance, by the OMC or the declining role attributed to the Community Method; the changing nature of the Comitology System from a watchdog tool for the Council into an instrument of deliberative supranationalism; until, that is, a new intergovernmental meeting rewrites (part of) the script. Associated with those changes are also the shifting fortunes of institutions and actors: some policy networks acquire more relevance while others are left floating without institutional anchorage and therefore lose their policy relevance; entire departmental structures are side-lined while others manage to recycle themselves by associating them with a new or refreshed policy initiative. Thus, traditional institutions like UNESCO, which used to supply expertise and prestige to cultural and educational programmes, are slowly supplanted by others like the OECD, while education ministries have functions taken away which are then passed onto more technical ministries dealing with economic issues or are absorbed wholesale into those ministries.

These changes end up producing ripple effects at the supranational and infra-national levels, where the various actors are forced to revise their strategies and frames of reference, producing eventually a systemic shift from one steady state to another. At that point in time, another policy cycle starts with new generations of players involved in the overall process. The renegotiation allows the collusive partnerships to regenerate themselves, teaches a lesson to those actors who have lost policy relevance and institutional anchorage, and redefines the existing sets of pay-offs available. Cycles can finally manage to interlink producing medium and long-term sequences like the one considered in this volume: the passage from a neo-corporatist consensus politics to a neoliberal one, and the more epochal Polanyian processes leading to the progressive commodification of land, labour, money, and, as we shall argue in the concluding chapter, knowledge.

A final insight brought about by the notion of the metagame is related to the inner tensions shaking the three-level game periodically. Unlike systemic and post-structuralist accounts, agency and politics remain crucial factors in explaining how order is produced and reproduced each time. Since the rationale underpinning the behaviour of the players engaged in the sets of nested games that make up the metagame is purely instrumental and concerns the acquisition/retention of wealth and power, crises are endemic; for the crystallization of a societal equilibrium entails a biased redistribution of resources and opportunities that becomes more evident with time and elicits the emergence of defensive countermovements willing to challenge the system. By kick-starting a crisis and forcing the renegotiation of a collusive partnership, those countermovements open windows of genuine opportunity for change before a new steady state is reached and the renegotiation process comes to a close. This means that social changes although interlinked are never fully interlocking, but they tend to generate contradictions that will eventually upset the system and expose its justificatory mechanisms to critique.

6.6 Conclusion

The goal of this chapter has been to explain the role international institutions and supranational authorities play in the dissemination of market solutions worldwide. As a first step, we discussed the contribution made by the good governance agenda. Then we focused on the EU and tried to show how the integration process has helped the sharing of the NPM template (and related strategies of customization) by its member states. In both cases, we noted several interesting factors at work sustaining the spreading and deepening of market reforms in PA and HE. First, the adoption of neoliberal ideas and managerial tools is not the result of coercive pressures from without, whether understood as an effect of hegemonic powers or impersonal systemic forces. We found that state actors are always the main market makers and prime-movers, and keen to exploit internationalization processes for their own ends. Those ends are related to the maximization of their positional power *vis-à-vis* other subnational units, which enjoy autonomous sources of legitimacy, able to challenge them. Market solutions and managerial techniques are tools they employ to (i) undermine their social and institutional competitors; (ii) impose reforms that help centralize decision making power and; (iii) escape democratic accountability by shifting operational responsibilities onto others. Second, we noted that the role international organizations and supranational authorities play in this self-serving struggle for power is that of 'enablers' rather than 'enforcers'. They supply willing state actors the means needed to sell market reforms to their national audiences and enact those changes against the fierce opposition of the domestic constituencies who are going to bear the full cost. Transnational corporations, NGOs and local elites are enticed to lend intellectual, political, and material support to such an enterprise because of the financial returns they can gain. Market reforms entail the enclosure and commodification of realms of the nation state that will assure them high returns at a very low level of risk. Finally, we argued that the collusive partnerships established by this coterie have an inherently competitive nature that pushes the various components to renegotiate their arrangements whenever stochastic shocks upset the *status quo*. Hence the periodic crises affecting the neoliberal social and economic order, and the remarkable ability of the social and political coalitions supporting it to regenerate themselves in spite of the dysfunctional outcomes produced by their collusive behaviour for society at large.

Applied to the EU, this interpretative scheme gives us the opportunity to understand both the relation between the integration process and the growing democratic deficit. Since the construction of a common EAS and EHEA is the outcome of cooperative enterprises involving national, supranational, and sub-national actors, we suggested that the best way to analyze their interaction is through a three-level game yielding multiple and overlapping collusive partnerships. The conflicts between national and supranational authorities are, from this perspective, related to periodic attempts to renegotiate those partnerships, rather than the need to preserve state sovereignty in the face of strong globalizing forces justifying delegation of state functions above, below, and sideways. Consequently, we propose a reading of the democratic deficit that emphasizes the collusive interplay between the governments of member states and EU institutions the goal of which is to reinforce top-down governability while undermining indirect forms of domestic control and accountability. If the state *per se* is not being eroded by the overall process of Europeanization, the set of changes it has set in motion are having deep and far reaching effects on its democratic architecture. And they are developments that, in our opinion, do not go in the direction indicated by the social and political theorists who have been mesmerized by the advent of new modes of governance. More pessimistically, we view those developments as contributing to the inception of a post-democratic age, which the worldwide diffusion of the NPM template is alas fuelling. By supplanting traditional mechanisms of accountability and electoral forms of representation, new modes of governance insulate those state actors that operate at the transnational level and attribute to them growing meta-regulatory powers. This explains why multiple attempts to involve societal actors in policy making and policy implementation by handing those activities to deliberative democratic fora is not generating bottom up forms of legitimation that can counterbalance the anti-European feelings rocking the EU at present. On the contrary, the freedom new modes of governance allow to meta-regulators located at different levels of the political fabric is promoting the rising of a novel fictitious commodity, emerging from the transformation of knowledge, and the social ways in which it is produced and transmitted. It is to this Polanyian shift that we shall turn our attention in concluding this work.

Notes

1 The same can be said about the US, where rising populist tendencies and social tensions are explained as due to neoliberal policies (Frank 2001). It is worth noting that here too it is possible to observe the introduction of forms of marketization that originated in Europe.

2 For instance, according to our reading of the integration process, intergovernmentalism and governance coexist. Thus, we try to connect the swinging from one form to another as the outcome of periodic attempts to counterbalance changing political conditions (i.e. the 2007 Treaty of Lisbon as an intergovernmental solution to the 2005 rejection of the EU Constitutional Charter). It is also evident to us that the swinging between modes of governance is accompanied by changes in the type of integration policy pursued. Thus, positive interventions aiming at restructuring a policy field are usually being followed by negative integration attempts to consolidate that same field. This dynamic perspective makes our framework different from more static representations of the diffusion process suggested in the literature on policy transfer (Benson and Jordan 2011; Börzel 2005; Bulmer *et al* 2007; Dolowitz and Marsh 1996, 2000; Radaelli 2003).

3 'The so-called Copenhagen criteria, which define (political, economic, *acquis communautaire*) access conditions for new member states, bear witness to the importance that the European Union attributes to the (good functioning of the) single market. The economic entry criterion requires future member states to possess functioning market economies that can face competitive pressures without imbalances' (Bongardt 2015: 758, endnote 1).

4 Olsen (2007: Ch. 11) suggests a different reading of the influence NPM has had in creating the EAS and of the role SIGMA has played in this. It is not clear to us on what evidence this statement is based. The specific literature we have consulted does not support this clear-cut distinction but is much more nuanced, connecting OECD's revisions to the need to retain both credibility and policy relevance (Pal 2008). Among the constellations of organizations sustaining this effort we also

found the *European Public Administration Network* (EIPAN), an informal network of the Directors General responsible for public administration in the member states of the European Union, the European Commission and observer countries steered by the ministers responsible for public administration (<https://www.eupan.eu/en/home/>), and the *European Institute of Public Administration* (<https://EIPA>), Europe's leading centre of excellence on European integration and the new challenges for public management (<https://www.eipa.eu/>), whose mission is to support the European Union and its member states and the countries associated with EIPA by providing relevant and high quality services to develop the capacities of public officials in dealing with EU affairs.

5 Online. HTTP: <https://www.ehea.info/> (accessed 10 December 2016).

6 Online. HTTP: <https://webgate.ec.europa.eu/fpfis/mwikis/eurydice/index.php/Main_Page> (accessed 10 December 2016).

7 Online. HTTP: <https://www.europarl.europa.eu/summits/lis1_en.htm?textMode=on> (accessed 10 December 2016).

8 Online. HTTP: <https://ec.europa.eu/programmes/horizon2020/ (accessed 10 December 2016)>.

9 To our knowledge, Koenig-Archibugi (2002, 2004) is the only author who has taken this hypothesis seriously and tried to carry out an empirical assessment of Wolf's 'new *raison d'etat*' theory in relation to the EU integration process.

10 For an analysis of the role played by the ECJ in this process see Weiler (1999: Ch. 5). Interestingly, national judicial systems are the only state institutions that have escaped neoliberal reforms so far and still enjoy significant autonomy from central government. Rather than refuting our reading, the reason why this is so, despite the explicit interest manifested by some governments in curbing the independence of their judicial systems (Italy above all), needs to be sought in the peculiar British context, where the absence of a formal, functional separation of powers along US lines gives central government great leverage on courts and tribunals. This means that the NPM template, as originally thought, does not contemplate its application to that realm. Hence the absence of an internationalization process national governments could use to justify reforming the system, for they lack the necessary *vincolo esterno* (self-binding commitments) needed to overcome strong domestic opposition.

11 Perhaps, the most blatant example of collusive relationship is the letter the ECB sent to Berlusconi government before the latter was replaced by a 'technical' cabinet led by Monti in 2011. In that letter Draghi and Trichet recommended several reforms of the labour market and pension system the aim of which was to make them more flexible and less financially burdensome. Later on, several journalistic investigations raised the suspect that the letter was in fact solicited from within the Italian government itself to overcome internal opposition against those very reforms, and that Draghi and Trichet were simply obliging. Eventually, those same recommendations were passed into law through the Job Act passed by Renzi government in 2014. See <http://www.ilsole24ore.com/art/notizie/2011-09-29/testo-lettera-governo-italiano-091227.shtml?uuid=Aad8ZT8D and http://www.ilfattoquotidiano.it/2012/05/12/lettera-della-vera-storia/227690/> (accessed 10 December 2016)

7 Conclusion

Is knowledge the new fictitious commodity?

7.1 Introduction

Since the latest financial crisis in 2008, we have witnessed the rise in popularity of Karl Polanyi's work. At the inception of the crisis, it was possible to detect a growing scientific interest in the double movement thesis in particular (Dale 2010). This was accompanied by the widespread – if short-lived – expectation of the demise of the neoliberal consensus and the arrival of another great transformation. Many assumed this great transformation would take the form of a second coming: the restoration of the post-war welfare state, including its Keynesian utilities and maintenance systems. Mainstream readings of the crisis presented it as an empirical refutation of neoliberal arguments for market solutions and a vindication of Keynesian stabilization policies (Akerlof and Shiller 2010; Skidelsky 2009; Taylor 2010). Financial rescue packages devised during several intergovernmental emergency meetings received, therefore, the support of left-wing intellectuals, opinion makers, and political parties and were positively presented as a relaunch of state activism in economic affairs. Almost a decade later, the expectation of a great transformation has evaporated, leaving many analysts busy looking for a plausible explanation of why it did not happen (Crouch 2011; Mirowski 2013; Streeck 2014). The surprising non-death of neoliberalism is, understandably, casting a shadow on Polanyi's double movement thesis (Dale 2012). However, it is not eroding the political faith in past welfarist solutions, nor denting the intellectual hegemony political economy has acquired within the social sciences. Notwithstanding the postmodernist search for a new politics related in Part I, state-driven protective measures aiming at harnessing the market still remain an integral part of political manifestos produced by opposition movements across the world.

In this final chapter, we want to engage in a reversed type of operation; namely, re-evaluate the heuristic role of Polanyi's double movement while casting doubts on the welfare solutions that he thought, and many others still think, would bring about a great transformation. We argue that the reading of Polanyi's double movement as a recursive cyclical phenomenon proposed in Chapter 1 gives us a better insight into both the nature of the current crisis and its failure to unravel the neoliberal consensus. In addition, we want to show that, given the theoretical and practical limits of past welfare solutions, these cannot represent the basis upon which to build a successful alternative vision of non-market society. In prospect, this means that the future resolution of the current crisis is likely to start a new cycle in what looks uncannily like capitalism's Groundhog Day. As such, we should expect not only the deepening of previous drives for the commodification of land, labour, and money, but also a full-blown attempt at commodifying novel fields of activity and social spheres. Knowledge is, in the context of the information age, the most likely candidate to be turned into another (fourth) type of fictitious commodity.[1] This, we shall argue, explains the tensions arising in those sectors engaged in the intellectual and administrative activities considered in Part II.

7.2 Polanyi's double movement and capitalism's Groundhog Day

Let us start by recalling the reading of Polanyi's double movement suggested at the outset of this work. In Chapter 1, we contend that there are at least three main historical episodes used by Polanyi to explain the unfolding of the double movement, each of them corresponding to the creation of a specific fictitious commodity:

1 The enclosure movement responsible for the attempt to commodify land leads to the establishment of the Speenhamland system.
2 The industrial revolution and the attempts to commodify labour are at the root of the Chartist Movement and subsequent political pressures for the regulation of the labour market.
3 The development of financial capitalism at the turn of the nineteenth century is finally responsible for the progressive era movements and the systems of social insurance developed after the First World War.

On each occasion, a countermovement arose in order to address the challenges posed by the commodification process, but unfortunately it managed merely to induce defective social accommodations responsible for the starting of a new cycle. Failure of the countermovement to stop the market experiment for good produces two main consequences: the deepening of the previous process of commodification and the starting of a new one having as its target some other social resource market forces strive to turn into a fictitious commodity.

As described by Polanyi, the process is threefold: (i) the rising of a countermovement willing to challenge the market order and re-embed the realm(s) subjected to commodification; (ii) the making of a grand political bargain between oppositional forces and ruling elites the goal of which is to protect society while retaining beneficial aspects of the market system; (iii) the progressive weakening of the protective policy regimes established as a result – due to growing unpopularity, and their eventual reversal by opportunistic market forces. Thus, the unravelling of the Speenhamland system is responsible for the beginning of the industrialization process and the commodification of labour, whereas the failure of the Chartist Movement marks the evolution of a financial type of capitalism pursuing the goal of commodifying money.

Although Polanyi is keen to show that in England the accommodations induced by recurrent countermovements helped preserve the country from the fascist experiences that devastated the continent in the 1930s, by no means did they manage to derail the market experiment once and for all. On the contrary, pro-market forces managed each time to weather the crisis, and were able to restart the experiment, increasing the risk for society and producing larger and more devastating social cataclysms. Thus, our conclusion is that the recursive nature of the double movements described by Polanyi follows an unmistakable vortex-like pattern. If this reading of the double movement is correct, it is not at all clear what warrants Polanyi's optimism in the ability of the then emerging welfare state to escape the fate of the previous historical solutions he acutely describes in his work. Even more puzzling is the support enjoyed by welfarist solutions nowadays, given the dismal track record of liberal attempts to embed the market in the post-war period. From our perspective, the problem is related to the fact, stressed by Polanyi, that liberal attempts at embedding the market are carried out in conjunction with others directed at emptying society of political content. The inability of postmodern social theory to unmask this cultural contradiction at the core of the liberal enterprise has not only impeded the development of a radical alternative to political economy, but has actively contributed to the success of the technocratic visions and mechanical solutions decried by Polanyi.

By the time the first paperback edition of Polanyi's work came out in 1957, he was based at Columbia University, busily carrying out the work in economic anthropology that was to give him an enduring reputation.[2] During this 13-year interval, he went back to the topic of the self-regulating market only once, in a 1947 paper titled 'Our obsolete market mentality', and did not use the opportunity offered by the 1957 editorial project to reassess his earlier work. The 1947 article published in the Jewish journal *Commentary* looks like a brief restatement of the main theses contained in his earlier book rather than a revision or an updating of the latter, and this despite the editorial footnote claiming that 'Karl Polanyi considers this article to represent his first significant advance over the thesis presented in *The Great Transformation*' (in Polanyi 1947: 109). The main novelties detectable in the article represent, at best, shifts of emphasis: first, the author contends that it is the trust posed in machines and technocratic fixes (rather than capitalism *per se*) that poses the main danger faced by human civilization;[3] second, a more sombre and less optimistic mood pervades Polanyi's reflections, notwithstanding his acknowledging of the many efforts to overcome the liberal utopia by welfare coalitions across the globe. Those shifts in emphasis seem to be conveyed by the title of the essay itself, implying the survival of a mindset that has outlived its time, and its subtitle (Civilization must find a new thought pattern) betrays distrust in the automatic rebalancing of social forces.

7.3 The rise and fall of embedded liberalism: a Polanyian reading of C. Wright Mills' work

While Polanyi appears no longer interested in analyzing the social and political developments of his own time from the standpoint of the double movement, at the time of the paperback edition of *The Great Transformation* a growing disenchantment with liberal attempts to embed the market was already evident; a clear premonition that the transformation was faltering and another capitalist cycle restarting. In the US, a thorough analysis of the shortcomings of the New Deal (as a form of embedded liberalism) was even proposed by a colleague of Polanyi at Columbia University, C. Wright Mills. Although there is no indication that the two had more than a fleeting acquaintance or were fully aware of each other's work[4], we contend that Mills' approach could be easily thought of as inspired by Polanyi's work and mistaken for an account of the unfolding of a new double movement, the one that will eventually yield the current neoliberal consensus. Mills' ethnography of American capitalism during the New Deal is no less bold, ambitious, and wide-ranging than the one carried out by Polanyi; it is framed in a radical language and uses conceptual categories derived from a similar mutualist tradition; and, like the latter, it was initially grounded in the belief that the US was on the verge of a great transformation. In the dozen years that followed the publication of Polanyi's masterpiece, C. Wright Mills produced a remarkable trilogy tracing the parabola of the American socialist dream.

The opening salvo was *The New Men of Power* (1948), where Mills engaged in the study of America's trade union leaders with the aim of uncovering 'who they are, what they think, how they will act in the coming crisis', as the book's dust-jacket has it. In so doing, he intended to develop a framework for (i) understanding labour organizations' role in promoting political and institutional change and (ii) assessing the real ability of popular movements to permanently shift the extant balance of power within American society. In the course of his research, Mills notes that American trade unions are undergoing a problematic process of bureaucratization responsible for the growing gap between leaders and rank-and-file members and he spells out the negative implications this will have for the political aspirations of the labour movement.

Three main aspects of the bureaucratization process are considered by Mills. First, he maintains that union leaders are strongly inclined to abandon confrontational syndicalist visions and adopt more cooperative economic attitudes. This is often a precondition imposed upon them by the government as a condition for being included in the tripartite committees to which policy making was delegated. Here they are joined by state officials operating not as neutral mediators but as allies of the corporate community representing the third component. As a result, any tiny concession unions manage to achieve is traded for a credible commitment to refrain from direct action and acts of class solidarity that could disrupt production and commerce. Second, Mills explains that the intensity and pervasiveness of direct class action is further constrained by the adoption of liberal forms of representation designed to professionalize union leaders and turn them into a specialized cadre operating on the supply side of the labour market. For him, this means turning the labour leader into 'a de facto businessman: a purveyor of labour as a commodity' (Aronowitz 2012: 106). Third, Mills contends that trade union leaders are induced to adopt a pluralist understanding of democratic politics at odds with the objective of building a nationwide independent labour party. Political activism at the local level is inevitably channelled towards supporting the reproduction of a two-party system representing only the urban middle classes.

Mills is fully convinced that any political settlement achieved under these conditions is both biased and ephemeral. To begin with, it is doomed to rest on the good will of economic and administrative forces subscribing to value systems incompatible with those of the working classes. The separation between politics and policy advocated by Roosevelt at the time is a case in point (Domhoff and Webber 2011); for in assuming that policy, as problem solving, is better left to experts and consultants with the necessary technical competence it makes social legislation dependent upon a liberal understanding of the social question and, consequently, of the good society. Moreover, Mills maintains that the actual effectiveness of this type of social legislation is also dependent on liberal constitutional mechanisms that remain outside the control of the labour force. Conservatives and corporations are in fact given the opportunity to either obstruct its application through the recourse to sympathetic courts, or exploit any lull in labour militancy to repeal, in part or whole, that legislation. Bureaucratized trade unions are, as a result, structurally unable to resist a conservative backlash, and risk being easily discredited and neutralized by their opponents. The passing of the 1947 Taft-Hartley Act is for Mills a stark illustration that the trade unions' moment has passed, that the labour movement has failed to shift the balance of power in American society, and that its decline as a political force is therefore a foregone conclusion.

It is on the basis of this gloomy assessment that Mills shifts his attention to the new social actors who are replacing the old working classes as a social force in post-war America. In *White Collar* (1951), Mills discusses the formation of specific subsets of the middle classes that are acquiring growing economic relevance. By using a rich set of social types, the study of the figure of the American white-collar worker is carried out at three distinct levels: the first is intent on analysing the structural changes at the root of this phenomenon; the second is committed to understanding the psychology that characterizes these actors and the set of values they subscribe to; the third is dedicated to investigating their modes of organization and the political leverage they can exert. In relation to the topics considered in this book, the crucial chapter is the one on 'Old Professions and New Skills (Ch. 6), where Mills presents white-collar groups as the outcome of the deepening of the commodification of labour, and of earlier attempts at commodifying knowledge. Here Mills

(1951: 112) proposes a distinction between old and new professions centred on the observation that 'much professional work has become divided and standardized and fitted into the new hierarchical organizations of educated skill and service'. In his account, most professionals are being turned into salaried employees with little autonomy, whereas the most entrepreneurial ones are assuming a more managerial role. In short, for Mills the old professions are undergoing a transformation similar to the one that affected crafts and trades during the industrial revolution, with the attendant proletarianization of those to whom are attributed largely technical functions.

The application of Taylorist techniques in professional realms left untouched by previous attempts to commodify labour is producing two main responses, consistent with Polanyi's double movement, that will determine the course of future developments. On one side, the social categories that are being proletarianized react by building their own trade unions and pressing for collective contractual agreements. As Aronowitz (2012, Ch. 4) explains in commenting on Mills's work, the new waves of union militancy that emerged in the 1960s and 1970s were mainly led by clerical employees and the salaried professionals (mostly teachers) working within an expanding public sector; it is their union representatives who will in time replace the exponents of the working classes in the neo-corporatist arrangements that were starting to spring up across the developed world at the time; and it is these that will be the target of state-driven neoliberal reforms since the 1980s.

On the other side, there is the rise of what Mills (1951: 140) calls the 'managerial demiurge', 'the professional entrepreneurs and the entrepreneurial professionals [who] seek to monopolize their positions by closing up the ranks'. They achieve this closure by strategies directed at commodifying knowledge and selling it on the market either as independent producers, or as agents of the corporate business world. We shall come back to this in the next section. Here we wish to point out that the developments described by Mills took place in a predigital era and cannot therefore be explained as the outcome of the technological innovations brought about by the information revolution. Technological innovations are simply opportunities used to push the process of commodification forwards and can work just as well with mechanical as with digital solutions; the typewriter just as well as the computer.

Given the psychological make up of white-collar workers, Mills claims that their political achievements would turn out to be even more ephemeral than those of the working classes. Their middle-class ideals make it extremely difficult for them to develop common, collective identities and unity of purpose: having no common roots or common goals they live in a state of permanent anomie, which they try to assuage through consumption; being individualists who exalt autonomy and independence, they tend to identify with the managerial demiurge and despise those at the bottom of the social ladder. It is this apolitical belief-system that explains the historical low level of unionisation among private sector white-collar groups on the one hand, and the disregard for issues unrelated to salary levels among the public sector's white-collar categories involved in trade union disputes. Combined with the bureaucratization processes noted earlier, this makes the political leverage of white-collar groups highly ineffective and their actions too self-regarding to promote wider forms of identification and solidarity. In the 1970s and 80s their trade unions will fragment, become engulfed in internal strife, and alienate public service users, giving neoliberal governments the opportunity to dismantle their power bases within neo-corporatist arrangements.

Mills closes his trilogy on post-war power in America with *The Power Elite* (1956), his most enduring (and controversial) book. Published the year before the paperback edition of Polanyi's book came out, in this work Mills describes the closing of the window of opportunity opened up by the Great Depression, which both authors believed could have led to a great transformation. Thanks to the war efforts and the political neutralization of the labour movement, a new American social order is generated, resting on three major institutions: a political directorate at the federal level located in the presidency; an economic elite whose power base is corporate America and their financial backers; the military circles dominating an American public sector upon which a wide-range of white collar categories depend:

> As each of these domains has coincided with each other, as decisions tend to become total in their consequences, the leading men in each of the three domains of power – the warlords, the corporation chieftains, the political directorate – tend to come together, to form the power elite of America.
>
> (Mills 1956: 9)

The elitist language used by Mills derives from but is not identical with the one used by Weber and other turn of the century authors who developed it (e.g. Michels, Mosca, Pareto, and Schumpeter). First, it is used as a critical tool rather than a realist jargon meant to justify liberal side-constraints on democratic politics. Second, it seeks to identify 'an intricate set of overlapping cliques [that] share decisions having at least national consequences' (Mills 1956: 18) – hence Mills's reservation about seeing the power elite as a ruling class or some sort of natural aristocracy.

The power elite identified by Mills not only has different characteristics than the one that was dominant during the Gilded Age, but it also operates according to a different logic. In the economic realm, corporate America has replaced both the robber barons and the old patrician families. Businesses are now run by hierarchical institutions in bureaucratic ways rather than by individual entrepreneurs and autonomous professionals. In the political realm, a process of centralization has increased the power and reach of federal institutions and the presidency in particular, and weakened the power of states and Congress alike.[5] A plutocratic rather than a democratic logic underpins decisions on major national and international issues. The war economy has, finally, created an expanding military apparatus free from previous constitutional controls and run by a largely self-regulating professional cadre of administrators. This last aspect is perhaps the most consequential for it highlights the ability of a sub-state system to acquire its own autonomy from the legal and political institutions that once controlled it. From this perspective, President Eisenhower's denunciation of the military-industrial complex a few years later is indicative of the fact that the collusive partnership Mills locates at the helm of the country remains competitive in nature, notwithstanding the overlapping interests and interconnections between its constituent parts.

Seated at the top of a new social hierarchy, this power elite is served by a managerial layer helping it to dominate a large mass of wage-workers, which includes both the old working classes who are being re-subjugated, and the white collar middle-classes, used as a social buffer to facilitate that subjugation. Mills also maintains that the recomposition of the power elite entails a shutting off of democratic opportunities at the top. Democratic politics and representative institutions operate now only at the meso-level, wherein managers and white-collar groups still compete among themselves, and pertains to middle-range issues affecting those constituencies. The defeat of the idea of industrial democracy supported by the more radical trade unions undermined the political agency of the working classes and made them dependent on the activism and solidarity of the liberal middle classes. Indeed, from then on political battles will be led by civic movements employing a language (rights discourse) and strategies (legal challenges) very different from those favoured by the labour movement, and about which Mills was less than enthusiastic. The fate of New-Left militancy that flared after Mills's premature death in 1962 will make his early assessment prescient. The 1960s and 70s militancy of the middle classes (students and white-collar people) will produce a degree of factionalism and inwardness far greater than the one that affected past popular movements and will eventually presage its self-destruction. In turn, this will cause both the implosion of the welfare coalition supporting the post-war settlement and the ascendancy of neoliberal perspectives able to 'rule the void'.[6]

7.4 Deepening commodification while broadening the reach of the market

Polanyi, as noted previously, and Mills share an unwarranted optimism about the ability of countermovements to produce a great transformation. This is part of a more general expectation that characterises the interwar generations on both sides of the Atlantic; one that was encouraged by the institutional actors seeking to shore up their own legitimacy in turbulent times. The disenchantment with the post-war settlement is largely connected to the growing realization that the welfare state fell far short of what had been promised earlier. It was not only socialism that was beyond the reach of the welfare state, but also democracy and the ideals of self-determination entailed by it. The constitutional moments experienced in America during the New Deal and in Europe after the war produced in fact a Schumpeterian form of representative democracy that turned it into a spectator sport excluding the citizen from any involvement in substantive political choices (Schattschneider 1960). Industrial forms of democracy were deemed to be out of the question;[7] and likewise well beyond the reach of any democratization process were other basic social institutions, which liberals located on the private side of the public–private divide. It is this sense of disappointment that fed the New Left and brought about repeated calls for participatory forms of democracy launched in the late 1960s and early 1970s.

To counter such widespread feelings, public rhetoric stressed instead the economic gains achievable through the proposed settlement and grounded embedded liberal arrangements in an economic calculus that traded political influence for material benefits – a solution that in Mills' opinion was more congenial to the white collar mindset. Obviously, once economic growth started to falter that utilitarian logic became unable to supply the legitimacy needed for actual existing liberal democracies to work properly (Habermas 1975).

The current advocacy of Keynesian policies and welfare solutions seems to rest on an assessment that uses an alien metric to measure past events. Viewed from today's vantage point, the post-war settlement induces nostalgic sentiments and produces positive cost–benefit analysis. However, today's vantage point is the outcome of three full decades of relentless neoliberal reform; it was not the one used by those who withdrew their support from the welfare state and cannot be used to understand the reasons responsible for the implosion of that system. This is especially true when it becomes clear that the social constituencies responsible for that implosion were ostensibly those that benefited from welfare policies. As the late Tony Judt (2010: 83–84) reminds us in what was to be his last work, 'the beneficiaries of that order – whether Swedish shopkeepers, Scottish shipworkers, inner-city African-Americans or bored French suburbanites – were increasingly resentful of their dependence upon administrators, local councillors and bureaucratic regulations'.

The strategic inclusion of the representatives of an expanding white-collar workforce into neo-corporatist arrangements (operating at the meso level) to which some policy-making power was delegated (concerning, again, middle-range issues) advocated by social-democratic forces to reinforce the stability of real existing democracies would in the end reveal itself as counter-productive. On the one hand, the neo-corporatist bodies called to rewrite the social contract would be unable to guarantee the voluntary compliance of their rank and file members, and risked themselves being delegitimized. On the other hand, the governments that were relying on those neo-corporatist arrangements felt they got little benefits when successful, but were held fully responsible in case of failure – hence our claim that the introduction of the NPM template in the public sector since the 1980s had as its goal reversing this situation: to shift responsibility downward and to channel decision-making power upwards.

These considerations lead us to conceive and use the expression neoliberal very differently from those who are engaged in more orthodox genealogical reconstructions. Neoliberal governments and policies are not seeking to engender a market utopia and attribute to the state an ancillary role. Rather, we use the qualifier neoliberal to identify instrumental and strategic uses of markets in order to accomplish goals that are genuinely political. From this perspective, the state is not an epiphenomenon but a *sui generis* entity with its own set of interests and relative autonomy. Thus, we reject the views that see states and markets as locked in a zero-sum game. On the contrary, we follow Polanyi in uncovering the role of the state as a market maker, market modifier, and first mover, and in particular emphasise its pivotal role in the sets of political and institutional changes discussed in Part II. It is upon this analysis that we mounted an all-out attack on recent developments in social theory supporting an allegedly epochal shift from modernity to some form of post- or second modernity. What the authors and schools of thought discussed in Part I identify as a paradigm shift, we metaphorically consider a new Groundhog Day for capitalism. The nature and logic of this recursive social pattern we attribute to state attempts to reaffirm their undisputed sovereignty whenever it is challenged by autonomous societal actors or other sub-state units with independent sources of legitimacy.

Our interpretation of Polanyi's double movement and parallel reading of Mills' trilogy on American power structure from a Polanyian perspective have this heuristic target in mind. This heuristic will be further developed here to explain the reasons behind the new wave of commodification experienced in the last three decades, and the current efforts to turn knowledge into another fictitious commodity. In both cases, we maintain that, consistent with past attempts, the objective is twofold: (i) to undermine the system of tangible and intangible commons from which societal agents and sub-state units derive their autonomy and legitimacy; (ii) to entice the corporate entities with whom governments establish collusive partnerships to achieve this goal.

7.4.1 The information society as digital Taylorism

The advent of the information society has produced a vast scientific literature committed to explaining the reasons behind it and the implications it will have for the world at large. Although this work is presented as mainly empirical, in reality it is often speculative, and thus highly dependent on the personal orientation of the author. Progressive analysts in general view the information revolution in positive terms, as an opportunity for human emancipation and inclusive forms of cyber-democracy (Kostakis and Bauwens 2014). Thus, empirical case studies having a controversial or limited scientific value are viewed as evidence of an epochal trend implicit in the changes we are witnessing. The most relevant example is the development of post-Fordism (Ash (ed.) 1994); a body of literature that emerged in the 1980s the aim of which was to show that the main tenets of the Fordist organization of labour are no longer valid and that productive activities are re-organizing according to an alternative logic. The understanding of this alternative logic rekindled the interest of social scientists in 'networks' as modes of organization alternative to both hierarchy and markets, as discussed in Chapter 2.

According to analysts like Castells (2005, 2009), the information revolution gave a new lifeline to networks by making it possible to overcome traditional problems connected with the acquisition and transmission of information in polycentric settings. Powell (1990) and Thompson (2003) have suggested compelling explanations purportedly showing what underlying features made networks superior forms of organization compared to both markets and hierarchies. DiMaggio (2001), Powell and DiMaggio (eds) (1991), Piore and Sabel (1984) proposed readings of the processes of decentralization and externalization observed in all developed economies that view those phenomena as the outcome of the adoption of a novel division of labour based on networking within heterarchies (cf. Stark 2009). The interests in networks and their underlying logic eventually caught the attention of political scientists and political sociologists; hence the proliferation of studies on governance as opposed to more traditional issues related to government (Rhodes 1997).

In tracing these theoretical developments, we argue that in reality they underplay both the differences between classic social thought and current social theory, and the profound influence that political economy still exercises on these postmodern accounts of social and economic change.[8] In spite of the fact that the theorists mentioned above wish to re-evaluate sociological approaches *vis-á-vis* political economy, we claim that, compared to classic social theory, contemporary social theorists have adopted a problematic type of social determinism that (i) neglects the political nature of social intercourse and (ii) ends up proposing a sociological version of spontaneous order no less problematic than its economic counterparts, from which it is ultimately derived.

In order to counter these tendencies, we went back to our modernist roots and use Polanyi and, latterly, Mills, two eminent exponents of that tradition of thought, to show how this modernist perspective can be employed to produce an alternative reading of the changes we are experiencing at present. In doing so, our inquiry builds on a host of alternative studies, some of them empirical some less so, which show that this alternative reading has a degree of plausibility superior to the one attributable to rival postmodern accounts. Admittedly, these alternative studies are part of a more fragmented and minoritarian endeavour within the social sciences. However, when the dots are connected they propose an interesting, if unsettling, picture of current events. The innovations that contemporary authors view as a potential tool for human emancipation are here presented as having the power to re-establish new and more subtle forms of subjugation. Informatization and digitization are the main cases in point. Far from showing that ICT is promoting a post-Fordist organization of labour, our inquiry arrives at a more dystopic conclusion: a renewed attempt to commodify labour, which has as its main target administrative, managerial, and intellectual activities that had successfully resisted previous attempts in the direction noted by Mills. Once again, we maintain that this endeavour is dependent on scientific managerial activities the ultimate goal of which is to arrive at what might be labelled 'digital Taylorism'.

The reforms introduced in PAs and HEIs under the aegis of the NPM template speak for themselves. By using different combinations of privatization, liberalization, and marketization, clerical and intellectual work is parcelled in discrete sequences and routinized; *ex ante* and *ex post* forms of assessments are then used to measure the degree of conformity of each civil servant and academic (as an individual and as a group) located along the production line. In this model of mass production, conformity is rewarded by allowing a tiny minority to move up the ranks, whereas non-conformity is strongly discouraged by the ease with which an individual could be replaced along the digital conveyor belt by a growing number of part-time and temporary workers seeking a more secure position:

> Digital Taylorism is not only deskilling many white-collar workers, but it also incites a power struggle within the middle classes, as corporate reengineering reduces the autonomy and discretion of some but not all managers and professionals. It encourages the segmentation of talent in ways that reserve permission to think to a small proportion of elite employees responsible for driving the business forward, functioning cheek by jowl with equally well-qualified workers in more Taylorized jobs.
>
> (Brown *et al* 2011: 81)

In comparison with previous forms of commodification affecting farmers and industrial workers, the novelty that characterises the process is this time due to the fact that it mostly affects white-collar employees. Although the process started much earlier and was already under way when Mills studied it in the earlier 1950s, it is only since the 1980s that a systematic attempt has been carried out in OECD countries; a goal that still remains at the core of the neoliberal programme of government. We argue that this is so because in the post-war period the welfare state (in both its Keynesian and neo-corporatist phases) managed to protect those categories quite effectively, at least in the public sector and neighbouring areas.[9] By assuming the role of the good employer and making PAs and HEIs largely self-regulating, clerical workers, middle-level managers, technicians, and salaried professionals in effect retained significant forms of autonomy that often set them apart from their private-sector colleagues. In turn, this privileged position attributed to them a position of leadership among white-collar workers in general, and was used as a benchmark for those working in the private sector; elements that in economic conditions of nearly full employment reduced the bargaining power of corporate businesses enormously – a factor already foreseen by a contemporary of Keynes, the Polish economist Michael Kalecki (1943), who has recently been rediscovered. This position of strength was reinforced by the fact that welfare policies were also able to generate new types of 'commons' that white-collar employees could exploit to insulate themselves from competition and retain an independent power base. This explains why the restarting of the commodification process in the 1980s has been carried out in parallel with repeated attempts at undermining the viability of those commons with the aim to enclose them.

7.4.2 Commodifying knowledge: stealing the common from the goose, once again

We have discussed the historical relevance of the commons and the reasons behind mounting enclosure movements elsewhere (Palumbo and Scott 2005). Here we want to recall some of the main points discussed to clarify the differences between past and contemporary experiences, as well as the role neoliberal political economists play in supplying the theoretical justification for launching new enclosure campaigns.

Commons are historical forms of social insurance used by local communities to protect themselves from adversity and assure a safety net for the most exposed members. In an agricultural society, forests, pastures, and arable land were the most relevant natural resources held in common to that end. These resources were supplemented by less tangible social practices allowing open access in specific periods (often after the harvest season), or reserved part of the community's wealth for selected categories of disadvantaged people (charity and social relief practices). In urban settings, artisan and professional groups also treated skills and technical knowledge as commons, and relied on a decentralised system of norms that minutely regulated access to trades, individual training, and the means for transmitting acquired expertise. As a set of common pool resources, commons helped integrate the individual income generated by market activities and shield those involved in them from natural or man-made events that disrupted business life and commercial ventures. In some cases, it was the access to commons that protected local communities and other social groups from political subjugation and persecution; for they supplied stable sources of funding even predatory warlords and imperial powers were keen to preserve. With the development of nation-states concerned with affirming stronger and permanent forms of territorial sovereignty, tangible and intangible commons assumed an increasingly contentious role, especially when used to resist the encroachment of central powers and bureaucratic administrative practices.

Modern movements of enclosure can thus be explained as due to the expansionary logic of state sovereignty rather than to the inherent efficiency of market arrangements advocated by political economists. 'Stealing the common from the goose' means in fact making the latter fully dependent on those feeding it, consequently restricting its freedom and ability for independent action. On this reading, strongly supported by Polanyi, the enclosure of forests and common land were means to restrain yeomen and cottagers; social constituencies able to stand up against both aristocratic landowners and absolute monarchs (Neeson 1993). A similar logic of control is detectable in industrial societies (Stanfield 1986: Ch. 5), where capitalists and robber barons replace warlords and landowners within national power elites.

Polanyi's account of the double movement attributes to successful counter-movements the ability to regenerate tangible and intangible commons that help check the commodification process. Within industrial society, the most tangible commons assumed the form of pension funds and other types of social insurance systems managed by labour organizations either directly or indirectly, and mutualist and cooperative activities making up the moral economy (Booth 1994; Fassin 2009; Götz 2015). Less tangible commons are related to labour legislation, collective bargaining systems, practices of code-termination and other democratic activities that give workers voice in managerial issues. This explains the relevance unionists and progressive thinkers like Polanyi attach to industrial democracy (against the language of rights advocated by liberals like T. H. Marshall (1997) [1949]), and Mills' negative assessment of the bureaucratization of traditional trade unions, or concerning the effectiveness of white-collar unionism. Despite the limitations noted above, the post-war settlement ended up producing new types of commons, having a growingly intangible nature, related to the ability of civil servants and salaried professionals to determine the terms and conditions of their activities, and influence the determination of their salary levels through collective bargain (Mau 2003).

Given the psychological make-up of the white-collar groups described by Mills, those achievements turned, in time, into privileges that slowly alienated the sympathies of both public service users and those employed in equivalent private sector roles. In the 1970s, growing discontent among the citizenry and mounting social instability made – as much noted at the time – liberal democracy highly susceptible to legitimation crisis, and set the conditions for the conservative backlash that allowed central governments to progressively dismantle the more problematic social arrangements obstructing top-down governability (Bowles and Gintis 1982; Wolfe 1977). This meant not only undermining trade unions and repealing labour legislation offering legal protection to disruptive categories of white-collar employees. It also meant enclosing the commons from which those societal actors derived their autonomy, and rolling back the neo-corporatist arrangements that gave them political leverage.

On the basis of this reading, in the previous chapters we have endeavoured to show: (i) that the twin process of enclosure-cum-commodification has affected specific categories within the public sector; (ii) that it is driven by a logic of political centralization-cum-managerial decongestion aiming to free central governments from social responsibilities and formal lines of accountability; (iii) that to this end collusive public–private partnerships have been established, allowing corporate businesses to enclose and commercially exploit the commons generated in the meantime. In passing, we have also pointed out that such a strategy of top-down governability has given licence to businesses to simultaneously; (iv) roll back the meagre advances made by private sector workers as well as; (v) externalize productive activities where the cost of labour is lower; (vi) use new technologies to enclose and exploit other global commons unaffected by previous waves. It is in this context that the worldwide development of intellectual property rights (IPRs) regimes may be located (May and Sell 2005). We shall show that IPRs along with academic publication offer an illustrative example of the new enclosure of common-pool resources to demonstrate our concluding point.

The reforms discussed in Part II, and in particular those affecting HEIs (see Chapter 5), exemplify the unfolding of this complex and multifaceted process, the means used to carry it forwards, and the role played by collusive partnerships involving global corporations, state actors, and international organizations (see Chapter 6). As in previous historical experiences, the process is highly contradictory in that it is based on the defence of individual rights to legitimize economic forms of exploitation, and on efficientist explanations used to justify setting artificial barriers to information flows crucial for social networks to function properly (Boyle 2003).

In academia, sustained attempts to marketize research in order to generate new funding streams has pushed all those involved in the social division of intellectual labour into a struggle to affirm their intellectual ownership of parts of the scientific enterprise. Individual researchers need to do that in order to demonstrate their productivity and meet the requirements imposed by multiple forms of assessment. HEIs encourage this sort of behaviour for the overheads they can extract, and are busy establishing start-ups and research parks dedicated to the commercialization of any patentable product. Corporations are interested in associating themselves with prestigious universities and research centres because that allows them to reduce their in-house research and development activities while maximizing the returns on those commercial ventures. Finally, central governments view all this as an opportunity to cut public budgets, promote economic growth indirectly and exploit, in the process, the system of assessments devised to measure the social impact of research to undermine the relevance of peer-review and, consequently, the autonomy of their own scientific communities. In this context, IPRs sought to protect individual authors are inevitably hijacked by the corporate actors operating within the cultural industry (a further theme brought to public attention by Mills).

The various attempts to separate and measure individual contributions to a common scientific enterprise are producing in fact a number of conflicting legal claims, which inevitably give the most powerful actors the opportunity to acquire exclusive entitlements. It is by now a common practice within the academic publishing industry to ask authors to relinquish their copyrights when they seek to publish in the major journals or with prestigious publishers, even if the contribution the latter makes to the scientific and editorial process is now negligible. With the advent of digital technology, publishers and journal repositories have been further given the option to appropriate the already available stock of past articles and books and charge exorbitant fees to the academic communities that produced that stock in the first place. This explains why the academic publishing industry is flourishing and assures returns sufficiently high to justify an ongoing process of consolidation in this sector worldwide. Competition leading to corporate consolidation is even fiercer in the bio- and life-science sector and in technological areas that can be commercially exploited more directly by using patent laws. The latter is an ever expanding legal body encompassing new artefacts, genetic material, natural compounds, production techniques, trade secrets, and, increasingly, collections of raw data. Rather than protect authors and scientists, IPRs are used to establish barriers on information flows and empower institutional gatekeepers and oligopolistic market forces (Boyle 2008). Rather than stimulate innovation and reward talent, they are supporting an expanding rent economy the feasibility of which depends entirely on the legal enforcement assured by national and international authorities (Baker 2016). As such, IPR regimes turn out to be doubly parasitical: first, they legalize the *de facto* corporate appropriation of common pool resources; second, they rest on external forms of enforcement whose burden is entirely born by the taxpayer (or other third actors).

The building of IPR regimes is a paradigmatic example of the way in which liberalization operates as part of the NPM template. To begin with, it relies on positive market integration policies requiring an active and centralized state system. Those positive policies are employed to carry out a three-pronged task: (i) upsetting pre-existing norms regulating common-pool arrangements by allowing free-riders to violate established practices; (ii) imposing a new legal framework that progressively displaces older conventions like 'fair use', and extends the limits of copyright legislation beyond reason; (iii) assuring an inflexible legal protection to sets of absolute and exclusive IPRs belonging to corporate entities. In the process, the communities which used to exercise regulatory power have their prerogatives taken away, and the whole system becomes centralized and run according to bureaucratic procedures enforced by anonymous administrators imposed from without.

The counter-reaction of all negatively affected interests is, in turn, dealt with in two ways. At a theoretical level, an increasing number of neoliberal think tanks and astroturf groups are enrolled to supply justifications appealing to any deontological and instrumental reason available. In doing so, past arguments used to justify property rights and the enclosure of the commons are freely recycled even when (i) rights are attributed to legal entities rather than physical persons and their enforcement requires the violation of traditional civic liberties; (ii) enclosure pertains to intangible cultural objects and practices that digital technologies are making non-depletable and reproducible at close to zero cost (Rifkin 2014). The upshot is a humourless 'comedy of the commons' that is replacing the melodramatic 'tragedy of the commons' staged in the past (Rose 1986). At a more practical level, state authority is systematically deployed to criminalize entire communities involved in a flourishing gift economy producing cutting-edge innovation and interesting forms of democratic experimentation. Hence the commitment of central governments and inter-governmental organizations to collibration strategies the goal of which is to raise the costs of collective action faced by antagonistic movements, and the reforming efforts chronicled earlier wishing to turn HEIs into assembly factories for the training of useful idiots (in the original Greek sense of the word 'idiot' used by Mills).

7.5 Freedom in a growingly complex information society

In Polanyi's account of the double movement, the reaction of society to the commodification of vital social resources and practices could produce two antithetical counter-reactions: progressive social movements wishing to preserve society from disruption while expanding freedom; regressive social movements committed to re-establish a mythological past harmony through authoritarian means. The 1930s fascist counter-revolution was for him caused by the failure of the progressive forces to achieve unity and endorse a democratic form of socialism – for which he lays the blame on both Soviet Marxists and liberal elites. This political outlook is shared by Mills, for whom the success of the American power elite is founded on the depoliticization of the organized labour movement (due to the bureaucratization of trade unions), and on the centralization of political power promoted by the Cold War (aided by a technocratic turn in the social sciences). In drawing inspiration from classic social thought, Polanyi and Mills endorsed two main aspects of this tradition: they wanted to resist the pretensions of political economists and the pressures exercised for a positivization of social research. Their objections against the alleged autonomy of the economic realm were based on the assumption that individual self-interest could not be taken as foundational and should not be allowed to trump other elemental motives. Against the notion of value-free social inquiry, they underscore the relevance of democratic ideals in addressing social problems, and the pivotal role intellectuals should play in engendering a free and just society.

Our reinterpretation of Polanyi's double movement and our reading of Mills's trilogy from a Polanyian perspective seeks to re-affirm not only the validity of their scientific endeavours for understanding our time, but also the importance of their political commitments for tackling the challenges we currently face. If the 2008 financial crisis has opened up a genuine window of opportunity, it is also clear that a positive outcome still depends on the conscious actions of progressive forces, and the ability of their intellectual exponents to clarify the nature of the choices we are called to make and the costs entailed by each. Since the start of the new century a multitude of social movements has sought to oppose the collusive partnerships supporting neoliberal programmes of government. The financial crisis and the austerity policies imposed in its wake have rekindled that social opposition and reinforced its progressive spirit. It is however becoming evident that the persistent failure of progressive forces to change the current neoliberal consensus could reinforce the appeal exercised by xenophobic arguments and Cesarist solutions (Mouffe 2016). Forced to operate in unresponsive political settings and unable to stop the drift towards postdemocracy, contemporary movements risk sharing the fate of their more illustrious predecessors. Before our window of opportunity closes, it is necessary to discuss once again what is the most suitable notion of freedom for a growingly complex informational society. And for us, the political tradition that inspired Polanyi and Mills retains a normative value that is worth exploring and updating.

That political tradition is made up of a variety of schools of thought and socialist movements equally distant from the liberal and Marxist traditions that dominated the twentieth century (Backer 1978; Hirst (ed.) 1993). What linked them was a commitment to engender a fully democratic society from the bottom up. Unlike liberals, this democratic vision is not dependent on individualistic values attributing foundational value to individual rights or preferences. Therefore, it does not conceive majority rule as an aggregative procedure and collective choice as a by-product of the maximizing activities of a plurality of self-seeking agents. Against Marxists, this socialist vision of democracy is founded neither on a philosophy of history nor on an epistemology able to identify true courses of action. As a result, it attributes to political activities a value autonomous from the economic realm, and perceives democratic participation as the way of living in a society that acknowledges autonomy as an ultimate goal. Given its set of radical political aspirations, liberals tend to dismiss this tradition by labelling it 'utopian', whereas Marxists seek to do the same by labelling it 'unscientific'. Historically, this tradition dominated earlier socialist movements up to the end of the First International – summarily brought to a close by the losing Marxist factions. Its final defeat as a political force in Europe arrived with the collapse of the Spanish Republic at the end of the 1930s – once again with the crucial contribution of Marxist factions loyal to Stalin. Thanks in part to Mills' efforts, this tradition inspired the 1960s New Left and the movements advocating participatory models of democracy ever since, to which patently belong those currently supporting calls for the introduction of cyber forms of democracy (Saco 2002; Wilhelm 2000).

Like the works of Polanyi and Mills, this tradition represents a large and rich conceptual and practical sediment that can be mined to recognize the alternatives available to us and the challenges we face in driving social choices in a progressive (rather than regressive) direction. It is also a tradition that warns us about relying too much on technology and technocratic solutions. If the ICT revolution is at all able to supply the means for overcoming some of the problems that beset networks in the past, as suggested by Castells (2005), the more recent experiences examined by that author (Castells 2015) show us that they seem to have an impact in helping people to mobilize more easily. Turning virtual mobilization into more stable forms of social aggregation and using the latter for shifting political dynamics in a specific direction are activities that still require conscious agents fully committed to acting as part of a politically engaged public, rather than players of a virtual interactive game. The final consideration we derive from our inquiry is that a politically engaged public cannot work effectively within the constraints imposed by liberalism, even in its more progressive version; for it lacks the ability to appreciate the reality of society and its political character. To borrow the words of Stanfield (1986: 150),

> If indeed the corporate-welfare state is the solution to the riddle posed by industrialism, then a positive theory of this response is needed in order to realize its promise. If it is not the solution the same intellectual effort is required in order to establish both its shortcoming and institutional alternatives. This is after all, the responsibility of the intellectual, to forge the concepts necessary to permit alternative institutional frameworks to come to view.

This is the spirit that has moved our inquiry, and this is the spirit in which we advance our invitation to explore once again the radical social and political tradition exemplified by Polanyi and Mills.

Notes

1 We saw a version of this argument – with respect to creativity – in the work of Nigel Thrift (e.g. 2008) – see Chapter 2. The possibility that knowledge constitutes a fourth 'fictitious commodity' in Polanyi's sense has been noted by Jessop (2007), but in a more Marxist reading than the one we offer here.

2 The 1957 paperback edition reproduces the American 1944 version of the book published by Rinehart & Company, Inc. In Britain a version of the book was published in 1945 by Victor Gollantz. Several differences can be spotted in these two editions. Mostly they are minor corrections, probably made by Polanyi himself for Victor Gollantz, as claimed by Fred Block in the editorial note to the 2001 edition. More substantial are the differences between the American and British editions concerning the structure of the last chapter. In the British edition Ch. 21 on 'Freedom in a complex society' is not only shorter than the American one, but also contains several new paragraphs. The paperback edition proposes instead a version of that same chapter which combines the original 1944 version with the 1945 British version and uses a modified pagination numbering for the last two pages 258A and 258B (which has been eliminated from the 2001 edition). We have not been able to find out the reasons for these editorial discrepancies.

3 'What appears to our generation as the problem of capitalism is, in reality, the far greater problem of an industrial civilization. The economic liberal is blind to this fact. In defending capitalism as an economic system, he ignores the challenges of the Machine Age. Yet the dangers that make the bravest quake today transcend economy. The idyllic concerns of trust-busting and Taylorization have been superseded by Hiroshima. Scientific barbarism is digging our footsteps' (Polanyi 1947: 117). Stanfield (1986, Ch. 5) correctly notes that markets and industrialization produce two distinct types of problem and points out that the one generated by industrialization depends on the fact that it takes place within a self-regulating market system.

4 According to Gareth Dale, they knew each other, but not well. Personal communication.

5 An argument elaborated much more recently by Theda Skocpol (2003).

6 To adapt the title of a survey of our current political condition (Mair 2013).

7 The principle of '*Mitbestimmung*' (codetermination) – i.e., the inclusion of *Betriebsräte* (work councils) in decision-making in private firms in post-war (West) Germany – represents a partial exception.

8 These differences are spelled out by Sayer (2000: 92): 'Networks, a recently popular object of study with some students of political economy (particularly in relation to "post-Fordism"), have often been seen in a more favourable light than markets and bureaucracies in as much as they combine cooperation with flexibility. However, they tend to have an instrumental rather than a moral rationale. Participants may share information, cooperate and suspend some kinds of short-term self-interested calculation, but the reason for doing so is a perceived correspondence between their own long-term needs and goals and those of the other members. Moreover, unlike bureaucracies, networks require no rules of procedural fairness, and can admit or exclude anyone, without any justification. Although the members may support each other, they do so for their own long-term benefit rather than for others' own sake or for the good of society, indeed they may be little more than a cartel.'

9 In the private sector, among the categories that came closer to achieving a similar level of protection was the journalists' one. For a study of the commodification process in that sector in the UK see Davies (2004).

Appendix 1

Table A.1 Major civil service policy initiatives carried out from 1979 to 2010

Year	*Initiative*	*Source*	*Objectives*
1979	Rayner's scrutinies (Efficiency)	PM Office (Thatcher)	Set of efficiency measures the goal of which was to detect organizational slack, suggest simplification of administrative procedures and make it possible 'to do more with less'. The scrutinies mobilized the creative and managerial ability of middle-rank officers and aimed at rationalizing both resources and the workforce
1980–1982	Abolition of Civil Service Department and of Priestley System	PM Office (Thatcher)	Set of measures intending to transfer the managerial powers previously exercised by the Civil Service on to the Prime Minister's Office and the Cabinet Office. They also pushed for abandoning the comparison between the private and public sector pay established by the Priestley Commission in the 1950s
1982	MINIS/Financial Management Initiative	Dpt. of environment (Heseltine)	Setting up of output measures for all departments, delegation of financial and personnel responsibility to line managers and informatization of administrative work
1984–94	Privatization of state-owned enterprises	Cabinet Office (Thatcher/Major)	British Airways (1981), British Telecom (1984), British Gas (1986), British Airports Authority (1987), Electricity (1987), Water (1989/91), British Rail (1993/94)
1987	Performance-related pay	PM Efficiency Unit	Introduction of performance-related pay (in agreement with unions) after pilot schemes started in 1985. Part of the salary of civil servants was to be linked to measures of their individual and collective productivity. Similar criteria were also devised in relation to career progression
1988	Improving Management in Government: The Next Steps. (Next Steps Programme)	PM Efficiency Unit (Robin Ibbs Report)	Creation of executive agencies responsible for the delivery of public services and policy implementation. Separation of policy design and implementation: departments focus on 'strategic' policy issues and the setting of performance targets, agencies given autonomy over implementation and management; agency head (director) on fixed-term contract and performance-related (and competitive) pay
1991	Citizen's Charter	PM Office (Major)	The initiative established that service delivery units needed to develop performance indicators and report on performance, increase of transparency and access to information. Also it attributed to departments responsibility for monitoring achievements and for periodically improving the standards of service established

Table A.1 (continued)

Year	*Initiative*	*Source*	*Objectives*
1991	White Paper *Competing for Quality* (Cm 1730)	HM Treasury	Establishment of market testing exercises according to which departments were asked to compare the cost of in-house tasks with market price by external providers to facilitate outsourcing. In time, market testing would also be applied to in-house providers in order to stimulate internal competition and used for developing quasi-markets
1994	Private Finance Initiative	HM Treasury (Norman Lamont)	Reform of public investment and procurement to encourage private investment and PPPs in infrastructure and maintenance. Since the original programme attributed all financial risks to the private sector, it was received with scepticism and remained dormant until it was relaunched by Gordon Brown in 2004
1994	Resource Accounting and Budgeting/Civil Service: Continuity and Change	PM Office (Major)	These reforms aimed at implementing new standards of accounting, introducing new senior civil service covering agency chief executives and embracing staff in grades 5 and above (to replace the existing Senior Open Structure for grades 1–3), and delegating managerial powers to departments and (within them) to more operative offices. At the same time, they re-stated the traditional lines of accountability of civil servants through ministers and cabinet
1998	Comprehensive Spending Review/Public Service Agreements (PSA)	HM Treasury/PM Office	Performance targets for departments linked to budget allocations; targets set in the process of bi-annual spending reviews; high priority targets in five areas monitored by the Prime Minister's Delivery Unit from 2001 to 2005
1998–2010	Privatization of Public services Programme	Cabinet Office	(i) direct: NATS, QinetiQ, BNFL, UKAEA and other PPPs; (ii) indirect: a) of the educational sector through PFI, education action zones (EAZs) and city academies b) of the NHS by the creation of trusts, the outsourcing of services and the recourse to private consultants and labour agencies; (iii) supportive: i.e. Royal Mail
1999	Modernizing Government/ Wiring Up	PM Office (Blair)	Overall reform programme dealing with the mechanisms of policy making and stressing the need for coordination and integration of governmental activities and departments following the accomplishment of the Agencies Creation Programme launched in 1988. In addition to joining-up government, it also stresses the need to establish partnerships between public sector and private sector organizations and develop extended forms of informatization to engender e-governance

Year	*Initiative*	*Source*	*Objectives*
1999	Civil Service Reform Report/ Bringing In and Bringing On Talent	PM Office (Blair)	Reform of pay and performance assessment; strengthening of external recruitment to improve leadership capabilities of public officials; redefinition of individual incentives aiming at rewarding talent
2003	Performance Partnership Agreements (PPAs)	Cabinet Office (Delivery and Reform Team)	Drawing up of formal documents stating the aims, targets and criteria of evaluation each department has to pursue. They are established in bilateral meetings between the senior civil servants instead of the department and a governmental team including Treasury and Delivery Unit personnel. Although the Delivery Unit is located in the Treasury, it answers directly to the Prime Minister.
2004	Private Finance Initiative (Mark II)	HM Treasury (Brown)	Relaunch of Major's 1994 policy initiative after a revision of the liability system that made the taxpayer the ultimate bearer of financial risk. Since then, it has been used as a 'privatization by stealth' tool in health, transport and education.
2004	Lyons and Gershon Review; Civil Service Reform: delivery and value	PM Office (Blair)	Review on efficiency of public sector working procedures, initiated major reduction of public sector workforce since 2005, stressed the use of ICT and automation for administrative procedures. Unlike the previous modernizing government programme, Civil Service Reform focused attention not on policy making but on policy implementation; hence the shift of attention from Whitehall to the departmental level
2004	Professional Skills for Government	Head of CS (Sir Andrew Turnbull)	As part of the government commitment to improve delivery services, the Head of the Civil Service launched a programme to improve the managerial skills of civil servants (as opposed to their policy advice skills) at all levels. The four sets of skills to be developed were: leadership, core-skills (financial and project management, strategic thinking and communication), job-related professional skills, broader experience across fields of activity
2006	Capability Reviews Programme	Head of CS (Sir Gus O'Donnel)	Review of department capabilities in three managerial areas (leadership, strategy, delivery). Its aim was to help departments act on key long-term development areas. The programme was designed to assess all major Whitehall departments against a common framework underpinning PPAs, to make the results public and accessible to all, as well as establish clearer lines of accountability.

Table A.1 (continued)

Year	*Initiative*	*Source*	*Objectives*
2006	UK government's approach to public service reform	PM Office (Blair)	Further step in the development of consumer choice within the public sector. The report recognized user choice of public service provider as a key component of the wider reform agenda alongside performance management, competition and capability
2009	Putting the Frontline First: smarter government	PM Office (Brown)	The programme contained little more than a series of cost-cutting measures to deal with the state sovereign currency crisis that followed the 2008 recession. The senior civil service was cut by 20% over the next three years, consultancy spending by Whitehall was cut by 50% over the same period, 123 government arm-length bodies were abolished or merged together and a number of staff were relocated outside London and South-East England to reduce costs
2010	Constitutional Reform and Governance Act	Lord Chancellor (Jack Straw)	For the first time, this Act gave a statute basis to the traditional conventions and practices regulating the appointment of civil servants and to the role of the Civil Service Commission established to oversee their application. It formalized and spelt out the values which had to underpin these activities (merit and professionalism) and those which had to be observed by civil servants when discharging their duties (integrity, honesty, objectivity and impartiality). It also regulated and strengthened the role of Departmental Boards establishing that they were to include high calibre non-executives brought in from the outside and be chaired by secretaries of state

Appendix 2

Table A.2 Major reform initiatives in HE since 1979

Year	*Initiative*	*Source*	*Objectives*
1980	Education (No. 2) Act	Mark Carlisle Dpt. for Education & Science	The Act gave the Secretary of State the power to cap the Advanced Further Education Pool so that the overall expenditure on public sector institutions could be brought under national control
1983	Education (Fees and Awards) Act	Keith Joseph Dpt. for Education & Science	The Act allowed the Secretary of State to require higher education institutions to charge higher fees to overseas students. The government granted university status to the Buckingham College, which became the first British private university
1985	Jarrat Report	Commissioned by the Committee of Vice-Chancellors and Principals (CVCP)	The report of the Steering Group on University Efficiency recommended the conversion of Vice-Chancellors to Chief Executives and the use of performance indicators to assess universities. It marked the first step towards the corporatization of university governance and led to the abolition of the tenure system by the CVCP
1986	Research Selectivity Exercise (pilot scheme)	University Grants Committee	The UGC separated institutional funding for research and teaching and started the pilot scheme of what would eventually develop into the Research Assessment Exercise (RAE)
1988	Education Reform Act	Kenneth Baker Dpt. for Education & Science	The Act started the process of incorporation of polytechnics in a unitary higher education sector and abolished both the UGC and the remaining forms of tenure in universities beyond the power of the CVCP
1989	Research Assessment Exercise	University Founding Council	First proper RAE requiring two publications per person and the list of publication output per unit; evaluation based on a 5-point scale

Table A.2 (continued)

Year	*Initiative*	*Source*	*Objectives*
1990	Education (Student Loans) Act	Kenneth Baker Dpt. for Education & Science	The Act discontinued the system of free university education and means tested maintenance grants; they were replaced by 'top-up' loans awarded on a means tested basis
1992	Further and Higher Education Act	Kenneth Clark Dpt. for Education & Science	The Act established the Further Education Funding Councils (FEFCs), removed further education and sixth-form colleges from local authority control, unified the funding of higher education under HEFCs, introduced competition for funding between institutions, and abolished the Council for National Academic Awards (CNAA); colleges and polytechnics were granted university status and degree awarding powers
1992	2nd round of RAE	Higher Education Funding Council for England (HEFCE)	In this round, the number of publications per person was increased to four; units were free to choose who to include in the exercise
1993	Teaching Quality Assessment (TQA)	Kenneth Clark Dpt. for Education & Science	Introduction of the TQA as a complementary means to RAE and establishment of the Higher Education Quality Council (HEQC) as a sector-owned quality assurance body
1994	Student quotas	Kenneth Clark Dpt. for Education & Science	Introduction of Maximum Aggregate Student Numbers (student quotas) for undergraduate places at individual institutions (before each institution was free to enrol all students they wanted)
1996	Education (Student Loans) Act	Gillian Shepherd Dpt. for Education & Employment	The Act extended the provision of student loans. Following the Vice-Chancellors' revolt of the previous year, the government also establishes the Dearing Committee to investigate alternative funding schemes. The Royal Agricultural College was the second private institution to receive degree-awarding powers

Year	*Initiative*	*Source*	*Objectives*
1996	3rd round of RAE	HEFCE	Evaluation based on a 7-point scale; besides publications, other assessment measures considered were: number of students, research income, peer esteem factors, research plans and general observation – the weighting for these other measures remained unspecified
1997	Dearing report	Royal commission	The report recommended charging undergraduate fees to cover teaching costs, along with the retention of maintenance grants
1998	Teaching and Higher Education Act	Estelle Morris Dpt. for Education & Employment	Following Dearing's recommendation, the government introduced an up-front fee of £1,000 to be paid by all home and EU students at UK universities starting their courses in 1998. Against Dearing's recommendation, the government abolished maintenance grants. Finally, it changed the loans system, which was to be income contingent as opposed to mortgage style; repayments would henceforth be automatically collected from monthly wages in a similar way to National Insurance Repayments. HEQC and the Funding Council assessment units were abolished and their function taken over by the Quality Assurance Agency (QAA)
1999	Performance Indicators Steering Group's First report	Steering Group	Production and publication for the first time of a set of indicators for institutional performance for the entire sector across the UK. Among these indicators were included statistical benchmarks
2001	4th round of RAE	HEFCE	The only relevant changes concerned the way to attribute publications between units belonging to personnel who have in the meantime changed institution
2003	Lambert Review	Royal commission	Commissioned by the Chancellor of the Exchequer to look at business–university collaboration

Table A.2 (continued)

Year	*Initiative*	*Source*	*Objectives*
2004	Higher Education Act	David Blunkett Dpt. for Education and Employment	The Act abolished upfront fees and replaced them with a deferred fee, the new fee was to be variable up to £3,000 with the universities themselves to decide how much to charge each student. The Act also granted decision making on tuition fee policy to the Welsh Assembly – Scotland enjoyed that power since the 1999 devolution
2005	National Student Survey		Introduction of the National Student Survey to measure the public satisfaction of students with their institutions. The results of the survey would be used to complement the assessments carried out through the TQA and RAE
2006	First implementation of top-up fees in England and Northern Ireland	John Denham Dpt. for Innovation, Universities & Skills	Despite being a variable fee, almost all English institutions chose to charge the full £3,000 fee. The government established the Office for Fair Access (OFFA) to monitor institutions' widening participation plans, and the Office of the Independent Adjudicator (OIA) to handle student complaints not resolved through institutions' procedures
2008	5th and last round of RAE	HEFCE	Specification of minimal weighting between the measure to use: 50% research quality, 5% peer esteem, 5% research environment
2009	A New Framework for Higher Education (a ten-year plan)	Lord Mandelson Dpt. for Business,Innovation & Skills	Main goals of the plan: a 'consumer revolution' to give students more information about courses and future earnings potential; a drive to make universities work more closely with industry in designing courses and funding them; a new focus on universities as engines of social mobility

Year	*Initiative*	*Source*	*Objectives*
2010	The Browne review, Securing a Sustainable Future for Higher Education	Royal commission	Six principles: more investment should be available for higher education; student choice should be increased; everyone who has the potential should be able to benefit from higher education; no one should have to pay until they start to work; when payments are made they should be affordable; and part time students should be treated the same as full time students for the costs of learning
2010	Tuition fees Research Excellence Framework (REF)	David Willetts Dpt. for Business, Innovation & Skills	Capping for tuition fees is raised to £9000 from 2012 (level set by 85% of universities). Announcement that the RAE was going to be redefined as REF and based on a new set of measures directed at measuring the social and economic impact of academic research
2011	Higher Education: Students at the Heart of the System	White Paper Dpt. for Business, Innovation & Skills	The document stated that the government intends to abolish direct funding streams to university, concentrate the funding for research further and relax the rules regulating the attribution of university title and granting of degree-awarding powers
2014	1st round of REF	HEFCE	65% research quality (established by bibliometrix indicators and peer-review where bibliometrix cannot be used); 15% peer esteem; 20% impact (assessed by the ministry)
2016	Fulfilling our Potential: Teaching Excellence, Social Mobility and Student Choice	White Paper Dpt. for Business, Innovation & Skills	The paper opened a public consultation for the setting up of a Teaching Excellence Framework (TEF). It also announced the government's intention to abolish the Higher Education Funding Council for England (HEFCE), the Office for Fair Access and the Office of the Independent Adjudicator, and replace them with the Office for Students

Bibliography

Abbott, A. (2001) *Chaos of Disciplines*, Chicago, IL: University of Chicago Press.

Adams, J. (2013) 'Collaborations: the fourth age of research', *Nature* 497(7451): 557–560.

Aguilera, R.V. and Cuervo-Cazurra, A. (2004) 'Codes of good governance worldwide: what is the trigger?', *Organization Studies*, 25(3): 417–446.

Ahmad, A.R., Farley, A., and Naidoo, M. (2013) 'Funding crisis in higher education institutions: rationale for change', *FormaMente*, 1: 15–42.

Akerlof, G. and Shiller, R. J. (2010) *Animal Spirits: How Human Psychology Drives the Economy, and Why it Matters for Global Capitalism*, Princeton NJ: Princeton University Press.

Albert, J.C. and Albert, S.E. (eds) (1984) *The Sixties Papers*, New York: Praeger.

Alderman, G. (2010) 'Reflections: change, quality and standards in British higher education', *Journal of Change Management*, 10(3): 243–252.

Allen, D. (2016) 'What is education for?', *Boston Review*, May 9. Available: <http://bostonreview.net/forum/danielle-allen-what-education> (accessed 30 November 2016).

Altbach, P.G. (2013) *The International Imperative in Higher Education*, Rotterdam: Sense Publishers.

Amadae, S.M. (2003) *Rationalizing Capitalist Democracy*, Chicago, IL: The University of Chicago Press.

Amin, A. and Thrift, N. (2013) *Arts of the Political: New Openings for the Left*, Durham NC: Duke University Press.

Anderson, G.L. (1998) 'Toward authentic participation: deconstructing the discourses of participatory reforms in education', *American Educational Research Journal*, 35(4): 571–603.

Anderson, M. (1978) *Welfare: The Political Economy of Welfare Reform in the United States*, Stanford, CA: Hoover Institution Press.

Ankarloo, D. (2002) 'Using Karl Polanyi as a stepping stone for a critique of the new institutionalist orthodoxy', *paper* presented at the CRIC Workshop: Polanyian Perspectives on Instituted Economic Processes: Development and Transformation, The University of Manchester, 23–25 October.

Ansell, C. (2006) 'Network institutionalism', in R.A.W. Rhodes, S.A. Binder and B.A. Rockman (eds) *The Oxford Handbook of Political Institutions*, Oxford: Oxford University Press.

Ansell, C. (2000) 'The networked polity: regional development in Western Europe', *Governance*, 13(3): 303–333.

Appadurai, A. (1990) 'Disjuncture and difference in the global economy', *Theory, Culture and Society*, 7(2): 295–310.

Aronowitz, S. (2012) *Taking It Big: C. Wright Mills and the Making of Political Intellectuals*, New York: Columbia University Press.

Ash, A. (ed.) (1994) *Post-Fordism: A Reader*, Oxford: Blackwell.

Backer, T.B. (1978) *The Mutualists: The Heirs of Proudhon In the First International, 1865–1878*, Cincinnati, OH: University of Cincinnati Press.

Baker, D. (2016) *Rigged: How Globalization and the Rules of the Modern Economy Were Structured to Make the Rich Richer*, Washington, DC: Center for Economic and Policy Research.

Ball, S.J. (2003) *Class Strategies and the Education Market: The Middle Classes and Social Advantage*, London: Routledge Falmer.

Barnes, S. (1996) 'England's civic universities and the triumph of the Oxbridge model', *History of Education Quarterly*, 36(3): 271–305.

Barnett, C. (2013) 'Review of Ash Amin and Nigel Thrift, Arts of the Political: New Openings for the Left', *Antipode*. Available: <https://radicalantipode.files.wordpress.com/2013/07/book-review_barnett-on-amin-and-thrift.pdf> (accessed 1 December 2016).

Barnett, R. (2003) *Beyond All Reason: Living with Ideology in the University*, Buckingham: The Society for Research into Higher Education and Open University Press.

Barnett, R. and Di Napoli, R. (eds) (2008) *Changing Identities in Higher Education: Voicing Perspectives*, London: Routledge.

Barry, N. (1982) 'The tradition of spontaneous order', *Literature of Liberty*, 5(2): 7–58.

Baty, P. (2005) 'Ratings drive hits teaching', *The Times Higher Education Supplement* (online), 18 March. Available: <https://www.timeshighereducation.com/news/ratings-drive-hits-teaching/194777.article> (accessed 29 November 2016).

Bauer, M.W. (2008) 'Diffuse anxieties, deprived entrepreneurs: commission reform and middle management', *Journal of European Public Policy*, 15(5): 691–707.

Bauerlein, M. (2009) 'Professors on the Production Line, Students on Their Own', *AEI Future of American Education Working Paper Series 2009–2010*.

Bauman, Z. (2005) *Liquid Life*, Cambridge: Polity.

Bauman, Z. (2000) *Liquid Modernity*, Cambridge: Polity.

Bauman, Z. (1995) *Life in Fragments: Essays in Postmodern Morality*, Oxford: Blackwell.

Bauman, Z. (1992) *Intimations of Postmodernity*, London: Routledge.

Bauman, Z. (1982) *Memories of Class: The Pre-History and After-Life of Class*, London: Routledge.

Becher, T. and Trowler, P. (2001) *Academic Tribes and Territories: Intellectual Enquiry and The Culture of Disciplines*, Columbus, OH: McGraw-Hill.

Beck, U. (2001) 'Interview with Ulrich Beck', *Journal of Consumer Culture*, 1(2): 261–277.

Beck, U. (1994) 'The reinvention of politics: towards a theory of reflexive modernity', in U. Beck, A. Giddens and S. Lash *Reflexive Modernization. Politics, Tradition and Aesthetics in the Modern Social Order*, Cambridge: Polity.

Beck, U. (1992) *Risk Society: Towards a New Modernity*, trans. Mark Ritter, London: Sage.

Beck, U., Giddens, A. and Lash, S. (1994) *Reflexive Modernization: Politics, Tradition and Aesthetics in the Modern Social Order*, Cambridge: Polity.

Beck, U. and Schnaider, N. (2006) 'Unpacking cosmopolitanism for the social sciences: a research agenda', *British Journal of Sociology*, 57(1): 1–23.

Beckert, J. (2011) 'Coordination through dissonance', *Socio-Economic Review*, 9(3): 606–612.

Beckert, J. (2009) 'The great transformation of embeddedness: Karl Polanyi and the new economic sociology', in C. Hann and K. Hart (eds) *Market and Society: The Great Transformation Today*, Cambridge: Cambridge University Press.

Bekkers, V., Dijkstra, G., Edwards, A. and Fenger, M. (eds) (2007) *Governance and the Democratic Deficit: Assessing the Democratic Legitimacy of Governance Practices*, Aldershot: Ashgate.

Bell, D. (1973) *The Coming of Post-Industrial Society: A Venture in Social Forecasting*, New York: Basic Books.

Bence, V. and Oppenheim, C. (2005) 'The evolution of the UK's Research Assessment Exercise: publications, performance and perceptions', *Journal of Educational Administration and History*, 37(2): 137–155.

Bence, V. and Oppenheim, C. (2004) 'The influence of peer review on the research assessment exercise', *Journal of Information Science*, 30(4): 347–368.

Benneworth, P. and Jongbloed, B.W. (2010) 'Who matters to universities? A stakeholder perspective on humanities, arts and social sciences valorisation', *Higher Education*, 59(5): 567–588.

Benson, D. and Jordan, A. (2011) 'What have we learned from policy transfer research? Dolowitz and Marsh Revisited', *Political Studies Review*, 9: 366–378.

Bevir, M. and Rhodes, R.A.W. (2010) *The State as Cultural Practice*, Oxford: Oxford University Press.

Billig, M. (2013) *Learn to Write Badly: How to Succeed in the Social Sciences*, Cambridge: Cambridge University Press.

Birch, J. (2015) 'Review of Giuseppe di Palma: the modern state subverted: risk and the deconstruction of solidarity', *Review of Politics*, 77(2): 330–332.

Bleiklie, I. (2012) 'Collegiality and hierarchy: coordinating principles in higher education', in A. Nelson and I. Wei (eds) *The Global University*, Basingstoke: Palgrave Macmillan.

Bleiklie, I., Enders, J., Lepori, B. and Musselin, C. (2011) 'New public management, network governance and the university as a changing professional organization', in T. Christensen and P. Lægreid (eds) *The Ashgate Research Companion to New Public Management*, Farnham: Ashgate.

Block, F. (2003) 'Karl Polanyi and the writing of The Great Transformation', *Theory and Society*, 32(3): 275–306.

Block, F. and Somers, M. (2003) 'In the shadow of Speenhamland: social policy and the old Poor Law', *Politics & Society*, 31(2): 283–323.

Blyth, M. (2002) *Great Transformations: Economic Ideas and Institutional Change in the Twentieth Century*, Cambridge: Cambridge University Press.

Boltanski, L. (1987) [1982] *The Making of a Class: Cadres in French Society*, trans. Arthur Goldhammer, Cambridge: Cambridge University Press.

Boltanski, L. and Chiapello, E. (2005) [1999] *The New Spirit of Capitalism*, trans. Gregory Elliott, London: Verso.

Boltanski, L., and Thévenot, L. (2006) [1991] *On Justification: Economies of Worth*, trans. C. Porter, Princeton, NJ: Princeton University Press.

Bongardt, A. (2015) 'The transformation of the Single European Market: from the Lisbon Strategy to Europe 2020', in J.M. Magone (ed.) *Routledge Handbook of European Politics*, London: Routledge.

Booth, W.J. (1994) 'On the idea of the moral economy', *American Political Science Review*, 88(3): 653–667.

Börzel, T.A. (2005) 'Mind the gap! European integration between level and scope', *Journal of European Public Policy*, 12(2): 217–236.
Börzel, T.A. (2002) 'Member state responses to Europeanization', *Journal of Common Market Studies*, 40(2): 193–214.
Bourdieu, P. (1986) 'The Forms of Capital', in J. Richardson (ed.) *Handbook of Theory and Research for the Sociology of Education*, Westport, CT: Greenwood.
Bowles, S. and Gintis, H. (1982) 'The crisis of liberal democratic capitalism: the case of the United States', *Politics and Society*, 11(1): 51–93.
Boyle, J. (2008) *The Public Domain. Enclosing the Commons of the Mind*, New Haven, CT: Yale University Press.
Boyle, J. (2003) 'The second enclosure movement and the construction of the public domain', *Law and Contemporary Problems*, 66(1–2): 33–74.
Breakwell, G.M. (2006) 'Leadership in education: the case of Vice-Chancellors', *Perspectives*, 10(02): 52–58.
Breiner, P. (2004) '"Unnatural selection": Max Weber's concept of Auslese and his criticism of the reduction of political conflict to economics', *International Relations*, 18(3): 289–307.
Brennan, J. and Williams, R. (2008) 'Higher education outside the universities: the UK Case', in J.S. Taylor, J.B. Ferreira, M. de Lourdes Machado and R. Santiago (eds) *Non-University Higher Education in Europe*, Dordrecht: Springer.
Brenneis, D., Shore, C. and Wright, S. (2005) 'Getting the measure of academia: universities and the politics of accountability', *Anthropology in Action*, 12(1): 1–10.
Brenner, N., Peck, J., and Theodore, N. (2010) 'Variegated neoliberalization: geographies, modalities, pathways', *Global Networks*, 10(2): 182–222.
Brenner, N. and Theodore, N. (eds) (2002) *Spaces of Neoliberalism: Urban Restructuring in Western Europe and North America*, Oxford: Blackwell.
Broadbent, J. (2010) 'The UK research assessment exercise: performance measurement and resource allocation', *Australian Accounting Review*, 20(1): 14–23.
Brody, H. (2007) *Hooked: Ethics, the Medical Profession, and the Pharmaceutical Industry*. New York: Rowman & Littlefield.
Brown, P., Lauder, H. and Ashton, D. (2011) *The Global Auction: The Broken Promises of Education, Jobs, and Incomes*, Oxford: Oxford University Press.
Brown, R. with Carasso, H. (2013) *Everything for Sale?: The Marketisation of UK Higher Education*, London: Routledge.
Brown, W. (2015) *Undoing the Demos: Neoliberalism's Stealth Revolution*, New York: Zone Books.
Brynin, M. (2013) 'Individual choice and risk: the case of higher education', *Sociology*, 47(2): 284–300.
Buchanan, J.M. and Tullock, G. (1962) *The Calculus of Consent: Logical Foundations of Constitutional Democracy*, Ann Arbor, MI: University of Michigan Press.
Bugra, A. and Agartan, K. (eds) (2007) *Reading Karl Polanyi for the Twenty-First Century: The Market Economy as a Political Project*, Basingstoke: Palgrave Macmillan.
Bukodi, E., Goldthorpe, J.H., Waller, L. and Kuha, J. (2015) 'The mobility problem in Britain: new findings from the analysis of birth cohort data', *British Journal of Sociology*, 66(1): 93–117.
Buller, J. and Flinders, M. (2006) 'Depoliticisation: a response to Burnham', *The British Journal of Politics and International Relations*, 8(2): 307–310.

Buller, J. and Flinders, M. (2005) 'The domestic origins of depoliticization in the area of British economic policy', *British Journal of Politics & International Relations*, 7(4): 526–543.

Bulmer, S., Dolowitz, D., Humphreys, P. and Padgett, S. (2007) *Policy Transfer in European Union Governance: Regulating the Utilities*, London: Routledge.

Bulpitt, J. (1986), 'The discipline of the new democracy: Mrs. Thatcher's domestic statecraft', *Political Studies*, 34(1):19–39.

Bundy, C. (2004) 'Under new management? A critical history of managerialism in British universities', in M. Walker and J. Nixon (eds) *Reclaiming Universities from a Runaway World*, Buckingham: The Society for Research into Higher Education andOpen University Press.

Burger, T. (1976) *Max Weber's Theory of Concept Formation*, Durham, NC: Duke University Press.

Burgoon, B. (2009) 'Globalization and backlash: Polanyi's revenge?', *Review of International Political Economy*, 16(2): 145–177.

Burnes, B., Wend, P. and By, R.T. (2014) 'The changing face of English universities: reinventing collegiality for the twenty-first century', *Studies in Higher Education*, 39(6): 905–926.

Burnham, P. (2006) 'Depoliticisation: a comment on Buller and Flinders', *The British Journal of Politics and International Relations*, 8(2): 203–206.

Burnham, P. (2001) 'New Labour and the politics of depoliticization', *British Journal of Politics & International Relations*, 3(2): 127–149.

Burris, V. (2004) 'The academic caste system: prestige hierarchies in PhD exchange networks', *American Sociological Review* 69(2): 239–264.

Burt, R.S. (2005) *Brokerage and Closure: An Introduction to Social Capital*, Oxford: Oxford University Press.

Cahill, D. (2011) 'Beyond neoliberalism? Crisis and the prospects for progressive alternatives', *New Political Science*, 33(4): 479–492.

Caporaso, J. and Tarrow, S. (2009) 'Polanyi in Brussels: supranational institutions and the transnational embedding of markets', *International Organization*, 63(4): 593–620.

Castells, M. (2005) 'The network society: from knowledge to policy', in M. Castells and G. Cardoso (eds) *The Network Society: From Knowledge to Policy*, Washington, DC: Johns Hopkins Center for Transatlantic Relations.

Castells, M. (2015) *Networks of Outrage and Hope: Social Movements in the Internet Age*, 2nd edn, Cambridge: Polity.

Castells, M. (2009) *The Rise of the Network Society: The Information Age: Economy, Society, And Culture Volume 1*, 2nd edn, Oxford: Wiley Blackwell.

Chang, H.-J. (2002) *Kicking Away the Ladder: Development Strategy in Historical Perspective*, London: Anthem Press.

Christiansen, T. and Gray, M. (2004) 'The European Commission in a period of change: a new administration for a new European Union?', *Eipascope*, 3: 20–24.

Cini, M. (2015) 'Good governance and institutional change: administrative ethics reform in the European Commission', *Journal of Contemporary European Research*, 12(1): 440–454.

Clarke, J., Newman, J., Smith, N., Vidler, E. and Westmarland, L. (2007) *Creating Citizen-Consumers: Changing Publics & Changing Public Services*, London: Sage.

Clauset, A., Arbesman, S. and Larremore, D.B. (2015) 'Systematic inequality and hierarchy in faculty hiring networks', *Science Advances* 1(1) 12 February, e1400005.

Available: <http://advances.sciencemag.org/content/advances/1/1/e1400005.full.pdf> (accessed 29 November 2016).
Cohen, M.D., March, J.G. and Olsen, J.P. (1972) 'A garbage can model of organizational choice', *Administrative Science Quarterly*, 17(1): 1–25.
Collinge, A. (2009) *The Student Loan Scam: The Most Oppressive Debt in US History*, Boston, MA: Beacon Press.
Collini, S. (2016) 'Who are the spongers now?', *London Review of Books*, 38(2): 33–37. Available: <http://www.lrb.co.uk/v38/n02/stefan-collini/who-are-the-spongers-now> (accessed 30 November 2016).
Collini, S. (2011) *What Are Universities For?*, London: Penguin.
Courpasson, D. (2000) 'Managerial strategies of domination. Power in soft bureaucracy', *Organization Studies*, 21(1): 141–161.
Cox, E.W. (1862) *The Law and Practice of Joint Stock Companies and Other Associations: As Regulated by the Companies Act, 1862*, 6th edn. London: John Crockford.
Cox, R.W. (2013) 'The corporatization of higher education', *Class, Race and Corporate Power*, 1(1). Available: <http://digitalcommons.fiu.edu/classracecorporatepower/vol1/iss1/8> (accessed 29 November 2016).
Craig, P. (2000) 'The fall and renewal of the Commission: accountability, contract and administrative organisation', *European Law Journal*, 6(2): 98–116.
Crouch, C. (2011) *The Strange Non-Death of Neoliberalism*, Cambridge: Polity.
Crouch, C. (2005) *Capitalist Diversity and Change: Recombinant Governance and Institutional Entrepreneurs*, Oxford: Oxford University Press.
Crouch, C. (2004) *Postdemocracy*, Cambridge: Polity.
Cummings, W.K. (2009) 'Teaching versus research in the contemporary academy', in RIHE International Seminar Reports 13, *The Changing Academic Profession Over 1992–2007: International, Comparative, and Quantitative Perspectives, Report of the International Conference on the Changing Academic Profession Project, 2009*, September, Research Institute for Higher Education, Hiroshima University: 39–55.
Currie, G., Humphreys, M., Ucbasaran, D. and McManus, S. (2008), 'Entrepreneurial leadership in the English public sector: paradox or possibility?', *Public Administration*, 86(4): 987–1008.
Dale, G. (2012) 'Double movements and pendular forces: Polanyian perspectives on the neoliberal age', *Current Sociology*, 60(1): 3–27.
Dale, G. (2010) *Karl Polanyi. The Limits of the Market*, Cambridge: Polity.
Davies, N. (2004) *Flat Earth News*, New York: Random House.
Dean, M. (2014) 'Rethinking neoliberalism', *Journal of Sociology*, 50(2): 150–163.
Dearlove, J. (1998) 'Fundamental changes in institutional governance structures: the United Kingdom', *Higher Education Policy*, 11(2–3): 2–3.
Del Favero, M. and Bray, N.J. (2010) 'Herding cats and big dogs: tensions in the faculty-administrator relationship', in J.C. Smart (ed.) *Higher Education: Handbook of Theory and Research, 25*, Dordrecht: Springer.
Denham, A. and Garnett, M. (1998) *British Think-Tanks and the Climate of Opinion*, London: UCL Press.
di Palma, G. (2013) *The Modern State Subverted: Risk and the Deconstruction of Solidarity*, Colchester: ECPR Press.
Diamond, P. (2015) 'New Labour, politicization and depoliticization: the delivery agenda in public services 1997–2007', *British Politics*, 10(4): 429–453.
Dicey, A.V. (1915) *Introduction to the Law of the Constitution*, 8th edn, London: Macmillan.

DiMaggio, P. (2001) *The Twenty-First-Century Firm: Changing Economic Organization in International Perspective*, Princeton, NJ: Princeton University Press.

Dnes, A. and Seaton, J.S. (1998) 'The reform of academic tenure in the UK', *International Review of Law and Economics*, 18(4): 491–509.

Dobbin, F., Simmons, B. and Garrett, G. (2007) 'The global diffusion of public policies: social construction, coercion, competition, or learning?', *Annual Review of Sociology*, 33: 449–472.

Dolowitz, D. and Marsh, D. (2000) 'Learning from abroad: The role of policy transfer in contemporary policy-making', *Governance*, 13(1): 5–23.

Dolowitz, D. and Marsh, D. (1996) 'Who learns what from whom: a review of the policy transfer literature', *Political Studies*, 44(2): 343–357.

Domhoff, G.W. and Webber, M.J. (2011) *Class and Power in the New Deal: Corporate Moderates, Southern Democrats, and the Liberal-Labor Coalition*, Stanford, CA: Stanford University Press.

Donoghue, F. (2015) 'Academic freedom, the "teacher exception", and the diminished professor', *Ethics in Science and Environmental Politics*, 15: 1–9.

Donoghue, F. (2008) *The Last Professors: The Corporate University and the Fate of the Humanities*, New York: Fordham University Press.

Douglas, M. and Mars, G. (2003) 'Terrorism: a positive feedback game', *Human Relations*, 56(7): 763–786.

Dowding, K. (1995) *The Civil Service*, London: Routledge.

Draca, M. (2014) 'Institutional corruption? The revolving door in American and British politics', *SMF-CAGE Global Perspectives Series*, Paper 1, October. Available: <http://www.smf.co.uk/wp-content/uploads/2014/10/Social-Market-FoundationInstitutional-Corruption-the-revolving-door-in-American-and-British-politics.pdf> (accessed 7 December 2016).

Drechsler, W. (2009) 'The Lisbon Agenda and public administration', in M.J. Rodrigues (ed.) *Europe, Globalization and the Lisbon Agenda*, Cheltenham: Edward Elgar.

du Gay, P. (2003) 'The tyranny of the epochal: change, epochalism and organizational reform', *Organization*, 10(4): 663–684.

du Gay, P. (2008) 'Without affection or enthusiasm. Problems of involvement and attachment in "responsive" public management', *Organization*, 15(3): 335–353.

Dumont, L. (1994) *German Ideology: From France to Germany and Back*, Chicago, IL: University of Chicago Press.

Dunleavy, P. (1991) *Democracy, Bureaucracy and Public Choice: Economic Explanations in Political Science*, Hemel Hempstead: Harvester Wheatsheaf.

Dunsire, A. (1993) 'Manipulating social tensions: collibration as an alternative mode of government intervention', Max-Planck-Institut für Gesellschaftsforschung, discussion paper 93(7). Avaliable: <http://www.mpifg.de/pu/mpifg_dp/dp93-7.pdf> (accessed 30 November 2016).

Durkheim, É. (1995) [1912]. *The Elementary Forms of Religious Life: The Totemic System in Australia*, trans. K. Fields, New York: Free Press.

Edgerton, D. (2006) *Warfare State: Britain, 1920–1970*, Cambridge: Cambridge University Press.

Ellinas, A. and Suleiman, E. (2008) 'Reforming the Commission: between modernization and bureaucratization', *Journal of European Public Policy*, 15(5): 708–725.

Elton, L. (2000) 'The UK research assessment exercise: unintended consequences', *Higher Education Quarterly*, 54(3): 274–283.

Enders, J. (2015) 'The academic arms race: international rankings and global competition for world-class universities', in A.M. Pettigrew, E. Cornuel and U. Hommel (eds) *The Institutional Development of Business Schools*, Oxford: Oxford University Press.

Enrione, A., Mazza, C. and Zerboni, F. (2006) 'Institutionalizing codes of governance', *American Behavioral Science*, 49(7): 961–973.

Esty, D.C. (2006) 'Good governance at the supranational scale: globalizing administrative law', *Yale Law Journal*, 115: 1490–1562.

Etzkowitz, H. (1990) 'The second academic revolution: the role of the research university in economic development', in S.E. Cozzens, P. Healey, A. Rip and J. Ziman (eds) *The Research System in Transition*, Dordrecht: Kluwer.

European Commission (2001) 'White Paper on European Governance', *COM*/2001/428. Available: <http://eur-lex.europa.eu/legal-content/EN/TXT/?uri=URISERV%3Al10109> (accessed 29 November 2016).

European Commission (2000) 'White Paper on Reforming the Commission', *COM*/2000/0200. Available: <http://eur-lex.europa.eu/legal-content/EN/TXT/?uri=CELEX%3A52000DC0200(02)> (accessed 29 November 2016).

European Council (2000) 'Lisbon Strategy for Growth and Jobs', Available: <http://cordis.europa.eu/programme/rcn/843_en.html> (accessed 8 December 2016).

Fassin, D. (2009) 'Les économies morales revisitées', *Annales. Histoire, Sciences Sociales*, 64(6): 1237–1266.

Ferguson, J. (2009) 'The uses of neoliberalism', *Antipode*, 42(S1): 166–184.

Filippakou, O., Salter, B. and Tapper, T. (2012) 'Higher education as a system: the English experience', *Higher Education Quarterly*, 66(1): 106–122.

Fischer, F. (2009) *Democracy and Expertize: Reorienting Policy Inquiry*, Oxford: Oxford University Press.

Flinders, M. and Buller, J. (2006) 'Depoliticization: principles, tactics and tools', *British Politics*, 1(3): 293–318.

Flinders, M. and Geddes, M. (2014) 'The silent revolution: a political history of the politics of patronage and reform', *Contemporary British History*, 28(1): 24–55.

Flinders, M. and Wood, M. (eds) (2014) *Depoliticisation, Governance and the State*, special issue of *Policy and Politics*, 42(2).

Foskett, N. (2011) 'Markets, government, funding and the marketisation of UK higher education', in M. Molesworth, E. Nixon and R. Scullion (eds) *The Marketisation of Higher Education: The Student as Consumer*, London: Routledge.

Foucault, M. (2004) *The Birth of Biopolitics: Lectures at the Collège de France, 1978–79*; ed. M. Senellart, trans. G. Burchell, New York: Picador.

Frank, T. (2001) *One Market Under God: Extreme Capitalism, Market Populism, and the End of Economic Democracy*, New York: Anchor Books.

Friedman, M. (1962) *Capitalism and Freedom*, Chicago: University of Chicago Press.

Fry, G.K. (2008) *Politics of the Thatcher Revolution: An Interpretation of British Politics 1975–1990*, Basingstoke: Palgrave Macmillan.

Fullbrook, K. (1999) 'The RAE and the post '92 universities', *History of Human Sciences*, 12(4): 123–124.

Fuller, S. (2009) *The Sociology of Intellectual Life: The Career of the Mind in and Around the Academy*, London: Sage.

Furlong, P. (2005) 'British higher education and the Bologna Process: an interim assessment', *Politics*, 25(1): 53–61.

Gambetta, D. (1988) 'Mafia: the price of distrust', in D. Gambetta (ed.) *Trust: Making and Breaking Cooperative Relations*, Oxford: Blackwell.

Gambetta, D. (1998) 'Concatenations of mechanisms', in P. Hedström and R. Swedberg (eds) *Social Mechanisms: An Analytical Approach to Social Theory*, Cambridge: Cambridge University Press.

Gassert, P. (2008) 'Narratives of democratization: 1968 in postwar Europe', in M. Klimke and J. Scharloth (eds) *1968 In Europe: A History of Protest and Activism, 1956–77*, Basingstoke: Palgrave Macmillan.

Gibbons, M., Limoges, C., Nowotny, H., Schwartzman, S., Scott, P., and Trow, M. (1994) *New Production of Knowledge: Dynamics of Science and Research in Contemporary Societies*, London: Sage.

Giddens, A. (1994) 'Living in a post-traditional society', in U. Beck, A. Giddens and S. Lash *Reflexive Modernization: Politics, Tradition and Aesthetics in the Modern Social Order*, Cambridge: Polity.

Giddens, A. (1991) *Modernity and Self-identity: Self and Society in the Late Modern Age*, Cambridge: Polity.

Giddens, A. (1985) *The Nation-state and Violence*, Cambridge: Polity.

Gilman, N. (2003) *Mandarins of the Future: Modernization Theory in Cold War America*, Baltimore, MD: Johns Hopkins University Press.

Ginsberg, B. (2011) *The Fall of the Faculty: The Rise of the All-Administrative University and Why it Matters*, New York: Oxford University Press.

Glaeser, E.L., Ponzetto, G. and Shleifern, A. (2007) 'Why does democracy need education?', *Journal of Economic Growth*, 12(2): 77–99.

Glasman, M. (1996) *Unnecessary Suffering: Managing Market Utopia*, London: Verso.

Goldfinch, S. and Yamamoto, K. (2012) *Prometheus Assessed?: Research Measurement, Peer Review, and Citation Analysis*, Witney: Chandos Publishing.

Götz, N. (2015) '"Moral economy": its conceptual history and analytical prospects', *Journal of Global Ethics*, 11(2): 147–162.

Gould, E. (2006) 'Professor or knowledge worker? The politics of defining faculty work', *Higher Education in Europe*, 31(3): 241–249.

Gould, T.H. (2012) 'The church and peer review: was peer-review fairer, more honest then than now?', *Journal of Scholarly Publishing*, 44(1): 36–60.

Graeber, D. (2015) *The Utopia of Rules: On Technology, Stupidity and the Secret Joys of Bureaucracy*, New York: Melville House.

Graf, L. (2013) *The Hybridization of Vocational Training and Higher Education in Austria, Germany, and Switzerland*, Opladen: Budrich UniPress Ltd.

Gramsci, A. (1971) *Selections from the Prison Notebooks*; ed. and trans. G. Nowell Smith and Q. Hoare, London: Lawrence and Wishart.

Granovetter, M. (1985) 'Economic action and social structure: the problem of embeddedness', *American Journal of Sociology*, 19(3): 481–510.

Greenaway, D. and Haynes, M. (2003) 'Funding higher education in the UK: the role of fees and loans', *Economic Journal*, 113(485): 150–166.

Greenwood, D. (2007) 'Who are the real "problem owners"? On the social embeddedness of universities', in A. Harding, A. Scott, S. Laske and C. Burtscher (eds) *Bright Satanic Mills. Universities, Regional Development and the Knowledge Economies*, Aldershot: Ashgate.

Gregory, R. (2009) 'NPM and the politics of accountability', in S.F. Goldfinch and J.L. Wallis (eds) *International Handbook of Public Management Reform*, Cheltenham: Edward Elgar.

Gruening, G. (2001) 'Origin and theoretical basis of New Public Management', *International Public Management Journal*, 4(1): 1–25.

Gualmini, E. (2008) 'Restructuring Weberian bureaucracy: comparing managerial reforms in Europe and the United States', *Public Administration*, 86(1): 75–94.

Guérot, U. (2016) 'The failure of the political centre ground: The EU and the rise of right-wing populism', *Eurozine*, 15 June. Available: <http://www.eurozine.com/articles/article_2016-06-15-guerot-en.html> (accessed 29 November 2016).

Habermas, J. (1975) *Legitimation Crisis*, trans. T. McCarthy, Boston, MA: Beacon Press.

Hagel, J. III, Davison, L., and Brown, J. S (2010) *The Power of Pull: How Small Moves, Smartly Made, Can Set Big Things in Motion*, New York: Basic Books.

Hajer, M. and Wagenaar, W. (eds) (2003) *Deliberative Policy Analysis*, Cambridge: Cambridge University Press.

Halsey, A.H. (1992) *Decline of Donnish Dominion: The British Academic Professions in the Twentieth Century*, Oxford: Oxford University Press.

Halsey, A.H. (1982) 'The decline of donnish dominion?', *Oxford Review of Education*, 8(3): 215–229.

Hamlin, A. and Pettit, P. (eds) (1989) *The Good Polity: Normative Analysis of the State*, Oxford: Blackwell.

Hamowy, R. (1987) *The Scottish Enlightenment and the Theory of Spontaneous Order*, Carbondale, IL: Southern Illinois University Press.

Hann, C. and Hart, K. (eds) (2009) *Market and Society: The Great Transformation Today*, Cambridge: Cambridge University Press.

Harding, A. (2007) 'Taking city regions seriously? Response to debate on "City-Regions: New Geographies of Governance, Democracy and Social Reproduction"', *International Journal of Urban and Regional Research*, 31(2): 443–458.

Harmes, A. (2001) 'Institutional investors and Polanyi's double movement: a model of contemporary currency crises', *Review of International Political Economy*, 8(3): 389–437.

Harvey, D. (2005) *A Brief History of Neoliberalism*, Oxford: Oxford University Press.

Harvey, M., Ramlogan, R., and Randles, S. (eds) (2007) *Karl Polanyi: New Perspectives on the Place of the Economy in Society*, Manchester: Manchester University Press.

Hassard, J., Mccann, L., and Morris, J. (2009) *Managing in the Modern Corporation: The Intensification of Managerial Work in the USA, the UK and Japan*. Cambridge: Cambridge University Press.

Haxhi, I. (2010) 'Explaining diversity in the worldwide diffusion of codes of good governance', *Journal of International Business Studies*, 41(4): 710–726.

Hay, C. (2007) *Why We Hate Politics*, Cambridge: Polity.

Hayek (1982) *Law, Legislation and Liberty: A New Statement of the Liberal Principles of Justice and Political Economy*, 3 Vols, London: Routledge.

Head, S. (2003) *The New Ruthless Economy: Work and Power in the Digital Age*, Oxford: Oxford University Press.

Heclo, H. and Wildavsky, A. (1974) *The Private Government of Public Money*, Berkeley, CA: University of California Press.

Heffernan, R. and Webb, P. (2005) 'The British prime minister: more than first among equals', in T. Poguntke and P. Webb (eds) *The Presidentialization of Politics: A Comparative Study of Modern Democracies*, Oxford: Oxford University Press.

Heidbreder, E.G. (2011) 'Structuring the European administrative space: policy instruments of multi-level administration', *Journal of European Public Policy*, 18(5): 709–727.

Helleiner, E. (2003) 'Economic liberalism and its critics: the past as prologue?', *Review of International Political Economy*, 10(4): 685–696.

Hennessy, P. (1990) *Whitehall*, London: Fontana.

Hennis, W. (2000) *Max Weber's Central Question*, 2nd edn, trans. K. Tribe, London: Threshold Press.

Hibou, B. (2015) *The Bureaucratization of the World in the Neoliberal Era. An International and Comparative Perspective*, trans. A. Brown, Basingstoke: Palgrave Macmillan.

Hibou, B. (2004) 'From privatising the economy to privatising the state: an analysis of the continual formation of the state', in B. Hibou (ed.) *Privatising the State*, trans. J. Derrick, London: Hurst & Co.

HirschmanA.O. (1997) [1977] *The Passions and the Interests: Political Arguments for Capitalism Before its Triumph*, 2nd edn, Princeton, NJ: Princeton University Press.

Hirschman, A.O. (1970) *Exit, Voice, and Loyalty*, Cambridge, MA: Harvard University Press.

Hirst, P.Q. (1996) 'Democracy and civil society', in P.Q. Hirst and S. Khilnani (eds) *Reinventing Democracy*, Oxford: *The Political Quarterly*/Blackwell.

Hirst, P.Q. (ed.) (1993) *The Pluralist Theory of the State: Selected Writings of G. D. H. Cole, J. N. Figgis and H. J. Laski*, London: Routledge.

Hix, S. (1998) 'The study of the European Union II: the "new governance" agenda and its rival', *Journal of European Public Policy*, 5(1): 38–65.

Hodgson, A., Spours, K., Waring, M., Gallacher, J., Keep, E. and Rees, G. (2011) 'Post-compulsory education and lifelong learning across the UK: moving from managed divergence to a new period of uncertainty', in A. Hodgson, K. Spours and M. Waring (eds) *Post-compulsory Education and Lifelong Learning Across the United Kingdom: Policy, Organisation and Governance*, London: Institute of Education, University of London.

Hofmann, H.C. (2008) 'Mapping the European administrative space', *West European Politics*, 31(4): 662–676.

Holligan, C. (2010) 'Building one-dimensional places: death by the power of audit', *Power and Education*, 2(3): 288–299.

Holmwood, J., Hickey, T., Cohen, R. and Wallis, S. (eds) (2016) *The Alternative White Paper For Higher Education. In Defence of Public Higher Education: Knowledge for a Successful Society: a response to 'Success as a Knowledge Economy', BIS (2016)*, The Convention for Higher Education, May.

Hood, C. (2007) 'Public service management by numbers: why does it vary? Where has it come from? What are the gaps and the puzzles?', *Public Money & Management*, 27(2): 95–102.

Hood, C. (1998) *The Art of The State: Culture, Rhetoric and Public Management*, Oxford: Oxford University Press.

Hood, C. and Dixon, R. (2015) *A Government that Worked Better and Cost Less?: Evaluating Three Decades of Reform and Change in UK Central Government*, Oxford: Oxford University Press.

Hood, C. and Dixon, R. (2010) 'The political payoff from performance target systems: no-brainer or no-gainer?', *Journal of Public Administration, Research and Theory*, 20(2): 281–298

Hooghe, L. and Marks, G. (2003) 'Unraveling the central state, but how? Types of multi-level governance', *American Political Science Review*, 97(2): 233–243.

Hummel, R.P. (2007) *The Bureaucratic Experience: The Post-modern Challenge*, Armonk, NY: M.E. Sharpe.

Hyslop-Margison, E.J. and Leonard, H.A. (2012) 'Post neo-liberalism and the humanities: what the repressive state apparatus means for universities', *Canadian Journal of Higher Education*, 42(2): 1–12.

Ireland, P. (2010) 'Limited liability, shareholder rights and the problem of corporate irresponsibility', *Cambridge Journal of Economics*, 34(5): 837–856.

Irzik, G. (2007) 'Commercialization of science in a neoliberal world', in A. Bugra and K. Agartan, (eds) *Rereading Karl Polanyi for the Twenty-first Century: Market Economy as Political Project*, New York: Palgrave Macmillan.

Jackson, B. and Saunders, R. (eds) (2012) *Making Thatcher's Britain*, Cambridge: Cambridge University Press.

Jasanoff, S. (2005) *Designs on Nature: Science and Democracy in Europe and the United States*, Princeton, NJ: Princeton University Press.

Jasanoff, S. (1990) *The Fifth Branch: Scientific Advisors as Policymakers*, Cambridge, MA: Harvard University Press.

Jenkins, A. (2004) *A Guide to the Research Evidence on Teaching-Research Relations*, York: HE Academy.

Jessop, B. (2007) 'Knowledge as a fictitious commodity: insights and limits of a Polanyian perspective', in A. Bugra and K. Agartan (eds) *Rereading Karl Polanyi for the Twenty-first Century: Market Economy as Political Project*, Basingstoke: Palgrave Macmillan.

Jessop, B. (2001) 'Regulationist and autopoieticist reflections on Polanyi's account of market economies and the market society', *New Political Economy*, 6(2): 213–232.

Johnson, B., Kavanagh, P. and Mattson, K. (eds) (2003) *Steal This University: The Rise of the Corporate University and an Academic Labor Movement*, New York: Routledge.

Johnson, P., Wood, G., Brewster, C. and Brookes, M. (2009) 'The rise of post-bureaucracy: theorists' fancy or organizational praxis?', *International Sociology*, 24(1): 37–61.

Johnstone, D.B. (2014) 'Tuition fees, student loans, and other manifestations of cost sharing: variations and misconceptions', in A. Maldonado-Maldonado and R.M. Bassett (eds) *The Forefront of International Higher Education: A Festschrift in Honor of Philip G. Altbach*, Dordrecht: Springer.

Judt, T. (2010) *Ill Fare the Land*, New York: Penguin.

Judt, T. (2005) *Postwar: A history of Europe since 1945*, New York: Penguin.

Kalecki, M. (1943) 'Political aspects of full employment', *Political Quarterly*, 14(4): 322–331.

Kallinikos, J., Hasselbladh, H. and Marton, A. (2013) 'Governing social practice: technology and institutional change', *Theory and Society*, 42(4): 395–421.

Kassim, H. (2004) 'The Kinnock reforms in perspective: why reforming the commission is an heroic, but thankless, task', *Public Policy and Administration*, 19(3): 25–41.

Kassim, H. and Le Galès, P. (2010) 'Exploring governance in a multi-level polity: a policy instruments approach', *West European Politics*, 33(1): 1–21.

Kassirer, J.P. (2004) *On The Take: How Medicine's Complicity with Big Business Can Endanger Your Health*, Oxford: Oxford University Press.

Keeling, R. (2006) 'The Bologna Process and the Lisbon Research Agenda: the European Commission's expanding role in higher education discourse', *European Journal of Education*, 41(2): 203–223.

Khurana, R. (2007) *From Higher Aims to Hired Hands: The Social Transformation of American Business Schools and the Unfulfilled Promise of Management as a Profession*, Princeton, NJ: Princeton University Press.

King, A. (1975) 'Overload: problems of governing in the 1970s', *Political Studies*, 23(2–3): 284–296.

King, R. (2007) 'Governance and accountability in the higher education regulatory state', *Higher Education*, 53(4): 411–430.

Klimke, M. and Scharloth, J. (eds) (2008) *1968 in Europe: A History of Protest and Activism, 1956–77*, Basingstoke: Palgrave Macmillan.

Koenig-Archibugi, M. (2004) 'International governance as new raison d'etat? The case of the EU common foreign and security policy', *European Journal of International Relations*, 10(2): 147–188.

Koenig-Archibugi, M. (2002) 'The democratic deficit of EU foreign and security policy', *The International Spectator*, 37(4): 61–73.

Kostakis, V. and Bauwens, M. (2014) *Network Society and Future Scenarios for a Collaborative Economy*, Basingstoke: Palgrave Macmillan.

Krackhardt (1998) 'Simmelian ties: super strong and sticky', in R. Kramer and M. Neale (eds) *Power and Influence in Organizations*, Thousand Oaks, CA: Sage.

Krause, E.A. (1996) *Death of the Guilds: Professions, States, and the Advance of Capitalism, 1930 to the Present*, New Haven, CT: Yale University Press.

Krimsky, S. (2003) *Science in the Private Interest: Has the Lure of Profits Corrupted Biomedical Research?*, Lanham, MD: Rowman and Littlefield.

Kwiek, M. (2008) 'Revisiting the classical German idea of the university', *Polish Journal of Philosophy*, 2(1): 55–78.

Lacher, H. (1999) 'The politics of the market: re-reading Karl Polanyi', *Global Society*, 13(3): 313–326.

LandryL. and Neubauer, D. (2016) 'The role of the government in providing access to higher education: the case of government-sponsored financial aid in the US', *Journal of Education and Work*, 29(1): 64–76.

Lapsley, I. (2009) 'New Public Management: the cruellest invention of the human spirit?', *Abacus*, 45(1): 1–21.

Lascoume, P. and Le Galès, P. (2007) 'Exploring governance in a multi-level polity: a policy instruments approach', *Governance: An International Journal of Policy, Administration, and Institution*, 20(1): 1–21.

Lash, S. (1994) 'Reflexivity and its doubles: structure, aesthetics, community', in U. Beck, A. Giddens and S. Lash *Reflexive Modernization: Politics, Tradition and Aesthetics in the Modern Social Order*, Cambridge: Polity.

Le Galès, P. (2016) 'Neoliberalism and urban change: stretching a good idea too far?', *Territory, Politics and Governance*, 4(2): 154–172.

Le Galès, P. and Scott, A. (2010) 'A British bureaucratic revolution? Autonomy without control or "freer markets, more rules"', *Revue Française de Sociologie*, 51, Supplement (Annual English Selection): 117–143.

Le Grand, J. (2007) *The Other Invisible Hand: Delivering Public Services through Choice and Competition*, Princeton, NJ: Princeton University Press.

Le Grand, J. (2003) *Motivation, Agency, and Public Policy: Of Knights and Knaves, Pawns and Queens*, Oxford: Oxford University Press.

Le Grand, J. (1991) 'Quasi-markets and social policy', *The Economic Journal*, 101(408): 1256–1267.

Lee, F.S. (2007) 'The Research Assessment Exercise, the state and the dominance of mainstream economics in British universities', *Cambridge Journal of Economics*, 31(2): 309–325.

Lee, F.S., Pham, X. and Gu, G. (2013) 'The UK Research Assessment Exercise and the narrowing of UK economics', *Cambridge Journal of Economics*, 37(4): 693–717.

Lemke, T. (2007) 'An indigestible meal? Foucault, governmentality and state theory', *Distinkion: Journal of Social Theory*, 8(2): 43–64.

Levien, M. (2007) 'India's double movement: Polanyi and the National Alliance of People's Movements', *Berkeley Journal of Sociology*, 51: 119–149.

Levi-Faur, D. (2005) 'The global diffusion of regulatory capitalism', *Annals, AAPSS*, 598: 12–32.

Lewis, M.S. (1991) 'The polytechnics: a peculiarly British phenomenon', *Metropolitan Universities*, 2(4): 24–34.

Lin, N. (2001) *Social Capital: A Theory of Social Structure and Action*, Cambridge: Cambridge University Press.

Lipsky, M. (1980) *Street-level Bureaucracy: Dilemma of the Individual in Public Services.* Russell Sage Foundation 2010.

Locke, W. (2014) 'Teaching and research in English higher education: the fragmentation, diversification and reorganisation of academic work, 1992–2007', in J.C. Shin, A. Arimoto, W.K. Cummings and U. Teichler (eds) *Teaching and Research in Contemporary Higher Education: Systems, Activities and Rewards*, Dordrecht: Springer.

Locke, W., Verbik, L., Richardson, J.T. and King, R. (2008) *Counting What is Measured or Measuring What Counts? League Tables and Their Impact on Higher Education Institutions in England*, Bristol: Higher Education Funding Council for England.

Logan, J.R. and Molotch, H.L. (1987) *Urban Fortunes: The Political Economy of Place*, Berkeley, CA: University of California Press.

Lohmann, S. (2004) 'Darwinian medicine for the universities', in R.G. Ehrenberg (ed.) *Governing Academia*, Ithaca, NY: Cornell University Press.

Lohmann, S. (2006) 'The public research university as a complex adaptive system', unpublished paper, University of California, Los Angeles. Available: <http://www.cabdyn.ox.ac.uk/complexity_PDFs/ECCS06/Conference_Proceedings/PDF/p88.pdf> (accessed 29 November 2016).

Lukes, S. (2005) *Power: A Radical View*, 2nd edn, Basingstoke: Palgrave Macmillan.

Lynch, K. (2015) 'Control by numbers: new managerialism and ranking in higher education', *Critical Studies in Education*, 56(2): 190–207.

Lyotard, J-F. (1984) *The Postmodern Condition: A Report on Knowledge*, trans. Geoff Bennington and Brian Massumi, Minneapolis, MN: University of Minnesota Press.

Maher, F.A. and Tetreault, M.K.T. (2007) *Privilege and Diversity in the Academy*, London: Routledge.

Mair, P. (2013) *Ruling the Void: The Hollowing of Western Democracy*, London: Verso.

March, J.G. and Olsen, J.P. (2006) 'The logic of appropriateness', in M. Moran, M. Rein and R.E. Goodin (eds) *The Oxford Handbook of Public Policy*, Oxford: Oxford University Press.

Marginson, S. and Considine, M. (2000) *The Enterprise University: Power, Governance and Reinvention in Australia*, Cambridge: Cambridge University Press.

Marinetto, M. (2007) *Social Theory, the State and Modern Society: The State in Contemporary Social Thought*, Buckingham: Open University Press.

Marquand, D. (2004) *Decline of the Public*, Cambridge: Polity.

Marshall, T.H. (1997) [1949] 'Citizenship and social class', in R.E. Goodin and P. Pettit (eds) *Contemporary Political Philosophy*, Oxford: Blackwell.

Martin, B. (1998) *Tied Knowledge: Power in Higher Education*. Available: <http://www.uow.edu.au/~bmartin/pubs/98tk/> (accessed 29 November 2016).

Marwick, A. (1998) *The Sixties: Cultural Revolution in Britain, France, Italy, and the United States, c.1958 – c.1974*, London: Bloomsbury.

Mattei, U. and Nader, L. (2008) *Plunder: When the Rule of Law is Illegal*, Oxford: Blackwell.

Mau, S. (2003) *The Moral Economy of Welfare States: Britain and Germany Compared*, London: Routledge.

May, C. and Sell, S.K. (2005) *Intellectual Property Rights: A Critical History*, Boulder, CO: Lynne Rienner.

McGettigan, A. (2013) *The Great University Gamble: Money, Markets and the Future of Higher Education*, London: Pluto.

McGuigan, J. (2016) *Neoliberal Culture*, Basingstoke: Palgrave Macmillan.

McRobbie, K. and Polanyi-Levitt, K. (eds) (2005) *Karl Polanyi in Vienna: The Contemporary Significance of The Great Transformation*, 2nd edn, Montréal: Black Rose Books.

Mead, L.M. (1986) *Beyond Entitlement*, New York: Free Press.

Meek, V.L., Goedegebuure, L., Santiago, R. and Carvalho, T. (eds) (2010) *The Changing Dynamics of Higher Education Middle Management*, Dordrecht: Springer.

Merton, R.K. (1973) [1942] 'The normative structure of science', in N.W. Storer (ed.) *The Sociology of Science: Theoretical and Empirical Investigations*, Chicago, IL: University of Chicago Press.

Miller, H.T. and Fox, C.J. (2007) *Postmodern Public Administration*, Armonk, NY: M.E. Sharpe, Inc.

Miller, T. (2012) *Blow Up the Humanities*, Philadelphia, PA: Temple University Press.

Mills, C.W. (1956) *The Power Elite*, New York: Oxford University Press.

Mills, C.W. (1951) *White Collar: The American Middle Classes*, New York: Oxford University Press.

Mills, C.W. (1948) *New Men of Power: American Labor Leaders*, New York: Oxford University Press.

Mirowski, P. (2013) *Never Let a Serious Crisis Go to Waste: How Neoliberalism Survived the Financial Meltdown*, London: Verso.

Mirowski, P. and D. Plehwe (eds) (2009) *The Road from Mont Pèlerin: The Making of the Neoliberal Thought Collective*, Cambridge, MA: Harvard University Press.

Moore, B. jr (1966) *Social Origins of Dictatorship and Democracy: Lord and Peasant in the Making of the Modern World*, Boston, MA: Beacon Press.

Moran, M. (2003) *The British Regulatory State: High Modernism and Hyper-Innovation*, Oxford: Oxford University Press.

Mouffe, C. (2016) 'The populist challenge', *openDemocracy*, 5 December.Available: <https://www.opendemocracy.net/democraciaabierta/chantal-mouffe/populist-challenge> (accessed 6 December 2016).

Mudge, S.L. (2008) 'State of the art: what is neo-liberalism?', *Socio-Economic Review*, 6: 203–231.

Mueller, F. and Dyerson, R. (1999) 'Expert humans or expert organizations?', *Organization Studies*, 20(2): 225–256.

Munck, R. (2006) 'Globalization and contestation: a Polanyian problematic', *Globalizations*, 3(2): 175–186.

Musselin, C. (2013a) 'How peer review empowers the academic profession and university managers: changes in relationships between the state, universities and the professoriate', *Research Policy*, 42(5): 1165–1173.
Musselin, C. (2013b) 'Redefinition of the relationships between academics and their university', *Higher Education*, 65(1): 25–37.
Musselin, C. (1996) 'Organized anarchies: a reconsideration of research strategies', in M. Warglien and M. Masuch (eds) *The Logic of Organizational Disorder*, Berlin: Walter de Gruyter.
Nafissi, M. (2005) *Ancient Athens and Modern Ideology: Value, Theory and Evidence in Historical Sciences: Max Weber, Karl Polanyi and Moses Finley*, London: Institute of Classic Studies, University of London.
Naidoo, R. (2008) 'Building or eroding intellectual capital? Student consumerism as a cultural force in the context of knowledge economy', in J. Välimaa and O.H. Ylijoki (eds) *Cultural Perspectives on Higher Education*, Dordrecht: Springer.
Nealon, J.T., (2012) *Post-postmodernism: Or, the Cultural Logic of Just-In-Time Capitalism*, Stanford, CA: Stanford University Press.
Needham, C. (2007) *The Reform of Public Services Under New Labour: Narratives of Consumerism*, Basingstoke: Palgrave Macmillan.
Neeson, J.M. (1993) *Commoners: Common Right, Enclosure and Change in England, 1700–1820*, Cambridge: Cambridge University Press.
Nemec, M.R. (2006) *Ivory Towers and Nationalist Minds: Universities, Leadership, and the Development of The American State*, Ann Arbor, MI: University of Michigan Press.
Newfield, C. (2008) *Unmaking the Public University: The Forty-Year Assault on the Middle Class*, Cambridge, MA: Harvard University Press.
Niskanen, W.A. (1971) *Bureaucracy and Representative Government*, New York: Aldine-Atherton.
Noble, D.F. (1998) 'Selling academe to the technology industry', *Thought & Action*, 14(1): 29–40.
Nussbaum, M.C. (2010) *Not For Profit: Why Democracy Needs the Humanities*, Princeton, NJ: Princeton University Press.
Oleinik, A.N. (2015) *The Invisible Hand of Power: An Economic Theory of Gate Keeping*, London: Pickering & Chatto.
Olsen, J.P. (2007) *Europe in Search of Political Order*, Oxford: Oxford University Press.
Osborne, T. (1998) *Aspects of Enlightenment*, London: UCL Press.
O'Toole, B. (2006) *The Ideal of Public Service: Reflections on the Higher Civil Service in Britain*, London: Routledge.
Özveren, E. (2007) 'Karl Polanyi and the modernity-versus-postmodernity debate', *The European Legacy: Toward New Paradigms*, 12(5): 549–564.
Page, E.C. (2015) 'Middle level bureaucrats: policy, discretion and control', in F.M. van der Meer, J.C.N. Raadschelders and T.A.J. Toonen (eds) *Comparative Civil Service Systems in the 21st Century*, Basingstoke: Palgrave Macmillan.
Page, E.C. (1985) *Political Authority and Bureaucratic Power: A Comparative Analysis*, Brighton: Harvester Wheatsheaf.
Pal, L.A. (2008) 'Inversions without end: The OECD and global public management reform', in R. Mahon and S. McBride (eds) *The OECD and Transnational Governance*, Vancouver, BC: UBC Press.
Palumbo, A. (2015) *Situating Governance: Context, Content, Critique*, Colchester: ECPR Press.

Palumbo, A. (2009) 'Due tipi di 'corporate governance': approcci manageriali ed etici a confronto', *Ragion pratica*, 33: 541–560.

Palumbo, A. and Scott, A. (2005) 'Bureaucracy, open access and social pluralism: returning the common to the goose', in P. du Gay (ed.) *The Values of Bureaucracy*, Oxford: Oxford University Press.

Park, E. (2013) 'From academic self-governance to executive university management: institutional governance in the eyes of academics in Europe', in U. Teichlerand and E.A. Höhle (eds) *The Work Situation of the Academic Profession in Europe: Findings of a Survey in Twelve Countries*, Dordrecht: Springer.

Parkin, F. (1979) *Marxism and Class heory: A Bourgeois Critique*, London: Tavistock.

Peck, J. (2012) 'Austerity urbanism: American cities under extreme economy', *City*, 16(1): 626–655.

Peck, J. (2010) 'Zombie neoliberalism and the ambidextrous state', *Theoretical Criminology*, 14(1): 104–110.

Peck, J., Theodore, N., and Brenner, N. (2012) 'Neoliberalism resurgent? Market rule after the Great Recession', *The South Atlantic Quarterly*, 111(2): 265–288.

Peet, R. (2009) *Unholy Trinity: The IMF, World Bank and WTO*, London: Zed Books.

Peters, B.G. (2002) 'Alternative models of governing', in E. Vigoda-Gadot (ed.) *Public Administration: An Interdisciplinary Critical Analysis*, London: Routledge.

Peters, B.G. and Pierre, J. (eds) (2004) *Politicization of the Civil Service in Comparative Perspective: The Quest for Control*, London: Routledge.

Peters, P.G. and Pierre, J. (2009) 'Governance approaches', in A. Wiener and T. Diez (eds) *European Integration Theory*, 2nd edn, Oxford: Oxford University Press.

Peters, T. (1992) *Liberation Management: Necessary Disorganization for the Nanosecond Nineties*, New York: Alfred A. Knopf.

Piore, M.J. and Sabel, C.F. (1984) *The Second Industrial Divide*, New York: Basic Books.

Plehwe, D., Walpen, B., and Neunhoffer, G. (eds) (2006) *Neoliberal Hegemony: A Global Critique*, London: Routledge.

Polanyi, K. (2001) [1944] *The Great Transformation: The Political and Economic Origins of Our Time*, 2nd Beacon edn, Boston, MA: Beacon Press.

Polanyi, K. (1947) 'Our obsolete market mentality', *Commentary*, 3(2): 109–117.

Polanyi, K., Arensberg, C. and Pearson, H.W. (eds) (1957) *Trade and Markets in the Early Empire: Economies in History and Theory*, New York: The Free Press.

Polanyi-Levitt, K. and Mendell, M. (1987) 'Karl Polanyi: his life and times', *Studies in Political Economy*, 22, Spring: 7–39.

Popitz, H. (1992) *Phänomene der Macht*, extended 2nd edn, Tübingen: J.C.B. Mohr; trans. Gianfranco Poggi, intro. Jochen Dreher and Andreas Gottlich (2017) *The Phenomena of Power: Authority, Domination, and Violence*, New York: Columbia University Press.

Portes, A. (2000) 'The two meanings of social capital', *Sociological Forum*, 15(1): 1–12.

Powell, W.W. (1990) 'Neither market nor hierarchy: network forms of organization', *Research in Organizational Behavior*, 12: 295–336.

Powell, W.W. and DiMaggio, P.J. (eds) (1991) *The New Institutionalism in Organizational Analysis*, Chicago, IL: Chicago University Press.

Power, M. (1997) *The Audit Society: Rituals of Verification*, Oxford: Oxford University Press.

Prasad, M. (2006) *The Politics of Free Markets: The Rise of Neoliberal Economic Policies in Britain, France, Germany, and the United States*, Chicago, IL: University of Chicago Press.

Pratt, J. (1997) *The Polytechnic Experiment: 1965–1992*, Buckingham: The Society for Research into Higher Education & Open University Press.

Professor X (2011) *In the Basement of the Ivory Tower: Confessions of an Accidental Academic*, London: Viking Penguin.

Przeworski, A. (1990) *The State and the Economy Under Capitalism*, Chur: Harwood Academic Publishers.

Puchala, D.J. (1971) 'Of blind men, elephants and international integration', *Journal of Common Market Studies*, 10(3): 267–284.

Putnam, R.D. (2000) *Bowling Alone: The Collapse and Revival of American Community*, New York: Simon & Schuster.

Putnam, R.D. (1988) 'Diplomacy and domestic politics: the logic of two-level games', *International Organization* 42(3): 427–460.

Radaelli, C.M. (2003) 'The Europeanization of Public Policy', in K. Featherstone and C.M. Radaelli (eds) *The Politics of Europeanization*, Oxford: Oxford University Press.

Radder, H. (ed.) (2010) *The Commodification of Academic Research: Science and the Modern University*, Pittsburgh, PA: University of Pittsburgh Press.

Raffer, K. (2011) 'Neoliberal capitalism: a time warp backwards to capitalism's origins?', *Forum for Social Economics*, 40(1): 41–62.

Rawls, J. (1971) *A Theory of Justice*, Cambridge, MA: Harvard University Press.

Reitan, E.A. (2003) *The Thatcher Revolution: Margaret Thatcher, John Major, Tony Blair, and the Transformation of Modern Britain, 1979–2001*, Lanham, MD: Rowman & Littlefield.

Rhoades, G. (1998) *Managed Professionals: Unionized Faculty and Restructuring Academic Labor*, Albany, NY: State University of New York Press.

Rhodes, R.A.W. (2007) 'Blair and governance', in R. Koch and J. Dixon (eds) *Public Governance and Leadership. Political and Managerial Problems in Making Public Governance Changes the Driver for Re-Constituting Leadership*, Wiesbaden: Deutscher Universitäts-Verlag.

Rhodes, R.A.W. (1997) *Understanding Governance*, Buckingham: Open University Press.

Rhodes, R.A.W. (1994), 'The hollowing out of the state: the changing nature of the public service in Britain', *Political Quarterly*, 65(2): 138–151.

Rhodes, R.A.W., Carmichael, P., McMillan, J. and Massey, A. (2003) *Decentralizing the Civil Service: From Unitary State to Differentiated Polity in the United Kingdom*, Buckingham, Open University Press.

Richards, D. (2008) *New Labour and the Civil Service: Reconstituting the Westminster Model*, Basingstoke: Palgrave Macmillan.

Rifkin, J. (2014) *The Zero Marginal Cost Society: The Internet of Things, the Collaborative Commons, and the Eclipse of Capitalism*, Basingstoke: Palgrave Macmillan.

Ringer, F. (1969) *The Decline of the German Mandarins: The German Academic Community, 1890–1933*, Cambridge, MA: Harvard University Press.

Robinson, E.E. (1969) *The New Polytechnics*, London: Penguin.

Robinson, E.E. (1968) 'Education as a social service', *Political Quarterly*, 40: 56–64.

Rose, C.M. (1986), 'The comedy of the commons: commerce, custom, and inherently public property', *The University of Chicago Law Review*, 53(3): 711–781.

Rose, N. (1999) *Powers of Freedom: Reframing Political Thought*, Cambridge: Cambridge University Press.

Rothblatt, S. and Wittrock, B. (eds) (1993) *The European and American University Since 1800: Historical and Sociological Essays*, Cambridge: Cambridge University Press.

Rowlinson, M. and Hassard, J. (2011). 'How come the critters came to be teaching in business schools? Contradictions in the institutionalization of Critical Management Studies', *Organization*, 18(5): 673–689.

Rudy, A.P., Coppin, D., Konefal, J., Shaw, B., Eyck, T.T., Harris, C. and Busch, L. (eds) (2007) *Universities in the Age of Corporate Science: The UC Berkeley–Novartis Controversy*, Philadelphia, PA: Temple University Press.

Ruggie, J.G. (1982) 'International regimes, transactions, and change: embedded liberalism in the post-war economic order', *International Organization*, 36(2): 379–415.

Sabel, C. (1995) 'Design, deliberation, and democracy: on the new pragmatism of firms and public institutions', *paper* presented at conference on Liberal Institutions, Economic Constitutional Rights, and the Role of Organizations, European University Institute, Florence, 15–16 December.

Sabel, C.F. and Zeitlin, J. (2010) *Experimentalist Governance in the European Union: Towards a New Architecture*, Oxford: Oxford University Press.

Saco, D. (2002) *Cybering Democracy: Public space and the Internet*, Minneapolis, MN: University of Minnesota Press.

Salaman, G. (2005) 'Bureaucracy and beyond: managers, leaders and the "post-bureaucratic" organization', in P. du Gay (ed.) *The Values of Bureaucracy*, Oxford: Oxford University Press.

Sanders, M. and Espeland, W.N. (2009) 'The discipline of rankings: tight coupling and organizational change', *American Sociological Review*, 74(1): 63–82.

Santiago, P., Tremblay, K., BasriE. and Arnal, E. (2008) *Tertiary Education for the Knowledge Society*, Paris: OECD.

Savage, M., Barlow, J., Dickens, P. and Fielding, T. (1992) *Property, Bureaucracy and Culture: Middle Class Formation in Contemporary Britain*, London: Routledge.

Sayer, A. (2000) 'Moral economy and political economy', *Studies in Political Economy*, 61(1): 79–103.

Scharpf, F.W. (1993) *Games in Hierarchies and Networks: Analytical and Empirical Approaches to the Study of Governance Institutions*, Frankfurt am Main: Campus Verlag.

Scharpf, F.W. (1996) 'Negative and positive integration in the political economy of European welfare states', in G. Marks, F.W. Scharpf and P.C. Schmitter (eds) *Governance in the European Union*, London: Sage.

Schattschneider, E.E. (1960) *The Semisovereign People: A Realist's View of Democracy in America*, New York: Holt, Rinehart and Winston.

Schön-Quinlivan, E. (2011) *Reforming the European Commission*, Basingstoke: Palgrave Macmillan.

Schostak, J. and Goodson, I. (2012) 'What's wrong with democracy at the moment, and why it matters for research and education', *Power and Education*, 4(3): 257–276.

Schugurensky, D. (2006) 'The political economy of higher education in the time of global markets: whither the social responsibility of the university?', in R. Rhoads and C. Torres (eds) *The University, State, and Market: The Political Economy of Globalization in the Americas*, Stanford, CA: Stanford University Press.

Schultze, G. (1992) *Die Erlebnisgesellschaft: Kultursoziologie der Gegenwart*, Frankfurt am Main: Campus Verlag.

Scott, A. (2013) 'Capitalism as culture and statecraft: Weber-Simmel-Hirschman', *Journal of Classical Sociology*, 13(3): 30–46.

Scott, A. (1997) 'Modernity's machine metaphor', *British Journal of Sociology*, 48(4): 561–575.

Scott, A. (1996), 'Bureaucratic revolutions and free market utopia', *Economy and Society* 25(1): 89–110.
Scott, A. and Pasqualoni, P.P. (2016) 'Invoking Humboldt: The German model', in J. Côté and A. Furlong (eds) *The Routledge Handbook of the Sociology of Higher Education*, London: Routledge.
Scott, C. and Hood, C. (2004) 'Higher education and university research: harnessing competition and mutuality to oversight?', in C. Hood, O. James and B.G. Peters (eds) *Controlling Modern Government. Variety, Commonality, and Change*, Cheltenham: Edward Elgar, 75–129.
Scott, J.C. (1998) *Seeing Like a State: How Certain Schemes to Improve the Human Condition Have Failed*, New Haven, NJ: Yale University Press.
Scott, J.C., Tehranian, J. and Mathias, J. (2002) 'Naming like a state: the production of legal identities proper to states: the case of the permanent family surname', *Comparative Studies in Society and History*, 44(1): 4–44.
Seabrooke, L. (2001) *US Power in International Finance: The Victory of Dividends*, Basingstoke: Palgrave Macmillan.
Seidl, D. (2007) 'Standard setting and following in corporate governance: an observation theoretical study of the effectiveness of governance codes', *Organization*, 14(5): 705–727.
Selznick, P. (1948) 'Foundations of the theory of organization', *American Sociological Review*, 13(1): 25–35.
Sennett, R. (1999) *The Fall of Public Man*, New York: W.W. Norton & co. Inc.
Sennett, R. (1974) *The Corrosion of Character: The Personal Consequences of Work in the New Capitalism*, New York: W.W. Norton & co. Inc.
Shane, S.A. (2004) *Academic Entrepreneurship University: Spinoffs and Wealth Creation*, Cheltenham: Edward Elgar.
Shattock, M. (2006) *Managing Good Governance in Higher Education*, Buckingham: Open University Press.
Shatz, D. (1996) 'Is peer review overrated?', *The Monist*, 79(4): 536–563.
Shin, J.C. and Kehm, B.M. (eds) (2013) *Institutionalization of World-Class University in Global Competition*, Dordrecht: Springer.
Shore, C. (2008) 'Audit culture and illiberal governance: universities and the politics of accountability', *Anthropological Theory*, 8(3): 278–298.
Shore, C. and Wright, S. (1999) 'Audit culture and anthropology: neo-liberalism in British higher education', *The Journal of the Royal Anthropological Institute*, 5(4): 557–575.
Simmel, G. (1996) [1911] 'Der Begriff und die Tragödie der Kultur', in Georg Simmel *Philosophische Kultur, Gesamtausgabe*, vol. 14, Frankfurt am Main: Suhrkamp Verlag.
Simmel, G. (1995a) [1904] 'Kant und der Individualismus', in Georg Simmel *Aufsätze und Abhandlungen 1901–1908*, vol. 1, *Gesamtausgabe*, vol. 7, eds R. Kramme, A. Rammstedt and O. Rammstedt, Frankfurt am Main: Suhrkamp Verlag.
Simmel, G. (1995b) [1903] 'Die Großstädte und das Geistesleben', in Georg Simmel *Aufsätze und Abhandlungen 1901–1908*, vol. 1, *Gesamtausgabe*, vol. 7, eds R. Kramme, A. Rammstedt and O. Rammstedt, Frankfurt am Main: Suhrkamp Verlag.
Simmel, G. (1983) [1886] 'Das Geld in der modernen Kultur', in G. Simmel *Schriften zur Soziologie*, eds H.-J. Dahme and O. Rammstedt, Frankfurt am Main: Suhrkamp Verlag.
Skidelsky, R. (2009) *Keynes: The Return of the Master*, New York: Public Affairs.

Skocpol, T. (2003) *Diminishing Democracy: From Membership to Management in American Civic Life*, Oklahoma, OK: Oklahoma University Press.

Smith, D. and Adams, J. (2008) 'Academics or executives? Continuity and change in the roles of pro-vice-chancellors', *Higher Education Quarterly*, 62(4): 340–357.

Sousa, S.B. and Brennan, J.L. (2014) 'The UK Research Excellence Framework and the transformation of research production', in C. Musselin and P.N. Teixeira (eds) *Reforming Higher Education: Public Policy Design and Implementation*, Dordrecht: Springer.

Springer, S. (2012) 'Neoliberalism as discourse: between Foucauldian political economy and Marxian poststructuralism', *Critical Discourse Studies*, 9(2): 133–147.

Springer, S., Birch, K., and MacLeavy, J. (2016) 'An introduction to neoliberalism', in S. Springer, K. Birch and J. MacLeavy, (eds) *The Handbook of Neoliberalism*, London: Routledge.

Stanfield, J.R. (1986) *The Economic Thought of Karl Polanyi: Lives and Livelihood*, Basingstoke: Palgrave Macmillan.

Stark, D. (2009) *The Sense of Dissonance: Accounts of Worth in Economic Life*, Princeton, NJ: Princeton University Press.

Steiner, P. (2009) 'The critique of the economic point of view: Karl Polanyi and the Durkheimians', in Hann and Hart (eds) *Market and Society: The Great Transformation Today*, Cambridge: Cambridge University Press.

Stoker, G. (2006) 'Public value management: a new narrative for networked governance?', *American Review of Public Administration*, 36(1): 41–57.

Stone, R.W. (2011) *Controlling Institutions: International Organizations and the Global Economy*, Cambridge: Cambridge University Press.

Storper, M. (2016) 'The neo-liberal city as idea and reality', *Territory, Politics and Governance*, 4(2): 241–263.

Strathern, M. (ed.) (2000) *Audit Cultures: Anthropological Studies in Accountability, Ethics and the Academy*, London: Routledge.

Streeck, W. (2014) *Buying Time: The Delayed Crisis of Democratic Capitalism*, London: Verso.

Streeck, W. and Thelen, K. (2005) 'Introduction: institutional change in advanced political economies', in W. Streeck and K. Thelen (eds) *Institutional Change in Advanced Political Economies*, Oxford: Oxford University Press.

Sugden, R. (1992) 'Naturalness and the spontaneous order of the market', in S. Hargreaves-Heap and A. Ross (eds) *Understanding the Enterprise Culture*, Edinburgh: Edinburgh University Press.

Tapper, E.R. and Salter, B.G. (1995) 'The changing idea of university autonomy', *Studies in Higher Education*, 20(1): 59–71.

Tapper, T. and Palfreyman, D. (eds) (2010) *The Collegial Tradition in the Age of Mass Higher Education*, Dordrecht: Springer.

Taylor, L. (2010) *Maynard's Revenge: The Collapse of Free Market Macroeconomics*, Cambridge, MA: Harvard University Press.

Teixeira, P., Jongbloed, B., Dill, D. and Amaral, A. (eds) (2004) *Markets in Higher Education: Rhetoric or Reality?*, Dordrecht: Kluwer.

Thaler, R.H. and Sunstein, C.R. (2008) *Nudge: Improving Decisions About Health, Wealth and Happiness*, New Haven, CT: Yale University Press.

Theisens, H. (2003) 'Statism by stealth? Market orientation in British higher education', in B. Denters, O. van Heffent, J. Huisman, and P.-J. Klok (eds) *The Rise of Interactive Governance and Quasi-Markets*, Dordrecht: Springer.

Thompson, G.F. (2003) *Between Hierarchies and Markets: The Logic and Limits of Network Forms of Organization*, Oxford: Oxford University Press.

Thorp, H. and Goldstein, B. (2010) *Engines of Innovation: The Entrepreneurial University in the Twenty-First Century*, Chapel Hill, NC: The University of North Carolina Press.

Thrift, N. (2008) 'A perfect innovation engine: the rise of the talent world', *Distinktion: Scandinavian Journal of Social Theory*, 9(1): 115–140.

Thrift, N. (2006) 'Re-inventing invention: new tendencies in capitalist commodification', *Economy and Society*, 35(2): 297–306.

Thrift, N. (2000) 'Performing cultures in the new economy', *Annals of the Association of American Geographers*, 90(4): 674–692.

Thrift, N. (1997) 'The rise of soft capitalism', *Cultural Values*, 1(1): 29–57.

Tight, M. (2013) 'Students: customers, clients or pawns?', *Higher Education Policy*, 26(3): 291–307.

Topan, A. (2002) 'The resignation of the Santer-Commission: the impact of "trust" and "reputation"', *European Integration Online Papers (EIoP)*, 6. Available: <http://eiop.or.at/eiop/texte/2002-014a.htm> (accessed 29 November 2016).

Trondal, J. and Peters, B.G. (2013) 'The rise of European administrative space: lessons learned', *Journal of European Public Policy*, 20(2): 295–307.

Trowler, P. (2010) 'UK higher education: captured by new managerialist ideology?', in V.L. Meek, L. Goedegebuure, R. Santiago and T. Carvalho (eds) *The Changing Dynamics of Higher Education Middle Management*, Dordrecht: Springer.

Tsebelis, G. (2001) *Veto Players: How Political Institutions Work*, Berkley, CA: University of California Press.

Turner, C. (2010) *Investigating Sociological Theory*, London: Sage.

Turner, D. (2015) *The Old Boys: The Decline and Rise of the Public Schools*, New Haven: Yale University Press.

Turner, D.A. (2011) *Quality in Higher Education*, Rotterdam: Sense Publishers.

Turner, R. (2008) *Neo-liberal Ideology: History, Concepts and Policies*, Edinburgh: Edinburgh University Press.

Urry, J. (2000) *Sociology Beyond Societies: Mobilities for the Twenty-first Century*, London: Routledge.

Vernon, J. (2011) 'Canary in the coal mine', *Times Higher Education*, 1 December. Available: <https://www.timeshighereducation.com/features/canary-in-the-coal-mine/418284.article> (accessed 29 November 2016).

Villadsen, K. and Dean, M. (2012) 'State-phobia, civil society, and a certain vitalism', *Constellations*, 19(3): 401–420.

Vogel, S.K. (1996) *Freer Markets, More Rules: Regulatory Reform in Advanced Industrial Countries*, Ithaca, NY: Cornell University Press.

Vreeland, J. R. (2007) *The International Monetary Fund: Politics of Conditional Lending*, London: Routledge.

Vreeland, J.R. (2003) *The IMF and Economic Development*, Cambridge: Cambridge University Press.

Wade, R. (1996) 'Japan, the World Bank, and the art of paradigm maintenance: the east Asian Miracle in political perspective', *New Left Review*, 217: 3–36.

Walberg, H.J. and Bast, J.L. (2003) *Education and Capitalism: How Overcoming Our Fear of Markets and Economics Improve Americas Schools*, Stanford, CA: Hoover Institution Press.

Walters, R. (2011) *Eco Crime and Genetically Modified Food*, London: Routledge.

Wang, S. (2008) 'Double movement in China', *Economic and Political Weekly*, 43(52) (27 December): 51–59.

Warner, M. (2015) 'Learning my lesson', *London Review of Books*, 19 March. Available: <http://www.lrb.co.uk/v37/n06/marina-warner/learning-my-lesson> (accessed 29 November 2016).

Warner, M. (2014) 'Diary: why I quit', *London Review of Books*, 11 September. Available: <http://www.lrb.co.uk/v36/n17/marina-warner/diary> (accessed 20 November 2016).

Warren, M.E. (2009) 'Governance-driven democratization', *Critical Policy Analysis*, 3(1): 3–13.

Washburn, J. (2001) 'The idea of the university: the corporate university or the high seminary of learning', Clemson Presidential Colloquium, Spring. Available: <http://firgoa.usc.es/drupal/files/Washburn.pdf> (accessed 29 November 2016).

Weber, M. (2005) [1906] 'The relations of the rural community to other branches of social science', ed. and annotated P. Ghosh as Max Weber on 'The Rural Community: a critical edition of the English text', *History of European Ideas*, 31: 327–366.

Weber, M. (1924) [1908] 'Methodologische Einleitung für die Erhebung des Vereins für Sozialpolitik über Auslese und Anpassung Berufswahlen und Berufsschicksal der Arbeiterschaft der geschlossenen Großindustrie', in M. Weber (ed.), *Gesammelte Aufsätze zur Soziologie und Sozialpolitik*, Tübingen: J.C.B. Mohr.

Weber, M. (2002) [1920] *The Protestant Ethic and the Spirit of Capitalism*; ed. and trans. S. Kalberg, Oxford: Blackwell.

Weber, M. (1994) [1919] 'The vocation and profession of politics', in *Max Weber: Political Writings*; ed. and trans. P. Lassman and R. Speirs, Cambridge: Cambridge University Press.

Weber, M. (1994) [1918] 'Parliament and government in a newly ordered Germany'; ed. and trans. P. Lassman and R. Speirs *Weber: Political Writings*, Cambridge: Cambridge University Press.

Weber, M. (1989a) [1894] 'Developmental tendencies in the situation of East Elbian labourers', in K. Tribe (ed. and trans.) *Reading Weber*, London: Routledge.

Weber, M. (1989b) [1919] 'Science as a vocation', in P. Lassman and I. Velody (eds) *Max Weber's 'Science as a Vocation'*, London: Unwin Hyman.

Weber, M. (1972) [1922] *Wirtschaft und Gesellschaft*, Studienausgabe, Tübingen: J.C.B. Mohr; English *Economy and Society*, two volumes; ed. and trans. G. Roth and C. Wittich, Berkeley, CA: University of California Press, 1978.

Weber, M. (1948) *From Max Weber: Essays in Sociology*, H.H. Gerth and C.W. Mills (eds), London: Routledge.

Weiler, J. (1999) *The Constitution of Europe: 'Do the New Clothes Have an Emperor?' and Other Essays on European Integration*, Cambridge: Cambridge University Press.

Weiler, H.N. (1993) 'Control versus legitimation: the politics of ambivalence', in J. Hannaway and M. Carnoy (eds) *Decentralization and School Improvement: Can We Fulfill the Promise?*, San Francisco, CA: Josse-Bass Inc.

Weiler, H.N. (1983) 'Legalization, expertise, and participation: strategies of compensatory legitimation in educational policy', *Comparative Education Review*, 27(2): 259–277.

Wildavsky, B. (2010) *The Great Brain Race: How Global Universities Are Reshaping the World*, Princeton, NJ: Princeton University Press.

Wilhelm, A. (2000) *Democracy in the Digital Age: Challenges to Political Life in Cyberspace*, London: Routledge.

Wilks, S. (2015) 'The Revolving Door and the Corporate Colonisation of British Politics', High Pay Centre. Available: <http://highpaycentre.org/files/FINAL_REVOLVING_DOOR.pdf> (accessed 29 November 2016).

Williams, D. and Young, T. (1994) 'Governance, the World Bank and liberal theory', *Political Studies*, 42(1): 84–100.

Williams, G. (2011) 'Will higher education be the next bubble to burst?', *The Europa World of Learning 2011*, London: Routledge.

Williams, J. (2006) 'The post-welfare state university', *American Literary History*, 18(1): 190–216.

Williams, M. and Waldron, J. (eds) (2008) *Toleration and its Limits*, New York: New York University Press.

Williamson, O. (2000) 'The new institutional economics: taking stock, looking ahead', *Journal of Economic Literature*, 38(3): 595–613.

Willmott, H. (2003) 'Commercialising higher education in the UK: the state, industry and peer review', *Studies in Higher Education*, 28(2): 129–141.

Willmott, H. (1995) 'Managing the academics: commodification and control in the development of university education in the UK', *Human Relations*, 48(9): 993–1027.

Wolf, K.D. (1999a) 'The new *raison d'état* as a problem for democracy in world society', *European Journal of International Relations*, 5(3): 333–363.

Wolf, K.D. (1999b) 'Defending state autonomy: intergovernmental governance in the European Union', in B. Kohler-Koch and R. Eising (eds) *The Transformation of Governance in the European Union*, London: Routledge.

Wolfe, A. (1977) *The Limits of Legitimacy: Political Contradictions of Contemporary Capitalism*, New York: Free Press.

Wolff, R.P., Moore, B. jr and Marcuse, H. (1965) *A Critic of Pure Tolerance*, Boston, MA: Beacon Press.

Wood, M. (2014) 'Depoliticization, resilience and the Herceptin post-code lottery crisis: holding back the tide', *British Journal of Politics & International Relations*, 17: 644–664.

Woodhall, M. and Richards, K. (2008) 'Student and university funding in Britain in devolved governments in the United Kingdom', in P.N. Teixeira, D.B. Johnstone, M.J. Rosa and H. Vossensteyn (eds) *Cost-Sharing and Accessibility in Higher Education: A Fairer Deal?*, Dordrecht: Springer.

Wren, D.A. (2005) *The History of Managerial Thought*, Hoboken, NJ: Wiley.

Wythe, W. (2015) *Redbrick: A Social and Architectural History of Britain's Civic Universities*, Oxford: Oxford University Press.

Yi-chong, X. and Weller, P. (2009) *Inside the World Bank: Exploding the Myth of the Monolithic Bank*, Basingstoke: Palgrave Macmillan.

Zaman, M.Q. (2004) *Review of The Academic Evidence on the Relationship Between Teaching and Research in Higher Education*, Research Report RR506, London: Department of Education and Skills.

Zgaga, P., Teichler, U. and Brennan, J. (eds) (2013) *The Globalisation Challenge for European Higher Education: Convergence and Diversity, Centres and Peripheries*, Frankfurt am Main: Internationaler Verlag der Wissenschaften.

Index

For Product Safety Concerns and Information please contact our EU representative GPSR@taylorandfrancis.com Taylor & Francis Verlag GmbH, Kaufingerstraße 24, 80331 München, Germany